Cambridge Studies in Social Anthropology

General Editor: Jack Goody

60

CULTURE AND CLASS IN
ANTHROPOLOGY AND HISTORY

For other titles in this series turn to page 203

This book is published as part of the joint publishing agreement established in 1977 between the Fondation de la Maison des Sciences de l'Homme and the Press Syndicate of the University of Cambridge. Titles published under this arrangement may appear in any European language or, in the case of volumes of collected essays, in several languages.

New books will appear either as individual titles or in one of the series which the Maison des Sciences de l'Homme and the Cambridge University Press have jointly agreed to publish. All books published jointly by the Maison des Sciences de l'Homme and the Cambridge University Press will be distributed by the Press throughout the world.

Cet ouvrage est publié dans le cadre de l'accord de co-édition passé en 1977 entre la Fondation de la Maison des Sciences de l'Homme et le Press Syndicate de l'Université de Cambridge. Toutes les langues européennes sont admises pour les titres couverts par cet accord, et les ouvrages collectifs peuvent paraître en plusieurs langues.

Les ouvrages paraissent soit isolément, soit dans l'une des séries que la Maison des Sciences de l'Homme et Cambridge University Press ont convenu de publier ensemble. La distribution dans le monde entier des titres ainsi publiés conjointement par les deux éstablissements est assurée par Cambridge University Press.

This is the first of three planned volumes on a theory of culture in history: the role of culture in the formation and transformation of systems of inequality. The second volume will focus on ethnicity, and the third will take up the issue of folk culture and state formation.

Culture and class in anthropology and history

A Newfoundland illustration

GERALD M. SIDER
College of Staten Island and
Graduate School and University Center
City University of New York

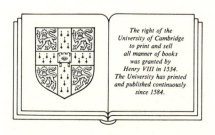

The right of the
University of Cambridge
to print and sell
all manner of books
was granted by
Henry VIII in 1534.
The University has printed
and published continuously
since 1584.

CAMBRIDGE UNIVERSITY PRESS
Cambridge
London   New York   New Rochelle   Melbourne   Sydney

EDITIONS DE LA MAISON DES SCIENCES DE
L'HOMME
Paris

Published by the Press Syndicate of the University of Cambridge
The Pitt Building, Trumpington Street, Cambridge CB2 1RP
32 East 57th Street, New York, NY 10022, USA
10 Stamford Road, Oakleigh, Melbourne 3166, Australia
and
Editions de la Maison des Sciences de l'Homme
54 Boulevard Raspail, 75270 Paris, Cedex 06

First published 1986

Printed in the United States of America

Library of Congress Cataloging-in-Publication Data
Sider, Gerald M.
Culture and class in anthropology and history.
Bibliography: p.
1. Newfoundland – Social conditions.   2. Social
change – Case studies.   3. Social classes – Case
studies.   I. Title.
HN110.N49S54   1985   306'.09718   85–14902

British Library Cataloging-in-Publication applied for.

ISBN 0 521 25403 5
ISBN 2 7351 0137 1 (France only)

In memoriam
Jay Pawa,
friend and colleague,
who knew most of all how history matters
in the daily lives of people, including our own

The aim of this book is to show how empirical categories – such as the raw and the cooked, the fresh and the decayed, the moistened and the burned, etc., which can only be accurately defined by ethnographic observation, and in each instance, by adopting the standpoint of a particular culture – can nonetheless be used as conceptual tools with which to elaborate abstract ideas and combine them in the form of propositions.

Lévi-Strauss,
The Raw and the Cooked

Whatever they loved to have roasted, he was to give to them raw; and whatever they wished to have raw, he was to give to them roasted.

Lord North,
testifying in the House of Commons in 1793
about the instructions given to the
naval governor of Newfoundland
concerning the treatment of the inhabitants

Contents

Acknowledgments   *page* ix
Map of Newfoundland   xii

Part One
Introductions   1
1 Anthropology and history, culture and class   3
2 The particularity and relevance of Newfoundland   12
3 Autonomy and the harness: the logic of merchant capital   34

Part Two
Domination, alliances, and descent   39
4 Regale and rule: the logic of paternalism and
   the emergence of village culture   46
5 When fishermen may starve: the Slade and Kelson Plan
   of 1825   58
6 The times of our lives: descent, alliances, custom,
   and history   74

Part Three
The politics of subsistence production:
hegemony at work in a collapsing state   97
7 The memorial of the merchants of Poole   107
8 A political holiday   129
9 We must live in hopes   158

Conclusion   187
10 Merchant capital and the cross-handed triumphs of tradition   189

vii

Contents

References   195
Index   201

Note: Eight unnumbered pages of photographs appear between pp. 96 and 97.

Acknowledgments

This book has been building over the past decade, and along the way I have accumulated a great many intellectual and personal debts to the people who have been so helpful.

First of all, thanks are due to Alf Lüdtke, Hans Medick, and David Sabean, of the Max Planck Institut für Geschichte, Göttingen, who in 1978 invited me to join their working group on history and anthropology. There have been four roundtable conferences organized by different members of this working group and cosponsored by the Institut and the Maison des Sciences de l'Homme: one on work processes, one on material interest and emotion in kinship, and two on domination. Each of these has served to introduce a variety of focused approaches to the conjunction of history and anthropology and has provided an opportunity to present and discuss aspects of the following study. Through the kindness of the director, Professor Rudolph Vierhaus, I spent several summers at the Institut, for extended discussions with my colleagues and with Robert Berdahl, Vanessa Maher, and William Reddy. My debt to this working group is far more than for insightful suggestions and specific clarifications, though these were plentiful.

In the course of developing this work I had the very rewarding opportunity of spending three months in Paris. Here I wish to particularly thank M. Clemens Heller for the invitation to the Maison des Sciences de l'Homme, and Professor Maurice Godelier for arranging the invitation to the Ecole des Hautes Etudes en Sciences Sociales and for the opportunity to give three papers in his seminar on anthropology and economics. In Paris my extended discussions with Maurice Aymard, Roger Chartier, Jean Chase, and Jean-Claude Schmitt were particularly helpful.

During 1980–1 I spent a year as a fellow of the Shelby Cullom Davis Center for Historical Studies at Princeton University, which was a major opportunity for writing and rethinking, with the time and space to explore new directions. My thanks to Professor Lawrence Stone, director of the center, for the hospitality of the center and for his own hospitality – and for the delightfully sharp arguments into which he drew me.

Central to the kinds of institutional support that I have received for this work has been a series of grants for field and archival research from the Institute of Social and Economic Research, Memorial University of Newfoundland. After my initial research in 1972, they have consistently and generously supported my further research trips, in 1974, 1976, 1980 (twice), and 1982. Each time they also provided an opportunity to present papers and discuss aspects of this work with Newfoundland scholars, from which has come much helpful information and advice. I am particularly grateful for the assistance I have received from Raoul Andersen, Steven Antler, Louis Chiaramonte, Rex Clark, James Hiller, Thomas Nemec, Rosemary Ommer, Robert Paine, George Story, and Wilfred Wareham, and from Keith Matthews, so unfortunately now deceased. My archival research in Newfoundland was assisted in major ways by Anne Hart and Nancy Grenville, of the Newfoundland Center of the Queen Elizabeth II Library at Memorial University; Philip Hiscock, archivist at the Folklore and Language Library at Memorial University; Ed Tompkins, who unearthed the Slade and Kelson Plan, and Howard Brown, both of the Newfoundland and Labrador Provincial Archives; and Heather Wareham, of the Maritime History Group Archives at Memorial, who also introduced me to her father, Freeman Wareham. Mr. Wareham was a major merchant in Placentia Bay, and he has been particularly open and helpful in our extended discussions, as was Joseph Smallwood, premier of Newfoundland for more than two decades after Confederation, who spent a very long morning discussing his policies of economic development with me after he had read two papers of mine quite critical of these policies. Professor George Story, who in the midst of our divergent interpretations of some points of Newfoundland history was consistently helpful and supportive, also deserves special thanks.

I also wish to thank the American Council of Learned Societies for a travel grant to Sweden in the fall of 1983, and for the opportunity to discuss the intersections of dominance and folk culture with Swedish colleagues working on the issue, particularly David Gaunt and Eva Österberg.

Much of this work was facilitated by the helpfulness of Dean Barry Bressler of the College of Staten Island, City University of New York, who provided released time from teaching and a variety of institutional support.

These thanks to the institutions and to the people within them do not sufficiently acknowledge the support, encouragement, and warm hospitality I encountered. In Dunnville, Placentia Bay, I was helped, advised, and made welcome by Bill and Mary Norman, Rita Barry, Patrick Barry, Bill

Acknowledgments

and Shirley Martin, Eric Shave, and Philly and Mary Vicount; in St. John's, the hospitality and helpfulness of Steven Antler and Sally Grenville were special and important.

At Princeton, also as Davis Fellows, Baruch Knei-Paz and Sarah Madden provided good companionship and advice during the formulation of the material in Part Three of this book. Ellen Antler, David Cohen, James Faris, Ashraf Ghani, Jane Schneider, Jurgen Schlumbohm, Dorothy and Edward Thompson, Eric Wolf, and Joan Vincent provided very useful help at key points in the analysis of the data, as did Judy Hilkey, who shared some of the field research with me.

In Germany, Helga and Alf Lüdtke, Doris Bachmann-Medick and Hans Medick, Ruth and David Sabean, and Adelheid and Manfred von Saldern were supportive and encouraging in ways that are beyond thanks, as has been Ursula Nienhaus, whose trenchant and friendly critiques led me to write a further, substantially different draft of this manuscript at a point when, having written several drafts already, and having tried the considerate patience of my editor, Susan Allen-Mills, beyond what even an author could consider reasonable, I was ready to stop. In this final rewrite Rhys Isaac and Andrea Bardfeld have provided excellent advice, and my sons, Byron and Hugh, essential cheer.

The extracts from the journals of Elizabeth Goudie that introduce Chapter 9 are used with the kind permission of the Honorable D. J. Goudie, and with thanks to Anne Hart, who alerted me to this document.

The photographs in this book, including the jacket photograph, are the work of Professor Louis Chiaramonte of the Department of Anthropology, Memorial University of Newfoundland. Both a scholar of Newfoundland social organization and a teacher of photographic anthropology, his images well repay study and thought, for they convey some of the subtleties of and the frameworks for social interaction in a way that goes well beyond what photography usually does. I am grateful for his willingness to include them in this book.

Special thanks to Robert Grumet for drawing the map of Newfoundland that appears on the next page.

New York   G. M. S.

xi

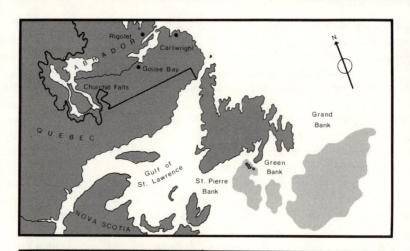
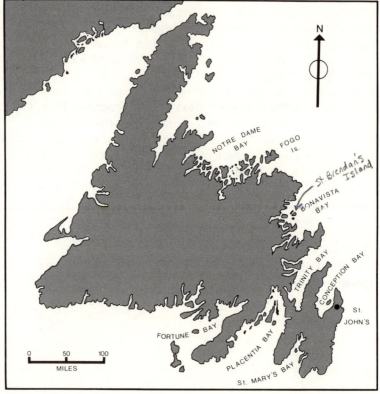

NEWFOUNDLAND

PART ONE

Introductions

1

Anthropology and history, culture and class

I

Most people, everywhere, think about the future. They think about growing up, or old; about their children, present, past, and to come; about their parents; about personal and public events, occasions, festivals, and holidays, coming and past; about issues that we abstractly call "economic trends" and "political processes"; about the condition of their material possessions in conjunction with their needs and wants; about their relations to and with other people, and what is happening in these relations. And they watch and listen to their kith, kin, and others grapple with the same topics – sometimes talking to each other about such issues directly, sometimes commenting on it all indirectly. In sum, people – even in so-called tradition-bound societies – conduct their day-to-day lives in ways that construct and invoke a knowledge, probably quite finely tuned and constantly adjusted, of the intimate, multiple interconnections of past, present, and future. And this knowledge grows out of and becomes somewhat distanced from, and yet is situated within, the concrete and specific material and social realities of daily life.

How is this "knowledge" created, invoked, and put to use? Does it matter? Does it have any substantial social import on any larger scale and in any larger arena than that of the individual adjustments and copings of individual lives? To point in a direction where we might start looking for ways to answer these questions: This knowledge is not, or not primarily, rational. It may be logical, internally consistent, and pragmatically rooted – it may, that is, possess all the attributes of what we might call rational knowledge, or it may not. But it is, more significantly, socially based in its origins and in its effects, and socially expressed – not just in individual activity but in the cycle of festivals, the ceremonies of life passages, the panoplies of power and deference. It is, in other words, what at least some

3

anthropologists call culture, although here delineated with more emphasis on its temporality, as people themselves perceive it, than anthropologists ordinarily find or look for. The question becomes: How does culture matter in situations of change?

There is very little in the way anthropology is done, or even more surprisingly, in historical methodology, that enables us to talk very clearly about the involvement of ordinary people in the transformations of their social lives. There are several versions of what might be called a hydraulic model of popular involvement in social change – press people down in one domain of their lives and they will pop up in another with even more force – but this perspective is primarily invoked to explain episodic upheavals, where the drama of the events conceals the lifelessness of the model. Such hydraulic explanations are of little use in understanding how people participate in the routine, but far more powerful and pervasive, transformations of their social world.

When social historians turn to anthropology (an increasingly popular tack in the past two decades) they have borrowed concepts, for example, from the study of custom and ritual; methodologies, particularly from kinship; models, the "gift" and "rites de passage" perhaps being the most popular; and even phrases, such as "thick description." The problem is that what is taken from anthropology is used *not* to do history but to *evade* doing history.

Edward Thompson stated this problem with particular force and clarity, although perhaps because he is a historian and not an anthropologist he did not at all see it as a problem:

When we examine a customary culture [the kinds of questions which must be asked] may often be concerned less with the processes and logic of change than with the recovery of past states of consciousness and the texturing of social and domestic relationships. They are concerned less with *becoming* than with *being*. As some of the leading actors of history recede from our attention – the politicians, the thinkers, the entrepreneurs, the generals – so an immense supporting cast, whom we had supposed to be mere attendants on this process, press themselves forward. If we are concerned only with becoming, then there are whole periods in history in which an entire sex has been neglected by historians, because women are rarely seen as prime agents in political, military or even economic life. If we are concerned with being, then the exclusion of women would reduce history to futility. [1978: 251]

Although for anthropologists Thompson is perhaps the most stimulating and methodologically influential of the social historians, this passage is painful. For it accepts rather than transcends the major issue of a historically focused anthropology: How do we understand the textures of social life as part not just of the being but the becoming of social life? And although Thompson ends the passage just quoted by observing that "the 'public' life arises out of the dense determinations of the 'domestic' life," the question is still how?

Anthropology and history, culture and class

Class is perhaps the core concept of social history; *culture* is certainly the central concept of anthropology. But although culture is central, anthropology has tended to set it aside when dealing with questions of change. When the focus is on why change occurs, the study of culture becomes irrelevant, and anthropology turns to "history" as a narrative sequence of events, or looks outside the society under study to the environment or to larger social fields, where the appalling dramas of social worlds in collision have held almost the entire stage. And when, on the other hand, the anthropological focus is on culture, as in symbolic studies, change becomes irrelevant or, at best and at worst, becomes reduced to the observation of transformations from place to place (e.g., Lévi-Strauss 1969), or in any one place the analysis of oscillations around a purportedly dynamic equilibrium (Leach 1954; Gluckman 1955, 1963).

II

When we attempt to use the anthropological concept of culture to analyze social-class formations and transformations, we encounter a profound difficulty. Either culture becomes derivative, an attachment to other, more "basic" political-economic processes, or culture appears to be autonomous, independent of the realities of social class. Giving labels to these pitfalls – *mechanical reductionism*; *idealism* – does not diminish the difficulty, as the problem did not originate in the relative importance we assign to culture and cannot be resolved by granting culture either more or less autonomy. Rather, the problem begins (but only begins) with the anthropological concept of culture itself, which is ahistorical, nonprocessual, and totalizing.

For those who work within, or close to, one of the marxist traditions, there is available a concept of class that is relational, processual, and specific. In such perspective, any particular social class can only be defined and understood in relation to other social classes, to the material forces of production, and to the property relations through which surpluses are formed, transferred, and transformed. The whole concept of class is dynamic, implicitly and explicitly focusing attention on the social-structural feature that generates process: the contradictions between the forms of property and the abilities and needs of the producers. By comparison, the concept of culture – as shared values, or as a system of values, beliefs, symbols, and rituals – lacks a dynamic and processual core.

Without any dynamic structure of its own, or at least without any we can see and understand, culture is bound to appear epiphenomenal, secondary, and derivative; simply a superstructure tacked on, and ultimately responsive to, a political-economic base. Moreover, lacking a specific dynamic structure that would give form and meaning to what is and is not culture, the concept becomes amorphous, vague, and totalizing in two

5

senses. First, it is a totalizing concept because everything becomes, or is considered, culture. There are material culture, symbolic culture, ritual culture, social institutions, patterned behavior, language-as-culture, values, beliefs, ideas, ideologies, meanings, and so forth. Second, not only is everything or almost everything in a society culture, but the concept is also totalizing because everyone in the society is supposed to have the same culture (as in the concept of culture as shared values) or at least to be measured by its standards (as in the concept of cultural deprivation or the subtler notion of subculture).

Because on the one side the concept of culture is totalizing and all-inclusive, culture appears to be independent – an aspect of the social system, an abstraction from the texture of social life unconnected to other aspects, other abstractions. Because on the other side the concept is neither processual nor dynamic, culture appears to be derivative from what is more clearly in motion.

This paradox of the concept of culture – that it can be either primarily independent or primarily derivative – haunts both nonmarxist and marxist analyses alike. Clifford Geertz has stated that culture is "independent but interdependent" with social organization (1973). Marxists, with a more specific set of labels, have not been much clearer about how the two are interconnected. In marxism this issue is an aspect of the base–superstructure problematic; that is, is the cultural-legal-political superstructure simply derived from the political-economic base? The solutions suggested in this theoretical tradition – that the base is a "final" determinant, but only a final one, or that there is a "dialectical" interaction between superstructure and base – leave the issue still very unresolved: Can we specify how and why culture has, or may have, its own (at least partly) separate historical dynamic, and can we specify a method for understanding the extent to which culture is determined by, determining of, or irrelevant to the changing (or relatively changeless) circumstances of daily life and productive relations?

It will not be possible to begin to answer this question if we simply seek to reformulate the anthropological concept of culture to make it more specific and more dynamic, although this is a major task of this book. Culture and class are, after all, simply abstractions from the same tissue of social life – abstractions made seemingly more concrete by the fact that many of the "natives" in class societies share these concepts with their observers – but they are just different abstractions from the same reality nonetheless. And the concept of class turns out to have its own difficulties, precisely because it shunts aside those aspects of social life pointed to by the concept of culture.

Nor can we simply add culture to class and so solve our problems with the concept of class. The intractability of the problems of understanding how class consciousness is shaped, or misshaped; what cultural hegemony is, and how it works; how to usefully conceptualize ideology; the "legitimacy" of power: The list of problems is, if not endless, sufficiently long and full of jargon to alert us to the possibility that we might not be able to take the marxist concept of class and paste onto it some cultural considerations.

Precisely because the concept of class is more historically dynamic and more analytically precise than is the concept of culture, it is more difficult to pin down its problems and to reformulate it accordingly. Moreover, political feelings attached to this concept are often fairly intense; tinkering with the concept of class can become a touchy issue. But it must be done, because as presently formulated it evades questions of cultural variation and the impact of culture on history. To understand the interconnections of culture and class, we must rethink both concepts.

In doing so, the purpose of this book is to root culture in the social relations both of production-appropriation (the framework from which comes the marxist concept of class) and of daily life and work, in ways that enable us not to reject but to go beyond the notion of culture as a system of "meaning," of "interpretation," of "values, beliefs, ideologies, and worldview, and the associated rituals, practices, and symbols." Our task here is to see culture not only with its own dynamic and volatile paradoxes, disjunctions, and contradictions, but also in the specific ways culture both takes from and gives to social relations shape, form, and meaning (and meaninglessness, etc.) – to see it as an active force in history.

III

Because of the centrality of the notions both of *contradiction* – fundamental antagonistic oppositions – and of *class struggle* in the marxist analysis of history, it has usually been assumed that class systems can ultimately be delineated by fundamental cleavages between antagonistic elements: workers versus owners; labor versus capital.

This assumption is close enough to being correct to make the marxist (or materialist and social-relational) approach to historical analysis exceptionally productive. A more subtle and complex appreciation of the antagonistic cleavages in a social system, however, will make the analysis of class even more productive. Briefly, and by way of introduction:

At the very end of Volume III of *Capital*, Marx finally addressed the concept of class directly. He wrote two pages – only a start – and then his manuscript breaks off.

In this last section he asks two questions:

7

1. "What comprises a class?"
2. "Why are wage-labourers, capitalists, and landowners the three great classes of England?"

He then makes three extraordinarily important points:

First, he says that the answer to the first question is the same as the answer to the second question. But this does not at all mean that the first question can or should (only) be answered empirically, specifically.

Second, he cautions that the answer to the second question is *not* that these are the major sources of income.

Third, Marx notes that even in the most highly developed economy of the time, England, the lines between the classes are blurred by intermediate classes and positions but states that this is irrelevant to an analysis of class.

I have no interest at all in guessing what Marx would have said had he lived to finish the chapter. Rather, I find the way the issue is posed fascinating, and potentially very significant. Why are the answers to the two questions about class connected, when the questions are dissimilar, the first seemingly totally abstract, the second seemingly completely empirical? I am interested in seeing what we can say by way of an answer to this based on what is now known, and in particular based on what an anthropological concept of culture might contribute to an answer.

Two possible answers to this linked pair of questions about class come to mind.

First (importantly, but theoretically straightforward and, surprisingly, not very significant in itself): These were the three classes with substantial access to state power, or that state power had to take into account; class has, and must have, a political dimension.

Second, and to my view the heart of the issue: The three classes that Marx names – labor, capitalists, and landowners – do not and cannot form any neat system. There is no single line of cleavage that can conceivably be drawn separating these three groupings into just two antagonistic camps. Rather, the alliances and oppositions must shift, and break, and shift again, each time re-forming in a new way. (Thus it would also not be possible to draw two lines of cleavage, separating three distinct and mutually antagonistic groups, for none of the cleavages could be stable.)

This means that social and historical processes *within* a class – as people reach out for, or turn away from, a range of potential alliances and oppositions, and as issues become understood and acted upon in ways that include and exclude in new combinations – are as crucial to defining what happens as are the struggles *between* classes. This is *not* to define class by class consciousness: Consciousness is only one of a multitude of events that occur within classes. It is, rather, to define a class – a class in history, as well as in the relations of production – by its internal dynamic as well as by its interclass confrontations and collusions. Further, the shifting and transient alliances and oppositions in a system of classes implies that the composition and internal structure of any particular class are fluid and dynamic – due not only to changes in the material basis and productive activities of the class but also to changing political and ideological claims, assertions, and practices.

It is precisely at this point that culture – a reformulated notion of culture – enters into the dynamic of class. *Not* because culture "happens" within classes, and class struggle between classes; not at all. Culture enters the dynamic of class because, as we shall see, it is where class becomes dynamic; where the lines of antagonism and alliance come together and apart.

IV

The problem that anthropology has had with cultural change is fundamental to the history of the discipline. The specter that has haunted anthropology since its inception is inequality, not so much within social systems as between them. This required anthropology, with substantial difficulty, to separate itself from its own social matrix of civilized elitism or racism and so to account for the strangeness of the other without making the other seem peculiar, or peculiarly inferior. In arguing for the validity of other lifeways, anthropologists have, from a variety of methodologies, argued for the integrity – the functional wholeness – of the ways of any particular society: how customs and social institutions fit in with each other, with the environment, and even with the fundamental structures of the human mind.

Critiques of functionalist theory in anthropology are by now too well known to be worth recounting, but these critiques have yet to lead to substantially successful resolutions of many of the more important problems they raise. To sum up this situation: The more effective of these critiques focus on the point that functionalist methodological approaches construct visions of social systems sufficiently well integrated to make it difficult to see how change comes from *within* the system. Loci of change are thus found externally – for example, in ecological considerations, or in so-called world-economy influences. Symbolic studies, for the most part, sidetrack this problem, and marxist studies, concentrating on systemic contradictions, leave largely untouched questions of how people alter their social relations in order to change the conditions of their existence.

Recent British social historiography, focusing in one of its perspectives on the now-popular concepts of *agency* and *experience* (as these concepts are rooted and shaped in the work of E. P. Thompson) has come close to confronting directly the problem of understanding the interconnections of social interaction and social change – and has done so in an approach that is gaining fairly wide popularity among anthropologists as well as social historians. However, the concept of agency – purposeful, socially influential

9

human activity formed out of people's experience – is too direct, too pragmatically rooted, and too conscious to merge very comfortably with any anthropological approach that has pondered the intricate interweavings and complex causal links that occur within the domain of culture.

To back out of the functionalist trap – apprehending culture in ways that constrain its liveliness and ultimately take its life – and to begin the task of constructing an alternative, we must do more than look for the tensions, disjunctions, paradoxes, and contradictions within a culture, or between different elements of a culture: the points where a culture does not form a functionally integrated whole. We must, rather, seek to discover how these disjunctions and contradictions are continually restructured within a culture – how they are generated and formed by the same processes that generate and form culture; how they are connected to social relations by the same processes that connect culture to the material and social realities of social life. For people act in terms of what they cannot understand, or understand in radically different ways, and in terms of relationships they cannot form, or sustain, or leave, as well as in terms of what "works," what they think they clearly understand and can probably do. From this perspective we may then better understand how time and history come also to be embedded in culture and class.

Above all, we must first understand – and this is the point of the quote from Lord North cited in the epigraph – that culture matters. Nothing is so pernicious and destructive to any conceivable understanding of the dynamics of social life as the notion that what anthropologists talk about are the quaint customs of the fuzzy-wuzzies. When Lord North said we give them raw what they want roasted, and roasted what they want raw, he at least did the people at the bottom of this system the honor of realizing, fundamentally, that what they wanted, or how they saw the world, was crucial to what they did or could be made to do. Let us, at the least, give no less due.

Understanding how culture (including its contradictions and disjunctions, its ambiguities and ambivalences) is generated and formed, and generates and shapes social relations, rather than seeing culture as something that is simply enacted, "participated in," "learned, shared, and transmitted," is the same problem, within anthropology, as the problem of social reproduction and transformation in marxist social history. The point is not, however, to give the same problem two different names or histories, nor to search it out and reveal it beneath two different guises, nor simply to seek to refashion the concept of class and culture so that they fit together better and are more helpful to each other. The point, ultimately, is strategic: to get a better handhold on a stronger lever. For that task we start by turning to Newfoundland, particularly while Newfoundland was in the grip of merchant capital, and in that context reexamine the formation and transformation of culture and class, and of domination and intentionality.

2

The particularity and relevance of Newfoundland

Constructing a historical anthropology from Newfoundland data is not like writing about Europe, America, or even Africa – when it can be assumed that most of the readers have in mind the broad outlines of the history and some data-organizing images of social-organizational patterns. In such circumstances one can jump right into the special argument. Here, to the contrary and by way of a start, it is necessary to sketch a silhouette and to show this silhouette moving through a few temporal frames. The second and third sections of this chapter, which introduce the relevance of the Newfoundland data to larger issues and arguments, also introduce new perspectives. But in the first section, some general points – generally known to those familiar with the region – need to be presented.

I

Around the island of Newfoundland, southward toward Nova Scotia, southeastward, westward into the Gulf of the St. Lawrence River, and especially eastward under the North Atlantic, there are a series of submerged islands, or "banks." The largest and most productive is the Grand Bank, which begins about fifty miles east of Newfoundland and is about as large as Newfoundland itself.

The Grand Bank lies under the intersection of the microorganism-rich, northward-flowing Gulf Stream and the mineral-rich, southward-flowing Labrador Current. The confluence of these currents over the sunlit bottom of the shallow sea makes the banks one of the richest fishing grounds in the world.

Sea life from the banks – the bait fish capelin, and especially the groundfish cod, halibut, flounder, and sole – spilling over into the bays, inlets, tickles, and sea arms that make up the six thousand miles of Newfoundland coastline has made possible a very productive "inshore," as well as a bank, fishery.

Each spring the capelin swarm into the bays of Newfoundland, and the cod follow them in. A century or more ago, when fish were very much more plentiful, the phenomenon of cod voraciously pursuing capelin was described in terms bordering on awe:

[The] vast surface [of Conception Bay] is completely covered with myriads of fishes . . . all actively engaged either in pursuing or in avoiding each other; the whales alternatively rising and plunging . . . ; the cod-fish bounding above the waves, and reflecting the light of the moon from their silvery surface; the capelins hurrying away in immense shoals to seek refuge on the shore, where each retiring wave leaves countless multitudes skipping up in the sand. [Anspach 1819: 354–5]

For two weeks or so, at the end of one year or the start of the next, the harp seals race down with the Labrador Current, as they once did by the hundreds of thousands, so close to the shore along the northeast coast and in the narrow channel that separates Newfoundland from Labrador that they can be caught with shore-anchored nets. Two months later – at the end of February or in early March, long before the capelin arrive in the bays – the seals swim back north to whelp on the pack ice that holds, with the winds and the current, against the northern coasts of Newfoundland until May at least. By the time the fishing boats could arrive from England the seals were mostly dispersed, but the winter residents could walk out on the pack ice to hunt the white-coat pups.

Since the 1500s, and perhaps a century before, Europeans of the Atlantic coast have been chasing fish, seals, lobster, and whales on the banks and along the coasts of Newfoundland, but focusing so intensely on codfish (whose flesh, low in fat, preserves best of all in salt) that in and around Newfoundland the word "fish" means "codfish." The Portuguese, who still came to the banks in sailing ships in the mid twentieth century, as they had done for three centuries, called Newfoundland *Terra Baccalau* – the land of the cod – an accurate, if unintended description of the long-standing restrictions the British tried to enforce on the use of the land.

By the mid 1500s English, French, Portuguese, Basque, and some Spanish and Dutch fishermen were coming out to fish the ocean banks and shores, leaving Europe in the spring, as the North Atlantic ice floes became less dangerous, and returning home in the fall, hopefully before the storms and fogs set in.

Cod can be preserved in salt in one of two basic ways. Caught out on the ocean banks, where it would rot before being landed, it was split, gutted, and stacked in alternation with thick layers of salt, or it was pickled in heavily salted brine. Such methods use a lot of salt and not much labor.

The English, lacking access to inexpensive salt, left the bank fishery mostly to the French and Portuguese and concentrated an increasing proportion of their effort upon the inshore fishery. Early each spring, as soon as they thought they could make it through the ice and storms (or even a bit sooner, for there were substantial locational rewards for being among the first to arrive), the great merchant houses in the West Country of England – particularly in Poole and the Devonshire ports – would send out boats to the Newfoundland bays. After stopping in southeast Ireland to pick up additional fishing servants and inexpensive food supplies, they would race to Newfoundland, pounding ice off the rigging as they went (Head 1976: chap. 1), for the first boat in any harbor each season could pick its spot to set up its fishing "rooms." Its captain became the "admiral" of the harbor for the season, hearing and judging cases – mostly petty cases, but also those affecting the labor terms and discipline of the "fishing servants" in the harbor (his own and others) and the rights of fishing boats against "trespass" (McLintock 1940: 52–5).

The sort of boat capable of crossing the North Atlantic was too large and too cumbersome around the rocky coasts to use for fishing. By the mid 1600s the fishing boats that came from England were, in fact, passenger, equipment, supply, and freight boats rather than craft from which much fishing was done. They carried dories and gear to Newfoundland, and often, in addition, they brought men who ran small, seasonal fishing establishments – "planters," who stayed in Newfoundland for several years, or "bye-boat keepers," who came out for the season with their own boats and gear and who hired labor. Always the "fishing" ships that came from England brought servants who signed on for the season, to work as they were told in return for a season's wage, fixed in advance regardless of the catch – a condition that generated, as we shall see, extraordinary tensions.

The first few weeks in Newfoundland would necessarily be spent constructing the equipment for the ship's room – a pier for offloading fish, with a shed on or near it for storing salt and fishing supplies, and space for heading, splitting, and gutting the cod as they were landed. The pier and the shed, together, were called the "stage." Additionally, a ship's room needed a place to spread large quantities of fish to dry. Where there was not sufficient shingle (pebble beach) for this, large racks of close-set poles, called "flakes," had to be built to spread the fish on.

In addition to the stages and flakes, crews needed cookhouses, places to sleep, and so forth. When all this was constructed, or repaired from prior years, the tasks were divided, some men going out to fish from small boats, others – men and increasingly some women – staying ashore to split, salt, turn, wash, resalt, stack, and restack the fish, allowing it to dry in the cool summer sun and shielding it from the rotting effects of rain and dew. This process, called "making the fish," took at least as much skill and about

14

the same amount of labor as fishing itself, but it used comparatively little salt.

Despite a very long coastline for its size – six thousand miles of shores around an island not quite three hundred miles wide and somewhat less than that at its longest northern extension – good shoreline is quite scarce in Newfoundland. Good shoreline: places that are not too steep to get to the boats; that are not so strewn with "sunkers" (submerged or half-submerged rocks) as to be extremely dangerous; that are protected from the full pounding of storms and ice, having enough level land to build shelters and, later, houses, and to dry thousands of fish; and, above all other considerations, that are near enough to the fish – which cluster, rather than disperse evenly along the coast – to make it possible to row out to the fish, fish all day long, and row back with a loaded boat.

The boats that came out each season from England thus raced to seize favorable spots, and coming back year after year to the same places, they soon denuded the surrounding woods of the timber necessary for building and for fuel. It would have made sense to stay in Newfoundland, at least for several years at a time, if not to settle then at least to maintain possession of a fishing locale, to preserve the structures necessary for fishing, and to minimize the time spent for construction each spring before the fishing could begin.

In the eighteenth century, ship captains increasingly left a few servants to "winter over" for just these purposes. Some planters set up their own establishments for fishing, furring, and sealing, retaining a few servants year-round and hiring more each summer season through the captains or merchant houses that provided supplies and took fish and pelts. But settlement in Newfoundland, particularly by servants or former servants who sought to establish their own fishing communities, was fairly rigorously, if increasingly ineffectively, suppressed at least until the third quarter of the eighteenth century; the property claims of the settlers were not fully legal until 1824.

There were several reasons why the British government, in partial, but at times antagonistic alliance with the West Country fish merchants, sought to suppress settlement – to the point of tearing down settler's stages and flakes, occasionally burning their houses, and less episodically but more systematically, denying them title to land or even civil (as opposed to naval) government. First, it was felt that full-time settlers would interfere with the seasonal, migratory inshore fishery by taking up the best rooms, by depleting the timber even further for fuel, for building, and as a consequence of clearing land for agriculture, and by catching fish that, instead of being sold in the Mediterranean countries to the advantage of English merchants and England's coffers, might be traded to New England skippers, or carried by Newfoundlanders to the Caribbean.

Second, Britain wished to protect not just its mercantile interests but its supply of trained sailors for the British navy. The difficult and dangerous waters of the Newfoundland fishery were regarded as the best of all naval training grounds – a "nursery for seaman," in the phrase familiar to all students of this particular colonial history. Throughout the eighteenth century British naval ships lay in wait off the coast of England to press-gang fishermen returning home, and England passed and stiffened laws requiring one-fifth of each fishing boat's crew to be "green" – new to the sea.

There was thus a strong impetus to jump ship in Newfoundland, and those who stayed behind at the end of the fishing season were occasionally joined by deserters from the naval ships sent out to patrol against settlement:

The commander of the [naval] ship *Hyperion* having lost, in less than two months [in 1813] thirteen men by this crime [desertion], had sought to make up his compliment by impressment. . . . But finding difficulties in the way of this, from the confessed impotence of the civil power, he laid his complaint before the Governor. He stated that there could not be less than 10,000 men in the island, in every respect eligible for His Majesty's service by sea, into which service they would inevitably find their way, if compelled to return to their homes at the expiration of the fishing season; but by staying behind, they were practically exempt from this liability. . . . The crime of desertion is practiced to a greater extent in this island than in any part of the world beside. [Pedley 1863: 285–6]

Moreover, settlers – particularly those on the northeastern shores – could do what seasonally migrant fishermen could not: hunt seals on the ice in the early spring. This gave the settlers an extra source of income, as it did also the merchant houses that, while encouraging suppression of settlement, bought pelts from the settlers.

Throughout the eighteenth century settlers struggled with the migratory fishery for place, space, and if not supremacy then sufficient order to go about the business of fishing. At the center of the struggle two figures stand out among the many participants: among the settlers the planter, and among the migrants the ship captain – or, if he be the first captain in the harbor, the "admiral."

The term planter had a variety of meanings for settlers and covered a broad range of situations. It was applied, in general, to residents of the island and to skippers of fishing boats. But primarily and more specifically it referred to a class of resident masters of small-scale fishing, furring, and sealing operations. At the bottom of this category were men who were planters because they were too poor to pay their passage out of Newfoundland and who could not be driven inland (Lounsbury 1934: 149–50). At the top were men who not only hired labor for fishing and furring but also dealt in supplies along a stretch of coast – supplies they had on credit from a merchant house in England, or later, in St. John's. Most planters were midscale in this range: They hired labor, and they and their families labored alongside their servants.

Planters were handicapped in their struggle with the migratory fishery by the higher prices they paid for provisions and labor (which kept them from under cutting prices), by their lack of power vis-à-vis the ship captains with whom they contested for rooms, and by the disorder and violence that episodically marked and continually colored this confrontation. A naval officer characterized this situation, and its implications for the fishery, in the early eighteenth century:

The masters of ships in Newfoundland generally endeavor to force their goods upon the inhabitants, especially the poorer sort, who generally pay dearest. Say they, if he makes a good voyage [i.e., if the inhabitant has a good catch for the season] we shall be all paid; and if he does not (says every one to himself) I will be quick enough to get my payment. By this means they [the captain-suppliers] have a jealous eye, the one over the other. If the fishing does not prove so good as was expected, some of these masters will fall upon them [the planters] before the fishing season is half over, take away their fish before half made; another comes and takes away his train [train-oil, i.e., cod-liver oil – a valuable part of the catch]; and many times there comes a third, who has more men than they, and takes it away from the former; he that has the most men is sure to have the greatest share. This is a common practice in Newfoundland. They never acquaint the admirals with this proceeding before they do it; neither do the admirals trouble themselves with it afterwards. But the consequence lies here; the planters' men will catch no more fish, because they have no hopes of getting any wages; and the planter is ruined, and all the rest of the creditors unpaid; who, if they had given him liberty to make his fishing-voyage, might have paid them all. The merchants of England have suffered exceedingly by this unparalleled thing, there being no precedent for it in the whole Christian world. I am fully satisfied that by this thing, and the multiplicity of liquors imported into Newfoundland yearly, the trade has suffered more than by the French plundering it so often in the late wars. [John Reeves (chief justice of Newfoundland, 1791–2) quoting Captain Taverner's Letter of Remarks, 20 March 1713–14; Reeves 1793: 77–8]

The planters, on the other side, had their strengths. During the eighteenth century they became increasingly more efficient than the migratory enterprise, and they provided essential services for this enterprise, from procuring bait, which they sold or traded to the arriving ships, to guarding and maintaining equipment left for the winter, and providing extra fish, oil, and pelts for the migratory fishery to carry back to Europe in the fall. They also had their own capacity to wreak havoc on the migratory fishery – stealing wood in the winter from stages and flakes for fuel and for their own buildings. There was also the question of their loyalty. They could, if pushed too hard, go over to the French who worked on the northwest, west, and parts of the south coast of Newfoundland and who contested possession of the coastline with England. Or they could leave the island altogether, for what came to be known as "the Boston states."

During the eighteenth century the resident population rose, if slowly, but the rapid collapse of fish prices at the end of the century led to the nearly total decline of the migrant fishery and tipped the balance in favor of the planters – a brief moment before the planters, as an emerging class, were wiped out.

At the start of the eighteenth century, the resident population of Newfoundland numbered a little more than a thousand, and comprised less than 15 percent of the summer population. By 1730 there were 3,500 residents, about one-third of the summer population. At the outbreak of the American Revolution, the residents numbered 12,000, half the summer population. Along with this increase in numbers of residents came a shift in their country of origin. In 1732, about 90 percent of the residents came from England, by midcentury the English had only a slight numerical edge over the Irish, driven from their homeland by famines and depressions (Head 1976: chap. 3; K. Matthews 1976: chaps. 10, 14; Handcock 1977; Mannion, 1977; Staveley 1977).

While the Newfoundland population rose, the migrant ships turned increasingly back to open ocean fishing on the banks, so that by the 1790s Newfoundland residents were almost entirely the primary producers in the inshore fishery.

The ending of the migrant fishery opened a double transitional period that lasted through the first three or four decades of the nineteenth century. The first transition was in the form of labor: from servants, brought in from England and Ireland or hired locally, to families, resident in Newfoundland, who organized their own work processes, owned their equipment, and sold their fish, not their labor. The second transition was in the form of payment, from a cash wage for the season that was specified in the servants' indentures or contracts, to a "truck" form of payment – a cashless barter of fish for shop goods – that was organized in such a manner as to raise questions about just whose fish the fisher families "sold" to the merchants. To explain how the truck form of payment was organized we must first say a few words about the problems it was designed to solve – that is, what was wrong with prior forms of payment (from the perspective of those who made the payments).

The fishery varied markedly from year to year, both in quantity caught and price received in Europe. Except for a few variables that effected prices – they rose during wartime and fell afterward – the variation in return at the end of the season was impossible to predict at the beginning. Catches could rise or fall by several magnitudes islandwide, regionwide, (i.e., from one large bay to the next), or locally, so that a fine season in one place might be a disaster a short distance away. In such circumstances fixed wages presented a number of problems for those who paid them. They were, to begin with, never sure that enough fish would be caught to cover the cost of their wages to their servants and the supplies used during the season. Fishing servants are not easy to supervise, particularly if a master operates more than one boat and the boats disperse each day. It was thus difficult in a good year to keep servants hard at work for the remainder of the season after they had caught enough fish to cover their wages. Paying the servants in shares of the catch, which had the advantages of ensuring effort and of spreading out the impact of a bad season, was tried and abandoned twice in the eighteenth century – at the beginning and near the end. Whatever its advantages, it had the marked disadvantage, for the planters and masters, of sharing too much of the rewards for a good year.

Although it was difficult or impossible to acquire sufficient labor in England unless fixed wages or shares were paid, Newfoundland residents had fewer options. Truck, the predominant form of payment in the Newfoundland fishery from the mid 1840s until World War II, imposed terms of trade on the fisher families that at least on the surface worked to the merchant's advantage in almost every circumstance. But truck created intense problems for the maintenance of government in Newfoundland, and it left the fisher families the power to "trespass" upon, and at times to bankrupt, the merchant, if not to negotiate with him.

In broad outline the truck system – payment in goods, not money – was based on a series of transactions that lasted at least one season and often more. In the spring a merchant advanced both production and consumption supplies to the fisher families with whom he dealt. These were usually basic supplies, in two senses: There were few frills, and they were essential. Salt, twine, nails, boots, jackets, flour, salt meat, tea, and lard: Such were the predominant goods. No price was put on these goods at the time they were advanced, but in return for the goods the fishermen, on behalf of their families, agreed to give the merchant the whole of their salt-cured catch in the fall – minus what could be fiddled away on the sly to a passing New England schooner – without any price being set for the fish the merchant would take in the fall.The uncaught fish became the property of the merchant at the beginning of the season when the merchant gave supplies; anyone else taking the fish was committing the criminal act of trespass. In August the merchant firms, meeting in St. John's, "broke the price" – established the general parameters of the prices they would pay for different grades of codfish and the "train oil," and the prices they would bill for the supplies advanced.

By controlling the prices for both supplies and fish, and by waiting until they had some idea how the season was going before they set these prices, merchants could control, within limits, how much of the rewards for a season's work went to the community of fisher families with which they dealt and how much they would retain for themselves. The prices were not adjusted family by family but prevailed throughout the community, although they varied somewhat from place to place and merchant to merchant.

The people in each fisher family, after turning over their catch to the merchant, balanced their account. If there was any surplus in their favor – if they turned over more value of fish in the fall than the cost of the supplies they took – they were paid this balance not in cash but in "winter supply." If there was no surplus or if there was a shortfall on their part, they could only hope that the merchant would "carry them on the books" until the next season and advance winter supply on credit. If he did not, they could be in serious danger of starvation unless they had traded some of their catch to a passing ship for a barrel or two of flour and salt pork – and had run, in so doing, the risk of being cut off if caught.

Until twentieth-century mining and lumbering operations, the interior of Newfoundland was almost entirely empty of permanent settlement. The basic pattern of settlement in Newfoundland can still be seen, although its outlines were sharper two decades ago. In the 1961 census (the last before the forced or assisted relocation of hundreds of communities began), there were about 1,000 communities in Newfoundland. Of these, 970 had fewer than 500 people; 800 had fewer than 300. Almost all were coastal, and during the nineteenth century more than nine-tenths of the labor force in these communities was engaged in the fishery. By 1933 the inshore fishery, prosecuted by families, still landed three-fourths of the total catch (Story 1969: 32).

Roads came only very recently to most of Newfoundland; on long stretches of the south coast they have not yet appeared. Apart from the region of the Avalon Peninsula around the capital city, St. John's, a few of the more populous regions of the northeast coast, and a portion of the west coast, there were no roads of any length between communities until after 1949, when Newfoundland abandoned its independence and confederated with Canada. For most of the small communities – called outports – access was only by sea, by sled in winter, and by the paths to nearby outports.

The outport fishery can be characterized by four descriptive terms: inshore, family, merchant, and village. It was primarily an inshore fishery – as opposed to fishing on the more distant and dangerous "middle grounds" or the ocean banks. The continual impoverishment of the fisher families, the fact that they built and owned their boats and nets, and the need to land the fish relatively fresh for it to be salt cured kept the range of operations to small-scale, close-by, one-day trips.

Here we might note that ecological anthropology, explaining social organization in terms of environmental factors, slights the basic point that social organization delineates – and defines – the environment from which appropriation can take place. There is a related form of Newfoundland history that argues that Newfoundland was always overpopulated, and increasingly so as the nineteenth century progressed. Whether this history is done by people that otherwise have much to contribute (e.g., Alexander), or by people with little grasp of Newfoundland history (e.g., Copes), this explanation is developed in the same manner: Every x number of years, say every five years, one takes the average catch for that period and divides it by the total population. As the per capita catch declines over time, this means that increasingly there are too many people. No one who does this kind of analysis then asks why it made sense for fishing boats to come to Newfoundland, in the mid twentieth century, from as far as Japan and the Soviet Union. Rather, the size of the catch Newfoundlanders caught is considered God-given; if it declines on a per capita basis, this does not measure forced impoverishment or exploitation or constrained development, or even the strength of community-based styles of fishing (all of which kept the Newfoundland boats small), or any factors that would be critical of the merchant classes or government policy, but rather too many people. Per contra, when I first started doing fieldwork in Newfoundland, in 1972, Newfoundland fisher families were getting two and a half cents a pound for codfish, headed and gutted; Norwegian fishermen were getting, in the same year, that price for the heads and the guts for mink fodder, and seven and a half cents a pound for the fish – and used a portion of the money to acquire better boats, and to equip them far better, than could Newfoundland fisher families. Newfoundland was overdominated, not overpopulated.

In any case, the fishery in Newfoundland was first an inshore fishery. It was also a family fishery, from the early nineteenth to the mid twentieth century, in that the family provided the fundamental organization of the work process: Male kinsmen crewed the boats; women, kin to these men, were the core of the"shore crowd" that "made" the fish cure. The village was the social unit from which the boat crews and shore crowds were drawn, and redrawn – reorganized – each season; the unit both of support and of competition between and among fisher families. The merchant – usually one to a village – organized and dominated the connections between the village fishery and the field of larger forces that took a part in, and of, the fishery.

The collapse of markets and prices in the Great Depression; the availability of wage labor at the large-scale construction projects during World War II; the opening of a market for frozen fish; the appearance of deep-sea trawlers, from a number of countries, that were so efficient they affected the inshore fishing stocks; the commitment of the Newfoundland provincial and Canadian federal governments to "forced growth" in the industrial sector and the abandonment of small-scale "old-fashioned" enterprise; and the emergence of opportunities to earn a more decent living, opportunities for the most part more apparent than real – all these together spelled the demise of the village fishery. It still persists, in a small way, far more for landing fresh fish for the freezing plants than for salt curing. The remains of the Newfoundland-based fishery are now centered in large-scale commercial ventures that hire labor for trawlers and plants.

II

In the first of a series of articles on Newfoundland (Sider 1976), I divided the Newfoundland fishery into three general periods. Named by the dominant form of labor, these were the servant fishery, from the seventeenth to the nineteenth century, the family fishery, from the early nineteenth century to World War II, and the factory fishery since. Although I still follow this basic periodization, my focus has changed from a *stage* model that emphasized a sequence of forms to a search for the underlying logic of Newfoundland social and cultural history, as this logic can be seen in a series of processes, and in the transformations between different kinds of processes. By "logic" I mean how things fit together, or do not, in ways that make for motion and change. This logic can be found in the irresolvable tensions, contradictions, and disjunctions of Newfoundland social organization and culture – and in why they are, or were, irresolvable.

In the servant fishery the two most significant irresolvable issues were the impossibility of disciplining the labor force and the destructive tensions between the migratory fishery and the settlers. Each of these conflicts encapsulated and expressed a far broader range of problems, and in each case the solutions attempted often set in motion a broader range of events.

The family fishery raised a further pair of irresolvable tensions that can be code-named *winter supply* and *capital formation*. On the surface, each of these was a simple confrontation with no winners. The struggle over winter supply took place first between the merchant and the fisher families – whether or not the merchant would give credit for a winter's goods – and simultaneously became a struggle between merchants and the government over who would feed the destitute, who were always a substantial portion of the active laboring population: not an underclass addition to this working population but a proper part of it.

The truck system, the dominant form of payment in the family fishery, inhibited and under certain circumstances prevented capital formation in the outports. This in fact may have been one of its most significant effects, for by suppressing capital formation it also prevented local alternatives to merchant domination from emerging. Fisher families, taking up their return in shop goods and production supplies, were severely limited in the acquisition of capital. Nor could the merchant invest his profits in his community, beyond building up his premises and extending his range of operations, without altering the structure of the fishery, which depended on people having only very few alternatives to fishing. The available economic activities, such as logging in the winter or sealing in the spring, were complementary to, rather than in competition with, the summer fishery.

The truck system, severely reducing the amount of cash in circulation in the outports, and just as significantly in its effects inhibiting the formation of capital by outport fisher families, was a major factor creating the "traditionalism" of Newfoundland outports. This traditionalism, which for villagers and for outsiders was both an appearance and in some ways a reality, was a characteristic (and indeed almost a definitional) feature of Newfoundland outports. The phrase, for example, "the traditional village (or family) fishery" is so often used that the words seem woven together. By way of introducing a number of related issues, it will be useful to look briefly at several factors, in addition to the truck form of payment, that lie behind this traditionalism. It will also help orient us within a complex array of issues to briefly introduce some of the irreducible tensions that lie, half hidden, within the social worlds and social processes pointed to by the concept of tradition. The focus will be on the particularities of Newfoundland; a brief and highly schematic comparison with similar issues in so-called peasant and tribal societies elsewhere provides a suggestive interpretive context.

One major part of the foundation of the traditional village fishery was the use of small boats, with handmade nets and traps, and hand-built shore facilities for equipment and for drying the fish. This small-scale technology was primarily imposed by the impoverishment of the village fisher families. To some extent, at least at some times and places, it may have been chosen as a way of resisting the longer trips away from home required by larger boats fishing further offshore, and as a way of resisting the emergence of differentiation within villages based on boat owners versus laborers (e.g., Stiles 1973). Associated with this small-scale technology is an organization of the work process within families and villages in a manner that emphasizes the kin connections of those whose work centers on catching and curing each boat's fish. Families organized the assembly of labor for the work process and the work process itself, and as we shall examine in some detail subsequently, the village was the locale for organizing the *reproduction* of the work process over time.

Control over the reproduction of the work process in fact is a key point in the maintenance of village-based social institutions and cultural practices. In some forms of merchant capital, such as the "putting-out" system of textile production in Western Europe in the eighteenth and nineteenth centuries, merchants controlled a very great deal of the work process itself, although the actual work took place in people's own houses and fields. Merchant control came through their dividing the work between increasingly specialized workers, delivering the particular goods to be worked on, and picking up the partly completed product for transfer to other workers. Even in such circumstances, while villages and families still *reproduced* the social relations of working and a substantial amount of the material preconditions for working, the village as a social unit maintained a certain autonomy, important even if partial, and the social and cultural ties of village life remained quite significant in shaping the lives of the inhabitants.

The "traditionalism" of Newfoundland outports was also, in part, an expression of a process that transferred economic and political power from the outports to the capital city, St. John's. Merchants had little room for investment in outports: They could develop their own premises – in a few market towns, rather substantially – and little else without interfering with their own fishery. None of the outports, not even the larger outport towns, had any form of municipal government whatsoever until the mid twentieth century: Political decisions and government administration took place in St. John's. Priests and ministers played occasional roles in village politics, but they were scarce in outport Newfoundland. Teachers were often very young, boarders in and strangers to the communities in which they worked. Apart from the merchant, there were few figures of power in rural Newfoundland and fewer social institutions through which political power could be expressed. Power was centralized in St. John's, berthed along the merchants' quays on one side of Water Street, and secured in the law offices, the Houses of Parliament, and the governor's mansion up the hill on the other side. The peculiar mixture of power and powerlessness that has characterized Newfoundland governments will be examined and discussed in Part Three, as will the point also at issue here: that the political powerlessness of the outports, both in a larger political field and over their own life conditions, conjoined with the autonomy of work and the centrality of kin, seems to have enhanced the sense of isolation and distance – the sense of being traditional, as opposed to modern. When Newfoundland outports were caught up in a government relocation scheme in the 1960s and 1970s, one of the major appeals to the people was to become "modern," to "give the children a chance" by moving into the twentieth century – a peculiar appeal to make to people so devastated by the depressions and wars of the twentieth century, and an appeal perhaps primarily effective among people who felt some substantial helplessness or powerlessness in their sense of distance from what has become socially significant.

The political powerlessness of the outports, though an important aspect of outport life, has been far from total. In the nineteenth century there were a number of major electoral riots in the villages, important enough to effect government; in the early twentieth century the fishermen's cooperative and union movement had a major impact; and outports cast the decisive vote for Confederation with Canada after World War II. But despite such episodes, political control remained external to the outports, and the social basis for the development of village political institutions was constantly undermined.

Twice in the nineteenth century an emerging outport "middle class" was broken and brought back within the ranks of common fisherfolk. At the outset the planters – especially the middlemen dealers in the fish trade – were wiped out by the large English and Jersey Isle merchant houses that began dealing with the resident families, turning them away from the migratory ship captains who supplied planters and servants. Although a few planters themselves became merchants in this transitional period, most did not. In the midst of the nineteenth century there was a brief flourish of village economic activity; on the northeast coast this was based on a schooner fishery that pursued seals in the spring and went to "the Labrador" for the summer cod fishery – in locally built boats, with local labor and local owners. Along the south coast, a bank fishery emerged, again expressing local enterprise.

During the last third of the nineteenth century all this locally based economic activity, which provided an alternative to fishing for the merchant, collapsed. Judge Prowse blamed "politics and steam" for the transfer of such larger-scale enterprise from the village outports and outport towns to St. John's (1895: chap. 16). Steam sealing boats did indeed play a major role, but neither these, nor the subsequent decline of the seal herds and cod stocks, can fully account for the destruction of this emerging outport capital formation. During this same period the large and powerful English and Jersey Isle merchant firms that had dominated coastal Newfoundland for more than a century also completely collapsed. Their place was taken by locally resident merchants whose success lay in exercising a much tighter control over the village fishery. "The business under one's own supervision is hazardous enough nowadays without leaving it to servants," Thomas Job wrote in 1864 (servants here meaning agents; Ryan 1971: 95, 83–97). This control structured within itself the transfer of capital formation from the outports to St. John's; simultaneously the outport merchant firms looked increasingly to the government to maintain the fishery from year to year by subsidizing the fisher families during the winter.

The continual reduction of internal differentiation in the outports – that is, the inhibiting of class formation – kept kinship and village institutions crucial both to mobilizing labor and, in general terms, to organizing daily life: These forms of social organization were seemingly more "traditional" than using cash wages and money payments to mediate and organize social and working relations. Even when money payments were made within the village – for example, for assistance from a craftsman skilled in boat repairs – these payments were subsumed within other social relations (Chiaramonte 1970).

But shifting the responsibility for winter supply to the government (a major expense along with the routine responsibilities of "modern" governments – roads, schools, hospitals, postal services, and so forth) created expenditure requirements that the government simply could not afford without developing an alternative economic base. The merchants had sufficient power in government to keep this from happening effectively enough to threaten their labor supply.

The outcome was an extremely brittle government, whose monopolization of the island's political processes barely sufficed to conceal its fragility. After a long series of governmental crises, during one of which the prime minister seconded the motion of no confidence in his own government, and after failing to sell a substantial part of its land (Labrador) to another government (Quebec), the Newfoundland parliament in 1934 voluntarily renounced its status as an independent dominion and asked Great Britain to take it back and directly administer it as a colony. In 1948, in a series of two bitter elections, the populace narrowly rejected continuing as a colony or returning to independence, choosing in the second election to confederate with Canada.

III

"Tradition" is a complex word in the English language. It has a range of meanings that share the notion of direct contact between people – something handed down or handed over. The primary meaning of tradition has come to be cultural; it usually refers to customary practices "handed down" from parent to child or, as it is often put, "from father to son." This was one sense of the term from the late fourteenth century in England onward. By the fifteenth century there was also a passive sense, "the trewe tradicion" (Raymond Williams 1976: 268–9, to which this discussion of the term is much indebted; see also the Oxford English Dictionary). But tradition also has had, particularly from the fifteenth through the seventeenth centuries, another meaning, more closely tied to the Latin meaning of handing *over*; that is, of surrender, betrayal.

There are, I think, important ways and specific contexts in which the two senses of the term come together. This conjunction of meanings can alert us to the antagonisms between generations – the demands of the present upon the past, of the future upon the present – demands exacerbated by the generally relatively worsening economic and political situation of the social units deemed traditional.

26

Particularity and relevance of Newfoundland

But there is another more historically and contextually specific way in which the societies that have been deemed traditional come to embed loss – surrender and betrayal – in the very act of *preserving* (and creating, developing, and expressing) their own traditions. This is rooted in the fact that most of these locally based societies, be they "peasant" or "tribal," exist in the context of domination. The very cultures that express their own ways, that provide their own meanings, and that delineate their own social relations are also, and simultaneously, relatively helpless, except perhaps episodically, against the forces of domination. The autonomy of village culture, like the autonomy of village social relations, is partial: partial in the sense of incomplete, and partial in the sense of "taking a part" – a side – that whether in opposition to or in collusion with the forces of domination cannot be wholly effective.

The fisherfolk of Newfoundland, neither peasants nor tribespeople, reveal key aspects of how such social forms are integrated into, shaped by, and participate in shaping larger social and economic processes. Particularly in the context of merchant capitalism, Newfoundland fisher families present thought-provoking similarities to tribal peoples on the one hand, and to a "classic" peasantry on the other. But there are some unique twists in the way fisherfolk are integrated into larger social systems, which reveal otherwise more hidden features of the processes of dominating tribal peoples and peasants, and extracting wealth from them. Moreover, by presenting an example of capital formation without an agrarian base, it becomes possible to see an agrarian base as a special case of capital formation (even though nearly universal). And by contrasting this special case with another – capital formation in a fishing society, with a "common-property, open-access" resource base – it will be possible to make some more general points about capital formation. The relevance of Newfoundland, in simple terms, is that it is a very special and unusual manifestation of a much broader set of social situations and historical processes.

For the century or more that the village fishery predominated (approximately 1830–1960), Newfoundland fisher families, like North American tribespeople producing fur or deerskins in a colonial context, sold the product of their labor, not their labor itself. They were constrained to produce a very specific salable commodity (for Newfoundlanders this was "light-salted, hard-dried" codfish) in as large a quantity as possible. Such constraints were twofold: the specific and focused suppression of viable alternatives to producing one or a very few specific commodities, which defined what they would do, and the severe disadvantages that they suffered in the terms of trade for supplies that became necessities, which defined how hard they would do it.

The domination that fisher families encountered was so severe that it permeated all other aspects of their social life. It shaped the outlines of their economic activity, keeping them poor and their equipment small-scale, and thus limiting the size of the potential catch. Moreover, the specific forms that domination took introduced specific competitive tensions within villages and families that played a key role in the shaping of family life and village culture. Yet for all the constraints and pressures that pervaded and shaped much of their social life, fisher families controlled their own social relations of work, built and owned their productive equipment, and wove the various threads of this self-determination within the fabric of their social life, alongside and crossing the strands of imposed poverty and need. The domination that outport people faced occurred at the point of exchange, not production, and thus despite its severity the fishing villages retained a certain autonomy, partial but crucial.

The autonomy of the fishing villages was rooted in their resource base. The sea is a common-property, open-access resource: It could not be taxed, enclosed, or alienated. This created major problems for the Newfoundland government by removing one of the usual revenue bases of western states. Furthermore, the common-property resource base created a situation where the upper classes could not get access to labor within the village through the mediation of property. Enclosure may have been crucial to the creation of both a rural and an urban labor force in England, as artificially high-priced land sales (based on manipulation of Indian land possession; e.g., Rogin 1975: chap. 4) were in continental North America, but no such devices as enclosure or foreclosure for individuating villagers and reaggregating them as a mass of workers were possible in Newfoundland. The common-property resource base, in sum and to begin, was part of the collective defense of the village against economic and political domination. But more is at stake in such forms of property than a defensive and insular potential.

Economists who discuss fisheries (including the seal hunt) as the pursuit of both a common-property and an open-access resource usually assume that the form of the resource is defined in nature, not by social relations. They assume that it is open-access and common-property because of the absence of titles and fences, and they argue that comparative advantage goes to the one who exploits the resource the fastest and most efficiently (e.g., Gordon 1954). In this view, the resource is open to all comers, so the one who takes the most the quickest gets what is to be gotten and leaves the others behind. Everyone must use this strategy, for anyone can. Economists have come to use this model to demonstrate the production of individualistic and competitive behavior, ruthless to the point of destroying the resource. This perspective may be adequate, even useful, for economics, but for a historical anthropology it conceals the most crucial fact of such resources and forms of property: They are resources (fish, seals, beaver, deer, ivory, etc.) and forms of property (territory) for which

28

membership in a community or collectivity is the precondition for access, and for which the capabilities of the community or collectivity (including the equipment, skills, organizational potential, and political power of those who have, or want, access) delineates what can be done with and to the resource.

Thus in Newfoundland fisher families had access to the sea on the one hand through a series of credit arrangements with merchants, including all that had to be done to make sure that fisher families *continually* needed merchant credit to get access to the sea. On the other hand, fishing required participation in a community in which were the skills to build and repair boats and nets, knowledge of the location of the fishing grounds and the process of the cure, the capacity and intent to cooperate in, or bitterly compete for, access to the grounds, and a willingness to come to each other's aid for some kinds of distress (but not, by far, all kinds). Most of all, the community continually reassembled, from families of changing composition and fortunes, the working groups that engaged in the fishery: units that were family based but rarely contained all or only the "eligible" members of one household.

This is the primary meaning of the assertion that the autonomy of the fishing villages lay in their resource base. By "resource base" I refer not primarily to the sea or to fish but rather to the social relations that provide access to the sea and bring the fish within the community. It is in this perspective that we may start to see some analogs between Newfoundland fisherfolk and tribal people with lineage, clan, or village lands.

Newfoundland fisherfolk were, in important ways, like Native American tribespeople in the fur or deerskin trade. Both sold the product of their labor, not their labor itself; both were dominated at the point of exchange, not production, and although constrained to produce a specific commodity in as large a quantity as possible within the limits of the continuing structure of domination, both controlled not only the social relations of work but the reproduction, over time, of these relations. And both formed, in the midst of a domination that was powerful enough to profoundly affect community social structure, communities that could define and incorporate a resource base and provide access both to the resources on the one hand and to the structures of exchange and domination on the other.

But tribal people in a colonial or colonized context are often marked – the word is chosen carefully – by a profound cultural difference between themselves and the dominant society; more precisely, by a cultural distinctiveness that is regarded as profound, particularly by their conquerors. This cultural distinctiveness is ordinarily assumed to be simply derived from an aboriginal precontact past. But there is far more to the *duration* of this distinctiveness in the colonial context than its precontact origins.

Moreover, much of the distinctiveness of "tribal" peoples is a creation of postcontact processes of incorporation and resistance, not precontact at all. (On the construction of divergence in the colonial context, see Sider 1986.)

This distinctiveness is an immensely complex topic, worth an entire book itself. Here it is necessary to illustrate and explore only one relevant dimension.

Native North Americans taught the Europeans to grow both tobacco and corn (maize), but it was unthinkable to allow them to participate in the rapidly expanding production of tobacco for export, or to become commercial maize growers for a domestic food market. Indians were only allowed to become commercial producers of *diminishing* resources – resources that declined, usually rapidly, from the onset of commercial production in any specific area. They could sell deerskins and beaver pelts, they could sell their bodies as soldiers, and they could sell their land. Once Indians became producers of diminishing resources it was relatively safe for the colonists to allow autonomous Indian cultures to develop and flourish – far safer than it would have been had the Indians been growing tobacco or corn for the market – for as the resources diminished and shifted westward, so too, it was thought, would the people and their ways of life.

The whole process of conquest and consolidation both elaborated and insisted upon the cultural differences between native and conqueror, and at the same time sought to destroy these distinctive native ways. The autonomy of native culture, far from being a simple derivative of the past, was an active reagent formed in the colonial crucible: simultaneously a justification for domination and a framework for incorporation (the ways that native people were *seen* as different from Europeans was part of how they would be used). In addition, it was a form of, and a framework for, native resistance to and collaboration with domination.

Peasants serve their overlords "according to custom" (Hilton 1975: 21); tribespeople serve precisely because their customs are different. In both cases, custom can become an arena of confrontation, but the structure of these confrontations will be profoundly different. For both peasants and tribespeople, custom can also construct a framework of collaboration; for both again, the structure of this collaboration will be profoundly different.

The classes – or "elites" – that dominate a peasantry are, or present themselves as being, both from the "same" culture as the peasants and from the elite center of this culture. The elites are thus supposed to politically, culturally, and economically serve the interests of the peasantry, as the peasants are supposed to serve the elites'; or both together are to serve some higher cause: "We know," wrote John Gower in the fourteenth century, "that there are three estates in which everyone in the world serves according to custom" (Hilton 1975: 21). On the other hand, the elites that

30

tribal people serve are utterly alien; the missionizing pretense does not offer to alter this fundamental incompatibility but to abandon it. Tribal people are offered the possibility of transforming or abandoning their culture to conform to their conquerors', which they cannot do and remain as a collectivity. Peasants are of course not made the same offer: Being more individualized, some might well accept.

This situation, in which tribespeople but not peasants are offered an opportunity to adopt the dominator's culture – even if the offer is fraudulent, and even if the offer is restricted to religion, basic styles of dress, and so forth – creates a major difference between tribespeople and peasants. Peasants, not being offered the elite culture (because they might accept the offer; or because there is nothing to offer, for peasant culture is supposedly both fundamentally the same as, and profoundly different from, the culture of their elites) – peasants, being excluded from and included in elite culture, can use their own folk culture to express confrontational claims upon their dominators, which tribespeople cannot do. Tribespeople can rise up, they can withdraw, they can develop their own cultural and social transformations of the domination that confronts them, and more – but they ordinarily cannot make influential or effective culturally rooted appeals to their colonizers – such as is done by peasants in the context of a "moral economy," or "just-price" uprisings. Newfoundland fisherfolk, in the nineteenth century, went back and forth between these two polarities.

The point here is not to force a simplistic distinction between peasants and tribespeople – that peasants could use their culture against their dominators and tribespeople could not (at least not during the colonial period). This is only a schematic suggestion to introduce a perspective, not an analytical model. It *is* important to realize that any cultural differences between peasants and tribespeople ought to be found not so much in the content of culture, and in how strange this content appears to us, but in the structure of culture – the way it participates in large-scale historical processes. The point here is, more usefully, to call forth for examination the different ways that folk culture enters into struggles over domination, is shunted aside, and returns to the fray in different forms.

When fishing boats first came from Europe to Newfoundland, the cod were so thick in the waters that boats were slowed in their passage and men could fish with weighted buckets – or so legend has it. There were, in any case, such enormous numbers of fish that the stock was not perceived as a diminishing resource. Fish might be cyclically abundant or absent in any particular place or year, but it seems to have been well through the eighteenth century and perhaps into the nineteenth before it began to become clear that fishermen could decimate not just a small harbor but the fish

31

stock itself. By the time that was realized, the native Beothuk Indians had been almost entirely, and purposely, exterminated.

I suggest that it was precisely the perceived nondiminishable nature of the resource that provided a major impetus for the Europeans to exterminate the Beothuks, rather than seeking to use them to procure the resource. Managing a fundamentally different people (or a people perceived as fundamentally different) who control a nondiminishing resource may well have been impossible.

The conjunction proposed here is admittedly speculative. The Beothuks had been fishing themselves, from oceangoing canoes, but no attempt was made to purchase fish from them. The Beothuks were hunted like deer, chased, and shot. West Country English and Irish servants, almost entirely without prior fishing experience, were brought in to do the work.

Whether it was regarded as unsafe, or even unthinkable, to allow native people to produce from a nondiminishing resource; whether the relevant and important experience that the English and Irish had was not fishing but serving – whatever the process was in the servant fishery, the customs and the culture of the fisherfolk became a key issue in the struggles to discipline their labor and to drive down the claims that they made for a portion of their product.

It was *not* in the context of this struggle to create and manage a *servant* labor force that the "traditional" and distinctive Newfoundland folk culture was born. Rather, it was after the servant fishery had collapsed, and the village and family-based fishery had developed, that Newfoundland folk culture became increasingly distant and distinct from the dominant cultural forms. In some ways Newfoundlanders, having killed the Indians – the "other" – became them, at least temporarily. In more enduring ways, Newfoundlanders became and remained like peasants confronting their masters in the domain of culture, but in confrontations in which it became increasingly clear – except for a moment or two – that the fisherfolk would lose.

Although it often seemed clear in Newfoundland who would and did lose, it was not equally clear who – or what – won. On the surface, this is the issue of the fragility of the Newfoundland state: Why the state, with no serious opposition from the "peasantry," and with no major sectoral battles within a divided elite, could not govern either very long or very effectively. Below the surface this turns out to be an issue of the role of the state in capital formation: a question both of the centrality of capital formation for the continuity of certain forms of state power and of the impossibility of substantial capital formation in Newfoundland. By capital formation is meant not the development of factories, industry, mines, and so forth. Rather, as capital is ultimately a relationship between owners and wage workers, what is at stake in Newfoundland in the context of capital formation is the formation of certain kinds of "modern" social relations. Why it was impossible to develop these relations in Newfoundland, and what that meant for the strength and continuity of state power, is altogether a different set of questions about "development" than why no factories moved to Newfoundland or, more recently, why all the ones that did failed so decisively.

The roots of this process of continually failing capital formation, as of all other processes introduced in this chapter, are to be found in the context of merchant capital. A brief chapter introducing and clarifying some general features of merchant capital is now necessary before proceeding to Newfoundland.

3

Autonomy and the harness

The logic of merchant capital

Merchant capitalism is probably the most pervasive and widespread context within which anthropology has found its classic and central examples. The "tribal," peasant, and semiproletarianized hinterland peoples who provide the great bulk of the ethnographic case studies by and large exist within – and in important ways are often the creation of – merchant capital. Using such conceptual perspectives as "acculturation," anthropologists have assumed there were certain general features or processes that marked the integration of hinterland societies into systems of domination, extraction, and control. These perspectives assume a directionality to the process of incorporation that is characterized by "loss," imposition, and "adaptation." To see more complex processes, with less uniform directionalities, in the history of hinterland societies – processes of both loss and creation, adaptation and distancing, collusion and confrontation – requires, rather than any concept like acculturation, some clarity as to how merchant capital works.

The basic features of merchant capital, as outlined here, are clear-cut:

The purchase of commodities from communities that generate these products through forms of work organization that they themselves control and supervise.

Domination at the point of exchange, not in production. The producing communities may have their own forms of domination within production; indeed merchant capital often encourages the emergence of traditional leaders in this context, but this is a different issue.

Community control over the reproduction of the local preconditions for production, including, for example, the reassembly of work crews year after year, the replacement of productive tools, and the reallocation of clan lands or family hunting territories. Much of this control, which of course is not complete, pertains to the social entailments of maturation, marriage, death, and inheritance and perhaps also shapes the kinds of products that will be produced, the intensity of the work effort, and so forth.

Incorporation of producing communities into larger social systems in a manner that, while bringing the communities within a larger and dominant social system, simultaneously emphasizes the social, cultural, and economic divergence of these communities from the centers of power and domination – either divergence within a single sociocultural system, as with peasants, or a more totalizing divergence, as with tribal peoples.

Taken by themselves, these basic features of merchant capital seem lifeless – just another list of essential characteristics. But between these different features, as they come together, there emerge fundamental and largely irresolvable tensions that are the life blood – and the bile – of merchant capital in motion. The same general pattern of fundamental tensions recurs in widespread and diverse contexts among both "tribal" and "peasant" societies, and expresses some general and basic features of the connections that form between producing communities and merchant capital. Moreover, the form these tensions take shows that the connection to merchant capital is both political-economic and cultural.

Three fundamental tensions are characteristic of the producing communities of merchant capitalism:

tension between the autonomy of work processes and the imposed constraints to produce
tension between the intensification of commodity-production relations and the massive variation in output or remuneration
tension between the tightening and intensifying of the bonds of alliance (and perhaps hierarchy) within the producing communities in the context of the pressures to produce for merchant capital, and simultaneously, the hollowing out – mocking, eviscerating – of these same bonds in the context of the increasing relative powerlessness and impoverishment of the producing communities

1. Tension between autonomy and constraints. The communities that produce for merchant capital ordinarily do so, as I have noted, through forms of work organization that they control and that they continually regenerate from within the community. The labor of production, from the point of view of the community, is self-directed. Characteristically, those who direct or coordinate this labor – for example, heads of households and of kin groups, clan leaders, village elders or leaders – have positions of respect and authority within what appears as a "traditional" framework of values and social organization. Yet their power – and often their authority – is in fact new, being enmeshed in and partly generated by the services of coordination and direction they provide for merchant capital. The position of these traditional village leaders within the village is made even more ambivalent by the fact that communities that produce for merchant capital invariably do so in the context of an imposed set of constraints that more or less force them to continual production on terms, and at a pace, over which they ordinarily have had but little influence.

The forms that these constraints-to-produce take vary widely from place to place, and at different periods of time, but they are usually severe. At times it is a need for a crucial commodity – for examples, the guns that in West Africa spelled the difference between whether one would take slaves or be taken slave, or that for Native North Americans were often also the only small chance for continual survival. In other contexts the pressure could be land shortages – driving a peasantry into a putting-out system of cottage production (Kriedte, Medick, and Schlumbohm 1981). Often the pressure was simply an imposed lack of alternatives to dealing with merchant capital in order to acquire a minimum but essential cash income. In any case it is often the same "traditional leaders" who coordinate the labor of production within the community that are a major point of articulation with (for, against) the imposed constraints.

The conjoining of these two diverse processes – the collective self-direction of the work to produce commodities, and the imposed constraints to produce – has a double impact within the community. First, it can hyperdevelop, or overdevelop, "traditional" forms of leadership in the community, giving the traditional leaders a power and an authority in the context of new production demands that they never had before, and it can simultaneously undermine and mock these leaders, reducing them to servants of the external (and hostile) demands. Often this same process occurs in resisting, as well as in complying with, the imposed demands, as "traditional" leaders get new powers in mobilizing resistance and then are eviscerated by loss, or by victories that turn hollow with new forms of integration to dominant extractive demands. The second, more general, impact of these two diverse processes is that seemingly traditional folk culture, flourishing in the context of merchant-capital production, becomes increasingly embellished and elaborated, and simultaneously much less autonomous than it appears to be to both its participants and to outside observers.

2. Tension between intensification of commodity production and variation in returns. The second, and perhaps the most powerful, tension within communities that produce for merchant capital emerges between the intensification of commodity-production relations and the routine, but often massive, variation in either output of a commodity, or price paid, or both. As the conjoining of intensifying production and varying output or reward may not at first seem like directly and powerfully antithetical pressures, it will take a moment or two to draw out the underlying logic.

In Newfoundland, and in many other locales, intensification of commodity-production relations came hand in hand with, and in large part was achieved by, an imposed specificity of product demand. The products that merchant capital demands from producing communities are ordinarily exceedingly specific. In Newfoundland, for example, it was not simply fish that were wanted but almost exclusively codfish cured in a particular way (called "light-salt, hard-dried"). The pattern of purchasing only one, or a very few, specific items from each of the communities with which it dealt is so characteristic of merchant capital that we have reason to suspect that much more is involved than what economists would call "locational advantages" in the production of these commodities, or than the convenience of merchant capital's operations. It may well be that this is a key element in the domination of merchant capital over its producers, and part of the package of constraining alternatives (to commodity production) in the communities.

Be that as it may, producing communities characteristically suffer massive variation both in supply and price for the commodities that they generate. Characteristically, these two forms of variation do not cancel each other out (prices rising when commodities produced fall). In Newfoundland, for example, the fishery could fail in a particular harbor, a major bay, or even a whole region or islandwide at the same time that prices were falling drastically.

What this means is that *a community was simultaneously increasingly tightly harnessed to the demands of merchant capital, by the specificity of product demand and the social rearrangements necessary to produce this product, and periodically thrown back upon its own resources to carry itself through periods of devastatingly low returns.* Moreover, we cannot assume that the forms of social organization and culture that develop in the context of production for merchant capital are adequate or even adaptable to the task of community self-sufficiency and subsistence production. To the contrary, the social forms that express this "autonomous" potential and generate the necessary tasks may be irrelevant to, or in bitter conflict with, the social forms of merchant-capital production.

However communities dealt with this difficult situation, it was *not* by the maintenance of "traditional" social forms and values tied to subsistence production and continuing in the midst of commodity production for merchant capital. For the apparently traditional social forms not only usually emerge in the context of merchant capital; it is precisely these traditional social forms that are bent into the service of production for merchant capital (if not directly created by this service). *It may in fact be specifically the need for "subsistence," without effective social forms for producing this subsistence, that throws the producing communities most violently into the arms of the state, or into mass emigration and so forth – creating a situation where the apparently traditional social forms are largely "about" production for merchant capital, and the subsistence needs are met by integration with larger social forms and forces – that is, by social forms that we would more readily and ordinarily call "modern" or "modernizing."*

3. Tension between intensifying and mocking the bonds of alliance and hierarchy. Community-based production of commodities for merchant capital is often extremely *labor-intensive*. This term, as used here, means not just a relatively low outlay for tools and machines ("capital goods") but also, usually, very long hours, intensely hard work, and an often underrated but extraordinary amount of skill necessary for production. In all these contexts, people are pulled together, more intensely insofar as they conjoin commodity production with other social and productive tasks.

But both the characteristic poverty and the specific forms of competitiveness introduced within the community by commodity production often make people incapable of meeting the demands and expectations for relationships that their own culture imposes upon them. Folk culture can thus take on, for its own participants, a special and illusory quality – becoming seemingly part of a special, glorified past, rather than part of ordinary, daily life – a quality heightened by widespread illusions about its traditionalism: the belief that certain practices are archaic or timeless, when they are in fact no older than the first flush of integration with merchant capital. Folk culture can thus both develop as central to the organization of local production and social reproduction and yet at the same time become increasingly abstract, increasingly cut off from the satisfaction of emerging needs and social-relational demands.

PART TWO

Domination, alliances, and descent

I

In 1819 the Reverend Lewis Anspach, missionary and historian, described the process of catching and curing fish in the inshore fishery. Saying only a few words about catching, his long and detailed description of the curing process hides within it many of the profound tensions of village life in the outports then taking shape.

... about the 10th of that month [June] the codfishery begins.

The boats used for this purpose vary in their sizes and in the number of their crews; some having only two hands, and these frequently boys and girls merely old and strong enough to handle the line: this is often seen in Conception and other bays when the cod-fish is plentiful. Most boats have four men, each with one line on each side of him, and these lines have two hooks. ... Each hook is furnished with such bait as the season affords. ...

The boat having taken her station on a ledge, or other shoally ground, each line being fastened on the inside of the boat, and the hooks baited, the man sits at an equal distance from the two lines which are committed to his care, moving them from time to time: as soon as the least tightness or motion is observed in the line, it is drawn up with all possible speed, and the fish thrown into the boat. ...

Cod-fish is also taken with nets called cod seines. These are cast some distance from the shallop, the rope being suspended by buoys made for that purpose, and placed at certain intervals, about an hour before sun-set; and two or three hours before sun-rise, all hands turn out to heave or haul them in. Sometimes the glut of fish in the nets is so great that the weight sinks the buoys under water. ...

When a sufficient quantity of fish has been taken to load the boat, it is then carried to the shore in order to be cured: this must be done within a certain time, not exceeding eight and forty hours; otherwise the fish will lose of its value in proportion to the length of time it is kept without splitting.

The place where the operation of curing the cod-fish is performed is a *stage* or covered platform erected on the shore, with one end projecting over the water, which is called the *stage-head* ... ; [it] has longers fixed horizontally at intervals, like so many steps, to facilitate the ascent to the stage. On the fore part of this platform is a table, on one side of which is the *cut-throat*, who takes the fish, cuts

41

with a knife the throat down to the nape, and then pushes it to the *header* on his right hand: the latter takes it in his left hand, and with the right, draws out the liver which he throws through a hole into a cask under the table; next the guts, which he throws through the *trunk-hole* in the floor of the stage into the sea: then fixing the neck of the fish to the edge of the table, which before him is semicircular and sharp, he presses upon the neck with his left hand to which a thick piece of leather, called the *palm*, is fastened for that purpose, and, with the right, gives the body of the fish which is uppermost a violent jerk which pushes it to the *splitter* opposite to him, while the head thus separated falls through an opening into the water. That operation requires such violent exertion that, beside the precaution of the palm . . . , the seat on which he is sitting has a strong round back, which assists in collecting all his strength for the effort necessary to separate the head from the body of the fish.

The splitter then taking the fish with his left hand, cuts it with his right, beginning at the nape down by the sound-bone to the navel; and giving the knife a little turn to keep as close to the bone as possible, he continues cutting to the end of the tail; then raising the bone with the knife, he pushes the fish so split into the drudge-barrow [a barrow that is carried, not wheeled], and the sound-bone into the sea through an opening close to him in the stage-floor. When the barrow is full, it is immediately carried to the salter, and another put in its place. The process of splitting is performed with considerable rapidity, though with the utmost care, because the value of the fish depends in a material degree upon its being correctly performed. . . . The tongues and sounds are sometimes reserved either for domestic uses or for sale; in this case so many of the heads and sound-bones as may be necessary for that purpose, are thrown aside and immediately taken up by some other person, so as not to give the least interruption or hindrance to the work performing at the table.

At the opposite end of the stage stands the *salter*, who, as soon as the drudge-barrow is brought to him, takes out the fish, one by one, and placing it in layers on one side of the stage, spreads on each with his hand some salt, taking particular care to apportion its quantity to the size of the fish and the degree of thickness of its several parts; this operation, which is continued until the *bulk* is of a proper size, requires particular attention, as if the bulk is too high the pressure of the upper layers will necessarily injure the fish in the lower layers. The province of the salter demands a perfect knowledge of this business and considerable experience and judgment; for everything now depends on him for the value of the whole voyage. If there is not sufficient quantity of salt put to the fish, it will not keep: if there is too much, the place where the excess is will look dark and moist; when exposed to the sun, it will be parched up, and when put back, it will be moist again and break in the handling of it; whereas, fish properly salted, when dry, will be firm and may be handled without breaking: the defect occasioned by an excess of salt is in Newfoundland known by the name of *salt-burnt*. . . .

In some parts of Newfoundland the operation of salting is performed in vats or deep oblong square troughs, with a spigot and fauset near the bottom to draw off the foul pickle. . . . The fish must remain four days in vats, and five or six days in bulk, before it has sufficiently taken the salt; and after that period, the sooner it is washed the better. For this purpose it is put into washing vats, generally seven or eight feet long, three feet and a half wide, and three deep. They first throw in two or three quintals [a quintal is 112 pounds], over which they pour a quantity of sea-water, gradually increasing the quantity of both until the vat is full. They then take up each fish separately, cleaning carefully back and belly with a woolen cloth, and next lay it in a long even bulk on the stage floor to drain. They resume the same process until they have washed such a quantity of fish as they can manage the next day. It may remain in drain-bulk no more than two days; if kept beyond that time, it will decay in weight, nor will it stand the weather so well, on account of the salt getting out of it.

The next day, or as soon after as the weather permits, the fish is spread out on boughs in the open air to dry, head to tail, the open side being exposed to the sun. This is done either upon a beach, or upon the ground which is called *laying-room*; but more generally upon standing flakes. These last are of two sorts, namely, hand and broad flakes. The former consist of a slight wattle, supported by posts, at such an elevation from the ground that a person standing can conveniently manage and turn the fish. The broad flakes consist of a set of beams, supported by posts and shores, or stout pieces of timber.... In some places these broad flakes are as high as twenty to thirty feet from the ground. It is said that a free circulation of air is of considerable service to the fish while drying; hence the high flakes are preferable to the low ones, or to beaches where, besides the want of circulation of air, the back of the fish is liable to be burnt, if spread after the sun has heated the stones. But when the fish is dry, and spread only to make it perfectly fit to be put on-board ship, beach or flake will serve equally well.

Towards evening of the first day, two or three fishes are placed one over the other, with their back upwards, to prevent the open side from being injured by the wet or damp. The next morning the fish is again spread as before, and towards evening made into faggots of five or six, proceeding in the same manner so as to increase the faggots to eight or ten on the third evening, and on the fourth to eighteen or twenty, always with the back upwards, as some larger ones on top in a slanting position, so as to shoot off the rain or wet that may happen to fall during the night. The fifth evening the faggots are much larger; the fish is then considered safe, and left in that state for a week, or even a fortnight if there is a want of flake-room for the whole voyage [i.e., the catch for the season] or the weather happens to be bad. It is next spread out again until about three or four o'clock in the afternoon of the same day, when it is put up into large circular piles, in the form of a round hay-stack, with the heads outermost, the backs upwards, and the whole covered with circular deal frames, or with mats, tarpaulins, or rinds [the bark peeled from trees] confined by large stones, in order to preserve it from the heavy dews which fall in the heat of the summer. It is left some time in that state, then again spread out, and the same day, lodged in stores or put on board the vessels. After the fish has been first spread on the flake, four good days out of seven (which is considered better than four consecutive good days, because it then works or, as the fishermen express it, *sweats* the better,) will be sufficient to save it from any material damage.

As a single drop of rain or fresh water may so affect a fish as not only to injure it materially, but also to communicate the infection to the whole faggot, pile, and even cargo, the state of the weather is watched with particular attention while the fish is drying; and on the least appearance of a shower, the fish is immediately turned back uppermost. As Newfoundland is subject during the summer to sudden showers, the hurry and confusion which these frequently create throughout the whole place can hardly be described, and are no small annoyance when this happens on a Sunday, while the people are at church: the flakes are then in an instant covered with men, women and children, busily employed in turning up the fish or in making it into faggots; the profits of the whole voyage, the means of paying the debts contracted, and of procuring supplies for the support of the family during the ensuing winter, may all depend upon the exertions of that moment.

Such is the precarious and uncertain nature of the cod-fishery, at the same time that the fatigues which attend it are very great.... During the heat of the fishery, under the most incessant hard labour, they have scarcely time to eat their meals, and hardly four hours rest in the four and twenty.

In some parts of the coast, the ledges are at so great a distance that much time is consumed in the passage from and back again to their respective harbours; and even in those which are more favorably situated, the fish does not equally abound in every part. It is sometimes found in the north and sometimes in the south of the island, at other times in the middle of the coast, according as it is driven by the winds or attracted by the smaller fish; so that some fishermen are nearly ruined, whilst others more fortunate make excellent voyages.

But even after the most successful catch, if any even the smallest quantity of rain or fresh water is suffered to lodge in any part of the fish whilst drying, unless some salt be immediately sprinkled upon the part affected; – or if the splitter has left too many joints of the bone, so that any particle of blood has remained in the fish; – or when there has been too great a quantity of fish in salt bulk, so that the whole could not be disposed of in proper time; – or when it has been exposed to bad weather on the flake; – or when the weather, while the fish was exposed to the sun, has happened to be hot and calm, and the flies have gathered and left blow-flies, and these have not been carefully removed in time with the fingers or small sticks of wood; ... It is also liable to become *sun-burnt*.... Again, when the fish after washing has been left too long before being spread out for drying, it is apt to contract a kind of *slime*, as well as if, after it has been carried [laid] out, there is a continuance of bad weather.... In order to remedy this defect ... it is again dry-salted, washed, and put out a second time; but even then it will, at best, be received only as of second quality. To mention one defect more, it may become *dun*, if left too long in the pile, which happens sometimes from want of sufficient store-room and of an opportunity to ship it off in proper time.... [Anspach 1819: 429–42, with added paragraph breaks]

II

There are three issues at stake here in Part Two:

1. It has become popular in contemporary social sciences, particularly in the analysis of the Third World, to regard "traditional" communities as forming reservoirs of cheap labor for capitalism or capital formation. Such communities are seen as carrying many of the costs of reproducing a labor force for the dominant powers (states, national or multinational corporations) – being at once nurseries, hospitals, refugee centers for the unemployed and unwanted, old age homes, and so forth, and in addition providing cheap commodities and a market for cheap industrial products. All these functions are seen as draped around a skeleton of a dying traditionalism maintained by an increasingly impoverished populace (e.g., Meillassoux 1975; the "dual economy" theorists).

This is indeed the surface appearance and the surface reality. But there are more fundamental processes at work in the logic of the connections between these apparently traditional communities and the political and economic powers that dominate them. Here we will need to pursue the

distinction raised in Part One, between commodity and subsistence production within these traditional communities, and begin to explore the fact
that traditionalism (of culture and of social organization) forms in the
context of commodity production, and that many of the most profound
and far-reaching alliances with political and economic domination form in
the context of the difficulties of subsistence production.

2. The second issue at stake in Part Two is related to the first; it concerns
the anthropological concepts of social structure and culture. We must reexamine the assumption, almost completely pervasive in anthropology, that
a society, however bounded, has *a* social structure and *a* culture. Putting
aside, for the moment, the difficulties of drawing boundaries around a
"social system" – even arbitrary but useful boundaries – and putting aside
also the less important issue of the difficulties of describing a social structure
or a culture, the notion of one structure and one culture in each social
system must itself be called into question. This can be done in ways that
clarify the problem of delineating the boundaries of a social system.

In the 1960s the assumption that there is one culture in a social system
faced a partial and weak challenge from the concept of "subcultures." This
notion was largely associated with the analysis of poverty, and it came to
an intellectual dead end in the "culture of poverty" concept.

Although the issue of conceptualizing culture will be most directly addressed in Part Three, Part Two will open the enquiry into the possibility
that multiple social structures and cultures coexist, at least in certain kinds
of social systems, and that this provides the analytical basis for understanding the dynamic of culture.

3. The third issue at stake in Part Two concerns the "invention of tradition" and the relation of tradition to class formation. Eric Hobsbawm
and T. O. Ranger, in an important recent book (1983) have collected a
number of essays on the recent emergence of apparently traditional social
forms – particularly in the period from the late eighteenth to the early
twentieth centuries. But they have overlooked the fact that this is the same
period that saw the emergence of class, in the modern sense and reality
of the term. This raises for us the difficult but significant question about
the relation between the invention of tradition and the formation of class
– a problem introduced in Part Two and discussed more specifically in Part
Three.

4

Regale and rule

The logic of paternalism and the emergence of village culture

Anspach described the work process of catching and particularly of curing the fish; we must now examine how production, in the larger sense, was organized.

The inshore small-boat fishery, prosecuted by the residents of Newfoundland, was dominated by merchant capital from its inception until World War II. It saw two periods of major technological change: the introduction of the cod trap – an enormous net box, particularly in use on the northeast coast – in the last quarter of the nineteenth century, and the advent of gas engines in the early twentieth. But the process of catching and curing salt fish remained about the same from the beginning to the end, and the technological changes did not have as powerful an impact as did the transformation in the organization of production that occurred in the early mid nineteenth century. This was the transformation from a servant to a family fishery.

Until the late 1700s Newfoundland had a very small resident population. However, a great many boats and fishermen came out from Atlantic Europe for a seasonal summer fishery, both inshore and on the ocean banks. The English, lacking access to the inexpensive salt necessary for the heavy salt cure of the bank fishery, for long periods left the open-ocean fishery to Portugal, Spain, and France and fished inshore, drying the fish for export using the sun, wind, and much less salt.

Since the sort of boat capable of crossing the North Atlantic was not suitable for fishing the shallow, often rocky coastal waters and the narrow reaches of the bays, by the mid 1600s the boats from England were more often passenger and supply boats, or "sack" ships trading in cargoes of supplies and fish, than they were boats for fishing (Innis 1954: chap. 5; K. Matthews 1973: chap. 9). The passengers in this seasonal, or migratory, inshore fishery were West Country English or, increasingly, Irish from Counties Cork and Waterford (K. Matthews 1973: chap. 9; Handcock 1977). They signed on as servants for the summer voyage, or for two summers and the winter between, to fish for a "planter" resident in New-foundland; or for a "bye-boat keeper," who came out seasonally with his servants and perhaps with his small boats and equipment tied on deck; or even for the ship captain himself. During the last half of the eighteenth century, Newfoundland residents were increasingly employed. But they were mostly employed as servants on the same sort of servant contracts as migratory laborers.

Fishing masters, whether resident planters, bye-boat keepers, or ship captains, owned the small boats and other gear necessary for fishing (although the ship captains were often only the employees of the English merchant firms that sponsored them and owned the equipment). The masters also controlled, by claim, access to the crucial areas of shoreline where stages and flakes could be built. Servants signed on with these masters for a fixed wage for the season's work, and they worked as they were told. For the first few weeks of a season all the servants worked to put the shore facilities and fishing equipment in order. Their tasks were then divided, some being sent to fish and others staying ashore to process the catch. The larger establishments also had various full-time specialists, such as coopers and female domestic servants.

Although in the larger operations the master functioned primarily as a manager, and in the smaller (which included many planters and almost all the bye-boat keepers) the master labored alongside his servants, in few cases did the master himself have the resources to offer servants a guaranteed wage for the season should the fishery fail, or to buy the supplies necessary to provision himself and his servants for the fishery. Planters, bye-boat keepers, and ship captains were very often the middlemen, and sometimes the agent-employees, between the large merchant houses head-quartered in West Country England (particularly in Devon, Dorset, and Jersey) and the servant laborers.

Each spring the planters and boat keepers usually received provisions, salt, and other supplies from "their" merchant in return for a guarantee that they would sell all their fish to him. Planters and boat keepers did not control either the price they paid for supplies or the price that they received for fish, and they contracted to pay wages before they knew what the season would be like. In good years planters made a lot of money. But they, not merchants or servants, bore the brunt of declines in fish prices or in the catch size, and in bad years they went bankrupt by the score. Hence when a servant made a contract with a planter, the supplying merchant also "signed the papers" of the servant, guaranteeing his wages should the catch fail, or fish prices in Europe fall, or the merchant's own price manipulations for supplies and fish bankrupt the planter. Labor could not be brought out from England in sufficient quantity on other terms.

In return for a guaranteed wage the servants agreed to work when and how they were told. A series of legal rulings and governor's decrees in the late eighteenth and early nineteenth centuries established that no wages at all were due to "disobedient" servants, even if they worked without failing to obey for almost the entire season.

On June 17, 1840 – at the end of the period of the servant fishery – Bartholomew McGrath, a planter, gave John Nowlan his "shipping paper" as servant for the season:

I have this day agreed with and shipped John Nowlan, from the date hereof until the last day of October next, in the capacity of Fisherman, Seaman, or otherwise for the good of the Voyage, and to do everything in his power for my interest, and after serving faithfully and honestly, without hindrance or neglect, I am to pay him as wages the sum of £20 currency... [JLC 1841: app. 39]

By 1840 merchants were finding other ways of doing business than guaranteeing wages, and Mr. Mudge, the merchant supplying Bartholomew McGrath, refused to sign McGrath's servants' papers. Several servants "threw their papers up" and would not sail. McGrath worked the season shorthanded, and in consequence had a poor catch. The record of the case, from the discussions in the Newfoundland Legislative Council, illustrates the importance of both the lien and "obedience":

The vessel returned on Saturday, October 17th; and on Monday the 19th [i.e., 12 days before Nowlan's service had expired], there was a dispute between him and McGrath [the planter]. Some Fish and [cod liver] oil belonging to a man named Burn had been landed that morning, and on the Defendant [McGrath] desiring Plaintiff [Nowlan] to help land the rest of the Fish, Nowlan refused, and not only refused to help himself, but prevented McGrath and his apprentice John Butler, from landing the Fish. In this resistance he was aided by one Abraham Clark, who was hired under like circumstances, and who is also suing the Defendant [McGrath]. Nowlan and Clark objected to the Fish being landed until they had security for their Wages. McGrath offered Nowlan half his Wages in goods, and the remainder when his time was up; but Nowlan, although he was willing to take half in goods (which he need not have done unless he was so disposed), still insisted on having security for the other half, and continued to refuse to land the Fish or let it be landed. Nowlan continued from time to time to go on board the Vessel, and was willing to do any work, except only as to the landing the Fish before he got security. But McGrath said unless he would land the Fish he was no servant of his. There were several disputes similar to the first, of which the most serious seems to have been one that took place 4 or 5 days after the first, when McGrath desired Nowlan to go about his business, saying he was no servant of his; and one that occurred a day or two before the last of October, when Nowlan and Clark, by force, kept down the hatches and prevented McGrath from getting the Fish out of the Vessel. Some conversations between Nowlan and McGrath were proved: On Saturday on which the Vessel returned to St. John's, McGrath told Nowlan and Clark that he should have enough to pay them their Wages, and almost to clear himself to his

Merchant, Mr. Mudge [i.e., to pay his bill for the supplies]. On the day but one after that, viz., Monday, 19th, the day of the dispute, when Nowlan asked for security, McGrath told him to go to Mr. Mudge; but Mr. Mudge declined paying Nowlan, and said he was no Servant of his, adding however that he had no doubt McGrath would pay him. On this, Nowlan asked McGrath what he was to do for his Wages? – McGrath replied, "Do what you can, do not blame me." These words were repeated two or three times, and then McGrath went ashore to Mr. Mudge's Counting-house, and on his return ordered the men to take the Fish out, which Clark and Nowlan refused to do, without security. At the last dispute, when Nowlan and Clark asked McGrath if he meant to baffle him out of his Wages? – McGrath said "I do! You are no servants of mine if you will not take the Fish ashore." Nowlan swore an oath that no one should take the Fish away. This was after McGrath had discharged Nowlan, and ceased to diet him. [JLC 1841: app. 39, reporting and discussing the case *Nowlan* v. *McGrath*, here with their names substituted for "plaintiff" and "defendant" in this quote from the "Statement of the Facts" of the case]

Nowlan's situation was impossible. As was noted by one of the three justices of the Supreme Court – to which this case had been brought, for it raised issues that marked the end of the servant fishery – had Nowlan unloaded the fish, as he was told, he could not have "followed the fish" to the merchant for his wages, for now it was only the planter, not the merchant, who owed the wages. Not unloading the fish made Nowlan a disobedient servant to whom no wages were due, even though he had only a few days left in his term of service when the boat sailed into St. John's. Nowlan received nothing at all for his work.

Not paying disobedient servants, at all or in part, was one of the many methods used to secure labor discipline during the servant fishery. But it was very often not possible for the master to observe his servants' "disobedience": When a small boat was sent out to fish, how could the master tell at the end of the day if few fish meant little luck or little work? And if the master was having fish cured at several locales along a section of coastline, how could he tell if a poor cure was due to bad weather or lack of effort? Not paying wages, however dramatic and however useful as a threat, was not necessarily effective in many day-to-day situations.

For masters and for the merchants who supplied the masters and who were required, until the early mid nineteenth century, to guarantee wages (a guarantee enforced, while it lasted, by the servants' lien on the fish they caught) two problems were crucial: how to ensure a maximum intensity of effort, that is, how to discipline labor, and how to pay wages if the catch failed. For servants, the problem was how to enforce their guaranteed wage; this was a problem even though "in the interests of the fishery," Newfoundland's naval, and then colonial, governors, and the Newfoundland legislature as well, actively supported servants' claims.

The problem of labor discipline emerged between all levels of the hierarchically organized servant fishery: between the merchant houses of

England (or later, of St. John's) and their resident local agents; between the merchants' agents and the planters and boat keepers, and between the planters and boat keepers and their servants. The problem was not diminished but intensified by the late-eighteenth-century shift from a fishery with predominantly migratory servants who came out each spring to a fishery with predominantly resident servants who lived year-round in the outport villages and hamlets. The problem persisted until the demise of the servant fishery and the guaranteed wage.

Planters and merchants had a limited number of strategies to secure labor discipline. One has been shown: the refusal to pay wages, either in part (called "deduction") or in full. It is difficult to gauge the frequency of this practice, but from the number of complaints by naval governors about destitute and abandoned servants flocking into St. John's for the winter (only some of whom were the products of a failed fishery, for this happened in good years and in bad), and from the persistent attempts by the governors to force masters to pay at least their servants' passage back to England, we know this practice was not uncommon. And we may suspect from such complaints that more was involved than simple discipline of the work process: it seems likely that abandoning servants was, at times, a way to increase the profitability or lower the costs of not very successful voyages. In such situations it would shade from a specific form of labor discipline into a diffuse form of terror.

Hugh Palliser, perhaps the most influential governor colonial Newfoundland had, attempted to make the guaranteed wage more effectively ensure effort by offering to permit adjusted wages (downward only) for those not meeting the standard of an average catch. Under the pressure of a bad year in the fishery, in 1767, he proposed that

an exact and true account of the whole quantity of fish taken this year, by Inhabitants and Boatkeepers who carry on fishing voyages by taking supplies from others, in each principal harbour distinguishing the quantity taken by each different kinds of Boats, viz., of 5, 4, 3 or 2 men, then the whole quantity taken by each kind of Boats be brought to an average and that average to be the standard or rule to judge how the people have done their duty in such Boats in each harbour or district as may be complained of, who according to this rule are liable to such abatements of Wages as shall appear equitable and just to me or my Surrogate, any particular circumstance also to be considered. [JHA 1837: app., pp. 521–2]

Putting aside the point that about half the fishing boats might fall below the average, this attempt was so ineffective that the following year Palliser simply declared:

Whereas the Servants of sundry Planters in Conception Bay [then by far the most populated and important bay in the fishery] have not been paid the wages due to them, for service the last year, nor their passages home provided for, they have been necessitated to stay in the country, in great distress during the winter.

Notice is hereby given to all such Planters, not to part with the produce of their present voyages, until the wages of all last and present year's servants are fully secured by engagements in writing, from able and sufficient persons [i.e., until a merchant actually signed a guarantee for the servants' wages the fish were not to be given to the merchant].

And all merchants and others are to take notice, that whoever receives any part of the produce of the present year's voyage, from any Planter, without giving sufficient security for the payment of wages due as abovementioned, such receivers will not be permitted to ship off any fish or oil from this country.

And all servants of Planters in Conception Bay are hereby authorized to *stop and detain on the rooms* [the piers and drying areas where the servants worked] *the produce of the voyages, till such security for their wages is given.* [JHA 1837: app., p. 519; emphasis added]

Except for including in the provision for guaranteed wages the servants of the year before, when the fishery had failed and many servants had been abandoned, destitute, there was little that was new in this provision. Servants already had been detaining fish, although not very effectively, and they had, as we shall soon see, the first lien on the fish they caught for their wages. As early as 1749 the right of servants to physically detain their fish was referred to as an "ancient custom," as was their first lien (the legal origins of these customs in Newfoundland are founded in the British Parliamentary Act, 10/11 William c. 25, 1698. See G. B. Rodney, JHA 1837: app., p. 527).

To detain fish – or for the smaller planters and boat keepers even to keep possession of their boats when confronted by a local merchant who thought their catch would not meet the credit extended – often took more power than servants and boat keepers could muster:

Whereas the principal Merchants, Traders and other interested in the Fishery, have represented to me, that their trade greatly suffers by the illegal practice of violence and force frequently committed by the merchants and traders residing in Northern and Southern Ports who have, and still continue, by force and violence, contrary to law and justice, to seize and carry away from divers inhabitants and boat keepers [their] (debtors) their fish, train oil, boats and craft, thereby rendering them incapable of prosecuting the fishery to the end of the season; all of which effects they keep to themselves in particular, without having any regard to other creditors, which force and violence, if not timely prevented, may be the ruin, not only of many inhabitants and fishermen, but of the trade in general.

The solution proposed by George Rodney, who penned the above for Governor Samuel Frazer, was ridiculous in the context of the magnitude of the problem and the intensity of the struggle between producers and creditors:

For preventing all such violent, unlawful and unjust proceedings, and the ruin of many useful subjects employed in the fishery, I have and do hereby strictly order that no person or persons whatever do presume to seize or carry away . . . any fish [etc.] . . . from the rooms of their debtors [bye-boat keepers and planters] but according to the ancient custom content themselves with such portion of their debts as shall be freely and voluntarily paid by the debtors. [JHA 1837: app., p. 520]

One of the major problems with allowing fishermen to detain their fish until their wages were paid was that the fish were not finished being cured all at one point at the end of the season; rather, they were cured in batches and often taken by the merchant throughout the last half of the season, well before the servants knew if they would be paid – although in bad years they might guess that they would not. Servants' wages were thus given first lien on the catch even when the merchant possessed the fish. In the oft-repeated words of Newfoundland courts, servants had the right to "follow the fish" to the merchant, and their wages must be paid in full before any other creditor could be satisfied.

The Newfoundland Supreme Court, in 1820, explained the logic of this lien:

The origin of this custom is to be found in the necessity of the thing, and the interests of the fishery are its best expositor. From the nature of the article of fish, and the method of curing it and sending it to market, it is the common practice of this Island to take it off the rooms at different times. . . . If the servant is to lose his lien by the removal of the fish, he must arrest it upon the rooms, the ruinous consequences of which proceeding require no comment. . . . Fish may be removed from the planter's rooms to the warehouse of the regular supplier without any detriment to the right of the servants, who are presumed to know and to be known to the supplier, as to their number, occupation, amount of wages, &c. [Decisions of the Supreme Court of Newfoundland, *Reports, 1817–1828*, p. 212; *Rourke v. Baine, Johnston & Co.*]

The servants' lien was enforced by the government in order to get labor, that is, to protect the interests of the fishery as a whole. It was also enforced so as not to have destitute servants abandoned on the island, for in the interest of the migratory fishery and the naval press-gangs, the governors and the large English merchant houses wished to constrain settlement. Enforcing the servants' lien gave them money for passage home, but the problem for merchants and planters remained: how to keep the lien from permitting fisherfolk to slacken their efforts – particularly after they had caught enough fish to cover their wages. For planters had themselves taken on credit far more than the wages the merchant guaranteed: They had also gone into debt for provisions and production supplies for the season.

One feeble attempt to enforce hard work lay in the structure of the lien and in the "law of current supply." The law of current supply meant that the fish caught in any season had to satisfy, in full, the wages due and the supply credit advanced for that season before any previous year's claims could be addressed. This meant that fisherfolk had to catch at least enough fish in any year to cover their wages that year: They could make no effective claims upon the past or future earnings of the merchant. Moreover, their lien for wages was *only* upon the fish that they caught: They had no claim for wages against merchants' or planters' capital goods.

The court itself explained the significance of this, not simply for labor discipline from the top down but also for having the servants watch each other's work efforts:

It is important to note that it is the fish made by the hirer [the planter or merchant], or in other words the produce of the master's fishery, which is made liable to all [his] servants in common, without any difference or preference in order of their claims. . . .

It is possible that the legislature, by making one man's earnings liable for another's wages, intended to give every servant a direct interest in the industry of his fellow-labourer, and thus to establish the most effectual guard against indolence. [Decisions of the Supreme Court of Newfoundland, *Reports, 1817–1828, Rourke v. Baine, Johnston & Co.*, p. 211]

This struggle over the lien often occurred between a relatively distant merchant, or merchant's agent, and the servants of a merchant's planters. Within the planter's operation, where the planter was involved in the day-to-day lives of his servants as well as in disciplining their work effort, another form of domination was crucial. This form, in several of its manifestations, has been termed *paternalism*. Understanding how it worked in Newfoundland, and perhaps elsewhere as well, entails first reexamining the sort of behavior delineated by this concept and then redoing the definition of the concept itself.

In the first of my published papers on Newfoundland (Sider 1976), I described the mode of operation of Captain George Cartwright, a planter from 1770 to 1796 on the Labrador Coast – then as now part of the Newfoundland fishery. Cartwright was master of a large and relatively prosperous fishing, sealing, and fur-trapping operation; he employed, from year to year, about twenty servants. In discussing the social relations of work in Cartwright's domain, I quoted from his journal and emphasized the occasions on which he beat and brutalized his servants, or treated them with haughty contempt:

Sunday, January 5 [1772]. All the people got very drunk today [this is during the twelve days of Christmas, a point to which we shall return in Chapter 6] and the cooper behaving in a very insolent manner, I gave him a few strokes with a small stick, upon which he had the impudence to complain of being so bruised as not to be able to eat his dinner. Charles relapsed, and was very ill again.

Monday, January 6 [1772]. I bled one of the sealers, and two of my dogs. The cooper refused to work, pretending he could not use his right arm; I gave him nothing but water gruel, and made a deduction from his wages for his neglect. [Cartwright 1792 (repr. 1911): 57–8]

Professor George Story, in a descriptively thick critique of this presentation of Captain Cartwright – to which I am much indebted, for it both forced a clarification and provided the basis for this reexamination of what paternalism is, and how it works – took me strongly to task for these "mischievous" and "marxist" selections from the data of the journal – in sum, for depicting Cartwright as "a kind of violent, grudging and truculent Scrooge, a northern Simon Legree, beating or bleeding men and dogs alike to establish and maintain the harsh master–servant relationship of eighteenth century vampire capitalism" (Story 1980: 14–18).

Per contra, Professor Story offers instance upon instance of Cartwright's kindness and benevolence to his servants. He quotes Cartwright's journal (1792 ed.) to show the number of times when, for example, Cartwright fed his servants "buttered hot rolls and coffee" and gave thèm spiritous drink (while grumbling about the servants' own, more autonomous, drinking – but only grumbling, not beating them):

Wednesday 11 [September 1771]. [The "leaving time" when the summer servants went back to England or Ireland, while other servants remained for the winter] According to the custom of this part of the world, as well as some others, all the people got very drunk today; because, some of their friends were taking their leave of them, and going away.
Thursday 12. All the people drunk again.
Friday 13. Not much work was done today; as the people were scarcely recovered from their late debauch. . . .
Tuesday 24 [December 1771]. At night Christmas Eve was celebrated in the usual manner, by the people getting very drunk.
Wednesday 25. I treated all hands with buttered hot rolls and coffee for breakfast. . . . I read prayers, and afterwards regaled the people with veal pie and rice pudding for dinner. . . .
Friday 14 [February 1772]. The people were all drunk as is usual on such occasions
. . .
Saturday 16 [March 1776]. This being St. Patrick's day, the people, as usual, got beastly drunk. . . .
Thursday 25 [December 1778]. This being Christmas Eve, I gave the people some brandy as usual, and they all got very drunk, in conformity to annual custom.
. . .
Wednesday 17 [March 1779]. I had reserved a small quantity of brandy for the people to celebrate St. Patrick's day with, and now let them have it for that purpose.
. . .
Thursday 19 [May 1785]. This being the Queen's birthday, I gave my people some cyder to drink to Her Majesty's health. . . .
Saturday 24 [December 1785]. This being Christmas Eve, we gave the people sweet cakes and cheese for supper, and made them a present of a bottle of rum.

Although Professor Story does not put our two perspectives on Captain Cartwright together – that is not his purpose – when we do so, when we simply merge the two views of Cartwright, we have before us a fairly standard depiction of paternalistic domination: the mixture of sternness and benevolence so characteristic of paternalism that it is taken as definitional.

But the point here is not at all to argue the relative strengths of the events on each side – literally the stick or the carrot; the few strokes or the few strokings – to judge which was more frequent or more significant. *Nor* is it at all the point to say that paternalism consisted of both, together and equally. For whatever the proportions, seeing this form of labor discipline as a mixture of warmth and wrath misses the major point.

The point is precisely to notice that the beatings were episodic and situationally specific, and that the benevolence was culturally delineated: It was specifically in the context of custom that Cartwright gave his servants buttered hot rolls and coffee. Going beyond food, over which he apparently had a virtual monopoly, it was specifically in the context of those customary occasions on which the servants themselves got drunk that Cartwright also provided them with drink – including both customs that he shared (like Christmas) and customs that he did not share but acknowledged (like St. Patrick's Day), but not including customs that he neither shared nor seemed to approve of (like the fall leaving time).

By the "cultural delineation" of Cartwright's benevolence, I do not mean that what – nor in this case even *when* – he gave was culturally prescribed, for we may doubt that there were any traditions firmly established in Newfoundland defining what masters should give to their servants. Rather, in the context of those customary occasions that were significant to both him and the servants and those that perhaps were more significant to him than the servants (like the Queen's birthday), Cartwright provided one of the major means for their celebration.

The food, if not the drink, conveyed a double message: He was the source of what they ate, and he was the source of special food for special occasions. In a context where labor served "by the custom of the fishery," and where servants and masters had their rights and claims adjudicated time after time in the courts by reference to the "custom of the fishery," it is not insignificant that masters would mediate, with so basic a symbol as food, servants' customary occasions.

Further, I suspect that this form of domination is not specific to Newfoundland, but that a reexamination of other expressions of paternalism – for example, on American slave plantations – would show a similar pattern of both episodic, situation-specific violence and custom-contextualized benevolence.

II

During the first four decades of the nineteenth century, the migratory-servant fishery collapsed with increasing speed. The servants' place in the labor force was taken by families resident in Newfoundland outport villages. The planters and boat keepers disappeared with the servants. Some planters became outport merchants or merchant's agents; some were reduced to being common fishermen; others just left. During this transition, the full-time residents outnumbered (and in size of catch outweighed) the seasonal migrants, so that the whole period of transition from servant contracts to truck payments was first marked by a transition from servants brought from England and Ireland to, increasingly, Newfoundland residents hired on servant contracts.

The event that summed up and expressed the end of the servant contract was the denial (first in practice and then in a series of court cases) of the validity of the servants' lien on their fish for their wages. Merchants refused to guarantee wages by the mid 1830s, planters lacked the resources to give their own guarantees, and the courts refused to continue the practice of having the first claim on fish be the servants' wages.

Throughout the late eighteenth and early nineteenth centuries, the servants' lien was constantly upheld by both the naval governors and the courts as the custom of the fishery. In a case concerning this lien that was brought to the Newfoundland Supreme Court in 1820, the court ruled (as I have noted): "The origin of this custom is to be found in the necessity of the thing, and the interests of the fishery are its best expositor."

But by the 1840s the custom of the lien was being denied, and custom itself was being defined as either nonexistent in Newfoundland or as local, particular, and irrelevant. In 1841, for example, Chief Justice Bourne of the Newfoundland Supreme Court denied that Newfoundland customs bound the law, inasmuch as they were simply local:

... for this usage [the servants' lien] is not a general usage or custom of the British Realm, but local and peculiar to Newfoundland. . . . It was argued [by counsel for the servant] that it was a general and not a particular custom, because it extended over the whole island: even that was not proved by evidence, but had it been so shown, it would none the less be a local or particular custom, which could be good only by special usage. To contend that it is a general law because it extends all over Newfoundland, would be like contending that the law of Gavelkind is a general and not a local law because it extends all over Kent. [*Nowlan* v. *McGrath*, JLC 1841: app. 39]

Six years later, another Newfoundland court denied the force of custom to bind the law – not simply because Newfoundland customs were local and particular but also because custom itself was now being denied to Newfoundland. The case again involved a servant's lien:

Lien is properly defined to be "a right to retain anything in possession until certain demands were satisfied." *Possession* is the essence of lien, and when that ceased, *lien* ceased also. Neither can the foundation of this claim be rested upon *custom*; no such custom exists, wanting, as it does, the grand essential of custom, viz., *prescription* – antiquity beyond memory of man. . . . There could be no prescription in a country that has only been discovered a few centuries. [Northern Circuit Court, *Decisions*, May 1846; *Moreen* v. *Ridley et al.*; emphases in original]

While the servant fishery lasted, customs were not only a point for the penetration of domination into the social and working life of a planter's servants, and not only a standard of reference for the courts' adjudication of claims. They were also a terrain of confrontation:

Regale and rule: logic of paternalism

At sunset the people ushered in Christmas, according to the Newfoundland custom. In the first place they built up a prodigious large fire in their house; all hands then assembled before the door, and one of them fired a gun, loaded with powder only: afterwards each of them drank a dram of rum, concluding the ceremony with three cheers. These formalities being performed with great solemnity, they retired into their house, got drunk as fast as they could, and spent the whole night drinking, quarreling, and fighting. It is but natural to suppose, that the noise which they made (their house being but six feet from the head of my bed) together with the apprehension of seeing my house in flames, prevented me from once closing my eyes. This is an intolerable custom, but as it has prevailed from time immemorial, it must be submitted to. By some accident my thermometer got broke. [Cartwright, 24 Dec. 1770; 1911: 58]

The end of the master–servant relationship in Newfoundland was also the end of the relevance of custom as a specific and direct point of connection between those who dominated the fishery and those who caught and made the fish. It was *in this precise context* that the "traditional" Newfoundland folk culture – and in less precise ways political ideology – was born.

It was also in this context that merchant capital, in the specific form under examination in this book, came into being in Newfoundland. The form of merchant capital that concerns us, particularly for its implications for the classic focuses of anthropological studies, entails more than merchants and trade: Its commodities come from quasi-autonomous producers who organize their own work processes. In Newfoundland this was the inshore, family fishery.

5

When fishermen may starve

The Slade and Kelson Plan of 1825

As the year-round Newfoundland population increased during the late eighteenth and early nineteenth centuries, resident merchants established themselves in the settlements, and predominance in trading supplies and fish passed from ship captains to resident merchants. These merchants were not independent; they were usually the agents of substantial merchant firms in West Country England or Jersey. In the first few decades of the nineteenth century, before the servant contract ended and the planters disappeared into the mass of resident fisher families, went back home to England, or themselves became merchant-agents, the resident merchants of Newfoundland dealt with several different categories of people: a few of their own servants and employees, planters and their servants, families, a few isolated individuals, and an occasional petty trader (an extra middleman in a small or isolated harbor).

For the most part, except for his own employees, the merchant referred to all these people as his "dealers," that is, the people with whom he dealt. He dealt with these people in a variety of ways – with fixed wages that were sometimes higher than usual if the person spent all the wages in the merchant's store (see, e.g., Kennedy wage books, NLPA), shares, a combination of wages and shares, and increasingly by truck.

One of the key features of the truck arrangement was that cash did not – and in some situations could not – enter into the relationship. When the fisher families took their supplies in the spring they had to agree to deliver their entire catch of fish in the fall; the merchant would then price both their catch and the supplies advanced the previous spring. The courts held, decisively, that a fisherman could not sell his fish to someone else – a passing schooner, another merchant, or a dealer – and pay his bill to the merchant in cash. The uncaught fish belonged to the merchant from the time when he gave credit.

In the spring of 1819, the St. John's merchant firm of Baine, Johnston

58

& Company supplied a fishing partnership that from the style of its name, Froud and Sons (and from having been formed as a partnership), clearly had aspirations of rising from the ranks of common fisherfolk – aspirations not likely to be realized while in the grip of their merchant. Froud and Sons sold thirty-five quintals of fish they had caught to a passing schooner-captain, A. Chambers. Baine, Johnston sued Chambers to get back "their" fish from him. They won, even though Chambers had gotten the fish from the fishermen. The court ruled:

It is certainly the right of the owner of any goods to dispose of them in any way that he pleases; but the gist of the case before the Court is, who were the owners of the goods in question? . . . This is a question of the greatest consequence to the trade and fisheries of this island, as at present conducted. . . .

The court then drew a sharp distinction between St. John's, the commercial capital, and the outports; a distinction relevant to the issue of ownership:

[The town of St. John's is] a market overt, an open and customary place of sale; in which it would be impossible to trace the private history of every boat-load of fish which may come to market. . . . But the same reasoning does not apply to the outharbours; they are unusual places of sale, and . . . the purchaser takes upon himself the risk of receiving fish in which another has a property. . . . He may buy fish at an outharbour, but he must buy it subject to all existing liens. [Decisions of the Supreme Court of Newfoundland, *Reports, 1817–1828*, pp. 219–20]

In a perceptive discussion of this case, Steven Antler points out that

the Court having previously ruled that physical catch, rather than any cash or goods equivalent, constituted repayment for supplies advanced, it remained for the Court to underline that third parties could not remain untouched by conditions imposed by the lien system. The ability of merchants to fix prices [and to dominate the village fishery!] was maintained by the court through the expedient of ruling that market transactions could not normally take place outside of St. John's. [S. Antler 1975: 65–7].

If the truck system seems to be starting to resemble debt peonage, it does – with the crucial difference that in the truck system the debtor can be turned loose (and often enough was) whether or not a debt was still owed. The fisher families had to give their entire catch to the merchant, but the merchant did not then have to give credit (food, to be specific) for the winter. As Thomas Holdsworth Brooking, a merchant on the northeast coast, testified in 1841 to the House of Commons in England:

Question: Under the old system [wages and shares, or a more generous amount of credit for winter supplies] you state that about three to one were [continually] indebted to you for credit?
T.H.B.: Yes . . . credit was given indiscriminately.
Question: But now you say it is one to three [on continual credit]?
T.H.B.: Yes, with our establishment, because we have drawn the cord tighter.
Question: What has been the effect of this restriction of credit upon the people?

> *T.H.B.*: I think it has made people more industrious and use greater exertions.
> . . . I think it is working very beneficially. [Great Britain 1841]

Denying credit, particularly for winter supply, was a complex matter. At the heart of this issue is the fact that merchants *had* to continue giving credit to at least *some* of the fisher families with whom they dealt, even though these families never, or hardly ever, caught enough fish to meet the cost of their supplies. They had to do this not out of kindness or concern for the possibility of starvation without winter supply, nor because other fisher families would turn their trade away from hardhearted merchants who let people starve, but for their own convenience and interest. Why this was so, how it worked, and the impact it had both on the fisher families that regularly met their bills and on social relations within communities – which always contained both successful and unsuccessful fisher families – is the problem now to be addressed. And the best starting point is a document penned in 1825 by Alex Bremmer, an agent who resided in the northeast coast outport of Catalina and managed the trade in that area for the English merchant firm of Slade and Kelson. This document specified who the firm should let starve, who they should "continue," and why. Bremmer called it a "plan"; for us it is more than that – it is a window into another world.

In the summer of 1825 the trade was in trouble. The prices paid for fish in Europe were down, the cost of supplies was rising, and the catch was poor. Slade and Kelson wrote to Bremmer. The firm's letter has been lost, but from Bremmer's reply we can tell that they asked him to restrict the trade to the best dealers – the planters, fisher families, and boat keepers who caught the most fish and used the least supplies. In his reply Bremmer made subtler and different distinctions about how the trade might be restricted and the profits increased.

His plan consists of five "statements." The first is a list of all the people with whom he regularly dealt and a description of them. The next three statements draw from this list, in order of decreasing importance, the people with whom it is profitable or necessary to trade. The last statement is a list of who should be turned out – admittedly to starve and perhaps to die. The plan ends with a "recapitulation," which reviews the five statements and further discusses their implications.

The entire plan follows. The numbers in the original document do not add up exactly to the totals given but have not been altered. Three minor changes have been made: First, the original document gives both the names of the dealers and the names of their servants in the first statement. I have retained the names of the dealers, so the cases can be followed from statement to statement, but for clarity of presentation have only given the number and gender of each dealer's servants. Second, in statements 2 through 5 I have changed horizontal rows of information to a listing. Third, the recapitulation, which restates several points made in the rest of the plan, is not given here in full. Otherwise, what once was, here is.

Statement 1st

Names of the Dealers in Slade and Kelsons Trade at Catalina Summer 1825, and their Servants and Sharemen with Number of Wives and Children Place of Residence & Remarks, &c.

Names of planters	Sharemen or servants		No. of wives	No. of children	No. of souls	Remarks
	M	F				
Ragged Harbour						Reside in Ragged Harb'r, are
1. John Feehan			1	3	4	the only regular dealers we
2. Mary Daily & her 3 sons					7	have there, generally pay their accts. & are fair in their dealings which is more than can be said of the other inhabitants of that settlement generally
Catalina						
3. Robert Baine			1	6	8	Has done poorly these last two
servants	3	1			4	years, but is an industrious man & deals honestly
4. Thomas Drake			1	3	5	Up till this year paid up very
servants	1				1	well, but is going to ruin now
5. Charles Duffet			1	9	11	Has hitherto paid, is very in-
servants	1				1	dustrious, & though sometimes troublesome about prices I consider him on the whole a good dealer
6. George Diamond Snr.			1	9	11	Supplied him this year on his
servants	1				1	promise to give up pickling [heavy salt]–cannot say much for or against him yet
7. John Mason			1	11 +	13	Does very poorly every year
8. Wm. Holloway			1	7	9	Does middling well hitherto
servants	2				2	
9. John House			1	10	12	A very industrious man some-
servants	1				1	what inclined to be honest & who I think may do pretty well yet
10. Matthew Mason			1	+	2	Like his brother always does
servants	1				1	poorly
11. Wm. Gould			1	5	7	I hold him in the same estima-
servants	3	1			4	tion as Duffet

Statement 1st (cont.)

Names of planters	Sharemen or servants M	F	No. of wives	No. of children	No. of souls	Remarks
12. Mary Neal & her two sons					5	If they keep honest I think they may get on pretty well yet
13. Wm. Shepherd			1	3	4	Of a very sulky temper under
servants	2		1	2	5	the constraint I have kept him supplied – has however nearly paid up his current accts since I have been here & if he faith-fully delivers his voyage this year it would be a pity to cast him off without a little for the winter
14. John Sutton			1	4	6	Has always done poorly & this
servants	3	1			4	year worse than ever of course
15. Wm. White Sr.			1	8	10	Never catches much fish, but
servants	1		1		3	generally gives us what he gets – is rather indolently inclined & I fear in these bad times will not be able to maintain his family

We have small accounts with almost everyone in the place [Catalina], but the above is what I consider the regular dealers

Bird Island Cove						
16. Wm. Chalk & Wm. Barnes			2	3	7	Will not I fear be able to main-
servants	2		1	4	7	tain their families in these times
17. John Chalk Sr. & sons			4	6	14	Do not see that they can make
servants	2		2	6	10	it out [pay their bill] if they have credit for winter diet
18. George Crew			1	6	8	Bad with him as with the rest
servants	5		1	2	8	but I consider that he deals fair. I hold him in favourable consideration
19. Thomas Cole			1		2	In independent circumstances
servants	5	1	2	7	15	
20. Thos. Clouter			1	5	7	In good circumstances. I con-
servants	7		2	3	12	sider him a better dealer than Cole because he has a large family and is a considerable consumer of goods
21. Richard Cole			1	4	6	Is very well off & I consider
servants	3				3	him a good dealer
22. Thos. Flynn & father & mother			1	3	7	No idea that he will be able to pay under the winter supplying system
servants	6		2	4	8	

Statement 1st (cont.)

Names of planters	Sharemen or servants		No. of wives	No. of child-ren	No. of souls	Remarks
	M	F				
23. Jno. Robert & Wm. Hobbs & father & mother			2	4	11	Have a little better opinion of these than of the former & not much
servants	5		2	6	13	
24. James Heile			1	7	9	Have the same opinion of & hold him in the same estima-tion as G. Crew
servants	4	1	1	1	7	
25. Menchiner & Stead			1	6	9	Will not make it out under the winter supplying system
servants	1				1	
26. John Miles			1	8	10	ditto
servants	2		1	1	4	
27. Nebuz. Tucker			1	6	8	ditto
servants	2				2	
28. White & Cole			2	8	12	Bad with them now, but have a favourable opinion of their in-dustry and honesty
servants	1				1	
George Smart resides in Catalina omitted			1	2	4	
			48	172	342	

In B[ird] Island Cove as well as in Catalina & Ragged Harbour we have a number of other small accounts but the above is the regular dealers–

Statement 2d

The Number of persons selected from Statement 1st who may be supplied under a *strict* adherence to Slade and Kelsons plan of doing business in Catalina for 1825, such as I judge able to pay their accts independent of bad voyages or other con-tingencies – the provisions I judge necessary for winter supply, and the number of souls that will be destitute of support the winter in consequence of acting on this plan.

Names of Planter, and Servant or Sharemen

1. Thomas Cole — Four or five sharemen, who may require credit to Amt £10 or £12 each
2. Thomas Clouter — Four or five sharemen who may require credit as above
3. Richard Cole — Two or three sharemen who may require credit as above

Quantity of Provisions Necessary for their Supply the Winter

27 Cwt Bread
14 Bls Flour
8 Firkins Butter
160 Ga's Molasses
required to be good quality and will amt to about £140

Number of Souls Without Support the Winter in Consequence of This Plan

Two hundred and ninety seven
viz. 297

Remarks

At this small extent of business the collection in middling voyages would probably be 600 quintals with Oil. It would require to transact it 1 agent & 6 or 7 hands viz. a boat's crew & 2 or 3 hands ashore. When reduced to this point it would I think be best to give up supplying any at Catalina, and let these come to Trinity if they would.

Statement 3d

[in the 3d & 4th statements the column "servants or sharemen" is left blank]

Adds to statement 2d such other persons as an *liberal interpretation* of S & K's plan might be credited moderately the winter, comprehending such as generally pay their accounts pretty fair to their suppliers, in respect of delivering their produce & c. and whose general habits of industry & economy render the supplying of them not much of a risk. With the provisions necessary for their winter supply together with the former, and number of souls destitute of support the winter in event of the plan being acted on in this manner.

Names of Planter

4. John Feehan
5. Mary Daily and Sons
6. Charles Duffet
7. William Holloway
8. William Gould

Quantity of Provisions Necessary for their Supply the Winter

52 Cwt bread
26 Bls flour
16 Bls pork
14 Firkins Butter
300 Gals Molasses
Worth about £270

Number of Souls Without Support the Winter in Consequence of This Plan

Two hundred & fifty two
viz. 252

64

When fishermen may starve: Slade–Kelson Plan

Remarks

I consider these better dealers than the former being larger consumers of store goods – The collection here would probably be 1300 quintals with oil. Would require no more expense for transacting than the former stage.

Statement 4th

Adds to statement 2d and 3d such other persons, as from their being considerably in debt cannot be supplied at all consistent with the terms of this plan, but whom I would recommend to a moderate supply on the grounds of their generally industrious habits & fair conduct in the trade, with the provisions necessary for their winter supply together with the two former &c&c.

Names of Planters

9. George Diamond Sr.
10. John House
11. Mary Neal & 2 Sons
12. Wm. Shepherd
13. Wm. Baines partners Chalk & Baines
14. George Crew
15. Jno., Rob't, & Wm. Hobbs
16. James Hill
17. White and Cole
18. Robt. Baine

Quantity Provisions Necessary for their Supply the Winter

102 Cwt bread
50 Bls Flour
28 Bls Pork
24 Firkins Butter
580 Gals Molasses
worth about £500

Number of Souls Without Support the Winter in Consequence of This Plan

one hundred and thirty
viz. 130

Remarks

[the left edge of the page is damaged and some words missing]

This is the stage at which I myself would recommend the business [to be] reduced to *at present*, both in regard to the planters themselves & the interest of the trade. Because as regards the former, a greater reduction then this so suddenly would occasion an immense degree of suffering and that this far at least these people from habits of industry & general fair dealing have a kind of claim to favourable considerations from the House although some of them have fallen behind. In regards the latter (the interest of the Trade) calculating that fish may be worth 9/ or 10/ [shillings per quintal] & that middling [catches?] happen again, I do not see that there can be much risk supplying these people – because it seems to me a convenient station to extend from again if times should warrant it, or to diminish from regularly in case of their continuing bad or becoming worse – Because from the bad times lately and [a gradual?] reduction that has taken place in this business a considerable [property?] has accumulated on hands in the shape of skiff and craft – [A greater?] reduction then contemplated here, or a sudden shutting up of this establishment would throw this property altogether out of use [...become?] a subject of wreck & plunder–

Continuing the business [as?] here contemplated will give the opportunity to draw something from this dead stock by hiring and selling [it] as opportunity offers to the people as other suppliers may happen to take them up.

The collection at this stage would probably be 2700 quintals with oil.

To transact it would require 1 agent & an assistant or boy as clerk shop or storekeeper and 1 or 2 additional labourers –

Statement 5th

Shows the number of persons selected from statement 1st who I cannot recommend to credit the winter under present circumstances on any grounds except that of extreme distress to which they will be exposed in consequence of being turned off; and which in a business point of view is in fact no recommendation at all.

Names of Planters	Sharemen or Servants	Remarks
Catalina		
Thomas Drake		Perhaps has means of support that I do not know of.
John Mason		
Matthew Mason		
John Sutton	two	
William White Snr.	one	
B. Island Cove		
William Chalk		
Jno. Chalk & sons	two	
Thomas Flynn	four	
Menchiner & Stead		
John Miles		
Nebuzaradon Tucker		

Quantity of Provisions that might *keep them alive* the winter
50 Cwt Bread   360 lbs Butter
20 Bls Flour   250 Gals Molasses
7 Bls Pork   worth about £190

When fishermen may starve: Slade–Kelson Plan

Number of souls without support the winter if these are turned off and no provision made for them

One Hundred and Thirty with George Vincent make one hundred & thirty four viz. *134*

Recapitulation

1. Total number of dealers in Slade and Kelsons establishment at Catalina 29
   With their wives, children, servants and sharemen &c they make up 346 souls

2. Contemplating reducing the business on credit to such only as are able to pay their accounts independent of bad voyages or other contingencies, there would remain to be supplied 3 dealers. . . . The necessary supply for the winter would be. . . . Confining the supply business to this extent would leave 297 souls without subsistence the winter.

3. Contemplating reducing the business on credit to those above described & certain other dealers not in quite such independent circumstances but yet as good if not better dealers than the former . . . The collection from these would probably be about 1300 qtls & to transact this business would require the same number of hands as before. Confining the supplying business strictly to this extent will leave 252 souls without support the winter.

4. Contemplating reducing the business on credit to those above described & certain other dealers, who though in debt, from their habits of industry and general fair dealing have a claim to favourable consideration in the Trade. . . . Confining the supplying business strictly to this estimate will leave 150 souls without support the winter.

5. The smallest number here contemplated to be turned off in the fall gives a great number to suffer from want the winter, and that many will perish seems to me almost certain, unless the Governing authorities do something for them – or Public subscription or something or other be done to avert the calamity – That Mr. Thompson or anybody else will supply them the winter is not at all probable – indeed I fear most of his dealers will be as bad off as those I am describing – It is extremely unfortunate for them that potatoe seed [which merchants supply on credit in the spring] was so scarce and dear this spring, so that they have not so much as usual of that article.

6. In these statements I am taking for granted that I succeed in getting the whole or greater part of the voyage – To whatever extent fish is smuggled away for provisions, so far of course will the amount of suffering from want be diminished, so that it is impossible to ascertain the exact amount of it till the collecting be over [shortly before the storms and ice set in]

Catalina, 20th Sept. 1825
[signed] Alex Bremmer

[NLPA. I wish to thank the very fine archivists of this collection, particularly Howard Brown and Ed Tompkins, who alerted me to this document.]

Domination, alliances, and descent

Three general features of this plan deserve comment.

The first feature appears in the sequence of the five statements, and it expresses the fact that the merchant houses could not afford to stay in business on the basis of the "good" fishermen alone. If they restricted their trade only to those dealers – planters, and as time went on, increasingly fisher families – who could be counted on to clear their bills each year, providing more value in fish than they took in supplies, or paying the balance in cash, there would be so few people in this category that all together they simply could not catch enough fish to make the merchant's business worthwhile. Bremmer's first, incidental suggestion, that if the firm wished to restrict its trade to just these dealers it should close up shop in Catalina and move to Trinity – a town down the coast that was its main port of trade – was not a viable solution: One cannot put all the good fisher families in one spot, to say nothing of the difficulties of moving fishermen from familiar terrain.

So the merchants, to build up the aggregate size of their catch and to increase the volume of supplies that they sold – for their profits were found at both ends of the trade – needed to include dealers who were not *regularly* able to clear their bills, and perhaps some who hardly ever did. It might at first appear to be "bad business" to continue to deal with people who were regularly behind on their credit, but it was crucial for the merchant to acquire a substantial number of fish and sell a substantial amount of supplies.

As everyone in this system well knew, and as we shall soon see, it was possible for the merchant to continue to deal with those who did not pay their debts in full if the losses on these people could be covered not simply by the gains of the trade as a whole but also specifically by raising the price of supplies for everyone, and lowering the price paid for fish to everyone, so that an entire outport village paid the same high price for supplies (approximately double the retail price of these commodities in England during the mid nineteenth century; Gunn 1977: 7), and received the same low price for fish. Beneath this surface equality among the fisherfolk, this system was specifically designed so that the substantial profits often made by the merchant from the good fishermen covered his credit losses on those less industrious, less skilled, or less lucky.

The second feature of the plan that requires comment is the significance of the attributes "industry" and "honesty" when deciding who would be kept on and who turned out. Industriousness is obvious; honesty in this context less so, and probably more significant for the merchant.

The opportunities for deception from below in this system were substantial. This was especially true before the late-nineteenth-century collapse of the large merchant houses that conducted their business through resident agents and before the emergence of more localized entrepreneurs

– resident merchants who owned the business and were interested in and capable of keeping a closer watch on community affairs. During most of the nineteenth century there was far more potential for deception, and fisher families were both under a lot of pressure to be dishonest and faced very dire consequences if caught.

The root of the potential for deception lay in the need of the merchant firms to disperse their activities along a stretch of coastline, partly to cushion the impact of localized variation in catches and partly to expand their range of operations as far as they could afford to credit: "Provided you furnish me with plenty of supplies and credit," William Kelson wrote to Mr. Slade in England (at this time – 1814 – probably as his agent), "our collections and dealings I have not the least doubt will be considerably more in the ensuing season than they were in the last" (Slade/Kelson Letters, Trinity 1809–25).

Expanding lines of credit usually meant enlarging the area within which one dealt. Where merchant trading areas overlapped, or even where they came close, planters and fisher families had room for negotiation and for deception: for selling some of their fish to a merchant other than the one that supplied them – a potential enhanced by agents who sometimes double dealt on their own employers. As Kelson reported to Slade, by way of explanation of his slightly more generous terms one year:

You will please recollect that there is a competition, that the Planters requires much humouring, and to which we must in many instances give way in order to prevent the encroachments of a certain character who is deeply interested in the Trade which he has some years conducted and which he in a greater or lesser degree divides with his employer. [Slade/Kelson Letters, Trinity 1809–25]

With two or more merchant houses in an area, the resident producers (planters or families) could not only bargain but deceive: They could sell part of their catch elsewhere, or take a full season's supplies from two different merchants and divide their catch between them, or give part of their catch to another planter or family who dealt with a merchant firm that gave a higher return (an act of collusion that the courts called "smuggling" – see *Connick* v. *Dooling & Co.,* 1819, Newfoundland Supreme Court, *Decisions* 1819–27, pp. 152–3 – a case considered by the court as having particular importance).

Merchants perhaps had to extend some credit, even in quite bad years, to keep a pool of fishing equipment and fisherfolk available for their future use. In the fourth statement we can see Bremmer trying to figure out an approximate base for his continuing business: " . . . I do not see that there can be much risk supplying these people – because it seems to me a convenient station to extend from again if times should warrant it, or to diminish from regularly in case of their continuing bad or becoming worse." While this need to extend credit to a substantial pool of people who in bad years would not be paying their bills probably did not give these people much, if any, leverage for their claims and needs, it was in fact a risky operation for merchants – particularly smaller ones, who would soon go bankrupt if their credit gambles failed. Such risks can create antagonistic relations between supplier and supplied, as the supplier seeks to enforce conditions that maximize the long-run potential for recovering his advances and more.

"Honesty," in sum, was a code phrase not just for an absence of deception but also for the centrality of control over the producers in this form of merchant capital. The resident fisher families and planters constantly faced the terror of being turned down for winter supply at the onset of winter, not simply for their own poor fishing, for which they might predict the response, but also for a variety of far less predictable factors, including the possibility that a merchant might just close up shop in an area. The denial of winter supply was invariably announced after the fish were collected. So fisher families, simply as a form of self-preservation, often tried to trade off some of the fish they caught to get a barrel or two of flour and some tea and molasses before giving the rest of the catch to "their" merchant. We do not know how often they did this, but it was often enough to be a major issue for the merchants. It was terror and domination, as much as honesty and what James Faris has shown (1972: 117–22) to be the "moral" claims of resident merchants upon the fish producers, that were central to constraining this "dishonesty."

Merchants knew what they needed even if they couldn't get it:

The supplying system . . . [is] an unsound system of doing business. . . . The natural exigencies of the supplying system . . . require that this island should be the exclusive property of one supplying firm, which should supply the able-bodied productive population in carrying on the fisheries of the island, under such close or exclusive rules, or legislation, as would preclude all . . . commercial competition and the modern rights of civil citizenship. [Murray 1895: 4]

The third feature of the Slade and Kelson Plan is by far the most generally important:

Two different and partly separate forms of community can be seen in this plan and found in the realities of social and productive life. One form of community is found in the plan's first statement, where the merchant groups his trade into three different named places with which he dealt – Ragged Harbour, Bird Island Cove, and Catalina – with brief comments on the characteristics of each of these places. And it is found again in the fifth statement, which groups the dealers who are going to be cut off, perhaps to starve, by the communities in which they live. These are communities of a particular place and physical environment: "communities of place and space," as they are here called. Each of these places offers to its inhabitants and to the merchant particular opportunities and constraints, each has a particular history, and each its own social life: people working together and negotiating such arrangements, competing for or sharing good fishing spots, marrying, raising children, being sick and in need, dying, celebrating, quarreling, helping each other in need, or not. . . . The "space" each of these communities occupies or creates is not simply physical but also social, historical, and to some extent intentional.

The second form of community found in the Slade and Kelson Plan is harder to see, but it is no less real. We may call it a "community of account," as distinct from a community of place and space. It appears in the merchant's plan in the second through fourth statements, which group people not by where they live but by how much they produce and consume, adjusted by their honesty and industry, and which set people one against another by the practice of squeezing the good fisher families to cover the losses of the less productive ones. (Keep in mind that a good deal of these losses can be paper losses only, for they are figured on the spread between manipulated prices.)

Permeated by the social relations and practical possibilities of communities of place and space – note the comment in the plan that most of the residents of Ragged Harbour were not "fair" in their dealings, which could refer simply to their greater poverty and need – the community of account comes to life in outport social organization and culture just as much as does the community of place and space.

The social relations of daily life and work on the one hand, and of appropriation on the other, though of course densely interwoven, are also separate and distinct: Each has its own history and dynamic of historical movement.

For a first illustration of this separation, I repeat the story of an incident that occurred in the early twentieth century – a story told across three generations, which took place in a village outport in Placentia Bay around the turn of the century:

I heard me father say one man came up to the door [of a merchant's house] and asked for a drink of water and he pointed to the water in the harbour and said, "plenty of water there." [Wareham 1975: 18–19; 1982: 45]

In Newfoundland outports it is rare for one house to be further than fifteen meters or so from another, the merchant's house included. It is even more rare for drinking water to be in short supply. The fisherman would not suffer from thirst before he could walk the few steps to another house. Nor was he asking for something that had any cost. To ask the merchant for a drink of water – precisely what everyone else in the community would freely and easily give to one another – was clearly provocative in the context of the inequality between merchant and fisherman. But it was more than a provocation. It was, openly and directly, the assertion of a claim: the claim that the fisherman and fish merchant belong to one kind of community, live by one set of community values, and participate in one social organization of their common humanity within which such small boons as a drink of water are freely asked and given.

The merchant had a different view. When he pointed to the bay – salt water and undrinkable – the *least* important statement he was making was about his contempt and his cruelty. The merchant was saying that in his view of the social order there was himself, the harbor, and between him and the harbor the fisherman, or a number of fishermen. For the merchant to have told the fisherman to get his drink of water from another house in the village would have been to admit defeat before the vision of the social structure that the fisherman had so provocatively presented: He would have admitted that the fisherman, or both of them, were part of a different kind of community than the one he sought to deal with, to dominate, to appropriate from, and in part to shape in this process.

This is not – not at all – to assert that two different community structures existed in Newfoundland in the context of merchant capital, structures that could be simply and neatly characterized by different forms and styles of interaction: a community of account (and of appropriation) characterized by relations of domination, and a community of place and space, of work and daily life, characterized by more egalitarian reciprocities. There are no such neat – or trivial – divisions in reality.

But it is useful to go beyond the pervasive assumption of anthropology, that the societies we study have *a* social structure and *a* culture, and that our task is to describe and analyze this. For there may be, at any one time, several different structurings of the social order. And what the social structure is may be open to contention and confrontation by the participants in the social system, not only in dramatic struggles but also in the very ordinary exchanges of daily life. These kinds of ordinary contentions and episodic confrontations have occurred within and between the fisher families of Newfoundland outports as well as between fisher families and the merchant, for they originate not in a struggle over the intensity of appropriation or domination but rather in the logic of production for merchant capital.

The Slade and Kelson Plan, after all, did no more than specify who should be turned out to starve and why. As powerful and dramatic as such statements are, the routine operation of the supply or truck system for those who were continued – kept on – within it was even more powerful. To see this, we need to look briefly at the social impact of truck: the system of advancing supplies in the spring against the catch in the fall, and then giving further supplies for the winter. In particular, we need to look past the surface appearance of truck, which seemed to be an arrangement between a merchant on the one hand and each of the several separate fisher families with whom he dealt on the other (an appearance reinforced by the practice of discussing the extent of credit for each fisher family privately; not in the open part of the store but in the merchant's office).

The Reverend Charles Pedley, Newfoundland missionary and historian, in 1863 heard and described how the truck system brought people together:

As . . . the voyage [the season's fishery] depended (in part) on causes beyond human control . . . a proportionate margin of profit had to be laid on the goods given out so as in case of success to compensate for the risk of failure; and also to make the gain from the man who did succeed cover the loss arising from the want of success in another man indebted to the same merchant.

The fisherman . . . knew that for the supplies for which he was indebted he had been charged an exorbitant rate, on the chance that he might not be able to pay, and therefore [he] scarcely felt the responsibility of the debt. . . .

But the worst effect of this system fell on the man who, more industrious than the others, was therefore as a rule more successful. . . . He knew that it fell on him to make good to the supplying merchant the failure arising from his less diligent neighbor. . . . [Pedley 1863: 205–6]

To unravel the broad range of effects that this had, both within the community and between the fisher families and their merchant, we shall first turn to look at the "traditional" outport culture that emerged, along with and after the truck system, following the demise of the servant fishery and the guaranteed wage.

6

The times of our lives

Descent, alliances, custom, and history

I

In 1849, twenty-four years after Slade and Kelson's agent at Catalina wrote his plan, while the system he described for credit and winter-supply decisions was flourishing, the Reverend Julian Moreton, an Anglican missionary sent to Newfoundland by the Society for the Propagation of the Gospel, arrived in Greenspond to minister to a flock dispersed along the shores of Bonavista Bay, the next bay to the northwest of Catalina. By this time the servant fishery was finished, and almost all the inshore fishing was done by the fisher families of the outports. Men, usually kinsmen, fished together; their mothers, wives, sisters, and young children salted and dried the fish, preparing them for fall delivery to the merchant.

On board ship at his departure, reminiscing upon thirteen years of ministering to these fisher families, most of whom were frightfully poor, Moreton wrote:

Having complete command of their time, these people are of a strange imperturbable habit. Unaccustomed to move at other men's bidding, they are hardly to be excited to action unless impelled by their own perception of need. *"When I see my own time,"* is a phrase continually in their mouths. Their very look betrays this feeling; and unless when for the moment they are eager after some advantage, their gait and every action seems possessed with a dignity, which would be ludicrous if it were not the token of so hurtful a temper. [Moreton 1863: 26; emphasis added]

Time belonged to the fisher families of outport Newfoundland: They made it their own as best they could, but they also lived within it, as they must. Hidden in this text, unannounced, alongside the idiom "When I see my own time," there is another idiom – at the point where Moreton uses a phrase to describe situations where fisherfolk move and act *without* dignity and self-possession: "unless when for the moment they are eager *after* some advantage" (emphasis added).

74

"After" is perhaps the most peculiar and poignant of the idioms of village Newfoundland. Sometimes it pertains to actions situated in the past, usually referring to intentions formed and completed, such as "All hands were after leaving her, cook and all. She was an old vessel, and they didn't like her" (DNE: 5). Usually, "after" implies a future, intended, or desired action, such as "I'm after going to the store," or "I'm after going to see the merchant," which means I will, or have to, or want to go to the store or to see the merchant.

The strangeness of using a word that means behind in time or place to refer to the future is illuminated by the fact that it is almost always used to refer to future encounters with the powerful and the dominant, or to situations where the poverty or helplessness of people is felt as a strong constraint: "Some poor fellers are after courting for six or seven years, just trying to get a little money to buy a house" (DNE: 5). "After": the past impaling the future.

To more fully see the fisher families of Newfoundland both fashioning time and held within it, we must go beyond the initial evidence of idioms and search for the logic of culture – expressed in and revealed by its movement over time and in history. In particular, we must look to the paradoxes of culture: its tensions and contradictions, rather than the interwoven content of culture-as-a-whole.

This is not to question the systematic connections between the disparate strands of culture but rather to change the notion of what the systematic connections are:

It is not possible to believe that the society which we study has a unity and forms a system, if one doubts at the same time the unity of its culture. But after that, it is necessary to identify its cleavages, its lines of opposition/contradictions, and also its exchanges which go across, in specific ways, the society studied and the field of its representations. [Schmitt 1981: 10; my translation]

II

Two customs in particular – and particularly in the distinction between their apparent and real divergences and correspondences – illuminate the paradoxes and contradictions of Newfoundland and folk culture. These customs, "mummering" (as Newfoundlanders call their form of mumming) and "scoffing," are both "times" in the most popular sense of that term in Newfoundland: the special events, the special and joyful occasions that punctuate daily life. (On times, see Faris 1968; Wareham 1982.) They are also both "parties" – occasions of drinking and merriment, music and dance. And for both, the threat implicit in the time is central to the custom.

For each custom I have previously published a detailed description and analysis (Sider 1976, 1984). The description of these customs in this chapter repeats briefly a few points of these essays – expanding here, deleting there. But by putting the two customs together, the analysis of each is substantially changed and pursued in new directions.

In almost all Newfoundland's small, isolated outports, for the twelve nights from Christmas to Old Christmas (25 Dec. – 6 Jan.), adult men and women have "janneyed up" – dressed in costumes that conceal their identity completely – and gone mummering from house to house.

Although mummers occasionally go alone, or in pairs, the loud banging at the hosts and victims' kitchen door with a split of stove wood from the porch, and the call "Mummers allowed in?" (uttered in unidentifiable, ingressive speech – the words spoken while breathing in, the way mummers talk if and when they will talk at all) usually signal the appearance of a group.

The knock is forceful, loud, and strange. In the small outports of coastal Newfoundland that, so long as mummering lasted, could usually be entered and left only by boat, and only visibly, only strangers and neighbors on commercial errands (neighbors become agents and strangers) usually knocked. Usual people – the people one knows and lives among – simply enter, at least as far as the kitchen, the first room in the house past the door and the largest and warmest room, the seat of both the family's own life and its hospitality. The appearance of the visitor is announced to the family within, if at all, by children and dogs.

Although mummers are always lifelong neighbors or kin, never strangers, the group and the people within it appear as strange as their knock, as unidentifiable as their ingressive speech. Men may be dressed as women, women as men, or masked with the head of a sheep or a circle of birch bark, scrawled and hanging with fungus and moss, steamed from a chunk of fallen half-rotted birch wood. Faces are always concealed by masks, veils, or paint; hands, in communities where people know and recognize the small details of each other, are hidden by gloves; posture and gait are altered. Even size may be changed by putting boards in boots or by stuffing one's costume with pillows and pads (Szwed 1969; Widdowson and Halpert 1969). The whole ensemble hovers at times on the edge of the far too fearful: for instance, a mummer at night coming down the road through his village, shortly after a shipwreck, dragging a spar and chains, and having the doors of the village barred. As likely, or perhaps more, it slithers from the fearful to the jocular: Yet mummers, crowding and banging on the porch, scary or jocular, always enter as the unknown.

To mummer well is to conceal and then reveal. Masked mummers stomping into a house tease and prod, fondle and pinch – men and women alike – dance, jostle, and prank, turning up chairs, shaking the stove: calling the tune with the force of their presence and dancing to it. As they perform they are questioned with increasing bravery, and pinched and prodded back, until bit by bit, one by one, they become known.

Once known they unmask and settle down as normal guests until all are known, at which time drinks are served and there is reestablished the usual, but festive, relationship between hosts and guests, reciprocal and careful of the customary niceties. At the point of reciprocity, when the hosts are invited to come around later and have a drink with – and from – the mummers, or to join the mummers on their rounds, they mask up again and go off to another house, or to a final party for the evening.

When starting down the paths that lace together the tightly clustered outport houses, mummers may begin in their usual groupings of kin and friends. But because the identification of one within a group may give away the identify of the whole group to the searching of the hosts (or, alternatively, a guess about the identity of the group may lead the hosts to the name of each person within it), groups often split up and recombine in the course of an evening, or from evening to evening.

For adults, but not for youths, it is crucial that they unmask before leaving and, upon unmasking, become guests: take a drink of liquor and perhaps also some food – social acts that demand the offer of reciprocity, even if the offer is not accepted. Adolescents may run out of the house without unmasking; an adult mummer must eventually drop the disguise – change back to being a usual person – even if unguessed. Jehovah's Witnesses, who do not drink, could neither mum nor host: Come back later and have a visit, they might call to the knock at the door, implying a visit with food; for central to mummering is the potential for reciprocal commitments that might follow the drinks.

A mummer, after accepting a drink, offers a return: Come for a drink; come and mum with us. The host, or hosts, have several options at that point. They can go mummering together, or they can go for a drink – and they can go for this drink either as mummers another night or, more seriously in its potential for new relations, they can go after the Christmas season ends, when they appear as themselves. Or they need not respond to the invitation, and because the occasion for making the invitation is special, there is no offense. Each year raises all possibilities, anew and differently.

Mummering is thus an opening – an opening for a series of new potentials for relations of reciprocity and integration that begin when the guests appear, their usual selves hidden to their hosts. To triumph over fear of the unknown and reveal your guests conjoins the possibility of seeing your guests with seeing them in a new light, with new possibilities for relationships. Why such possibilities are important we shall come to soon.

In scoffing, on the other hand, the guests are not hidden to, but *from*, their "hosts" – the host is not present at the party and never fully knows whom he or she is hosting or even when until after the party is over, if ever. For a scoff, in one sense of the term, is a party where the guests all bring and eat food that they have stolen from people who are not invited.

The word "scoff" has several different meanings in outport Newfoundland. In the first, more ordinary, sense a scoff means a dinner – almost always a family dinner – that the family makes from its own food and that is a particularly fine meal. In the second sense it refers to a party for people from several different families, for which all the food is stolen – or "bucked," as Newfoundlanders say, meaning something slightly different than simple stealing.

To generalize from a variety of forms this party scoff takes: The food is not taken from a person who is actively disliked, nor from a stranger in, nor a newcomer to, the community. It is not taken from the one prosperous and powerful person in the community, the fish merchant, nor from other figures of externally based power: doctors, schoolteachers, nurses, or resident government officials, if any such be present. Nor can the food be taken from someone who is poor and particularly needy. And it is not bucked from one's parents, brothers, or sisters, though late adolescents, just starting to scoff, may steal from their grandparents.

The food is taken from another fisher family living in the same community – and a lot of food is taken: a quarter of a deer, or some moose meat, or a live sheep, perhaps, or a bunch of chickens, and always also some vegetables, pulled from the garden or the root cellar. Never fish, never anything destined for sale to the merchant, and never anything, such as salt beef, bought from the merchant. The people from whom one bucks food are the only ones in the community who could themselves buck food: The community would not allow bucking by strangers, merchants, newcomers and outsiders, the very poor, or the morally marginal. One takes from people like oneself foods that they have themselves produced – hunted or raised – and that they themselves are planning to eat. (For a description of scoffing, see Faris 1968; 1972: 162–3. Also see Sider 1984.)

A lot of food is taken – enough to hurt, anger, or enrage the people from whom it was bucked, and enough to provide an exceptionally fine meal for the three, four, or five couples at the party, with a substantial amount usually left over for the person who "gave" (called, actually) the party. The couples, or sometimes the single men, and occasionally women at a "woman's scoff" who come to the party soon learn from whom each has bucked the food – that is, at whose expense the party is being given – and there is much merriment among them: a lot of sexual teasing, verbal and physical, drinking, dancing, playing cards, singing songs, telling tall stories and jokes, and eating, on and off, throughout the evening. And at some point late in the evening, in the midst of this scoff, they all sit down together for a large and fine meal from the bucked food – a meal that like

The times of our lives

the whole party, and like the dinner that a whole family enjoys from its own food, is also called a scoff.

During the next few days, as the victims of the bucking realize not just what happened but who is likely to have done it, there will be some hard looks and perhaps some hard words, much grumbling, perhaps some threats, occasionally a ballad composed about the villainy of the culprits, and plans made to get even. "Second plunder," people say, "is the sweetest" (Faris, 1972: 162).

"A regular time," people would say, approvingly, of a well-done scoff party; except that it is not all that regular a way of behaving in these usually quiet villages of rather reticent people. Occasions for playful merriment are scattered throughout the year – the "Christmas times," weddings, some festival days, and just parties and dances, in houses, in church, school, or "Orange Order" (the Loyal Orange Association – a Protestant social and political organization) halls. But bucking for a party is special to these scoffs (and to one other occasion, Bonfire Night, when burnables, not food, were taken; see Sider 1984). Such scoffs usually take place during a limited period in the fall of the year and are very special indeed, considering how careful, exact, and specific people ordinarily are about the obligations they owe and that are owed to them.

Louis Chiaramonte, for instance, in a very observant analysis of the interchanges of obligation in a south-coast outport (pseudonymously called Deep Harbour) noted the following incident:

A man was attempting to unload a dory engine onto a wharf. While he was struggling with it, two passing men stopped to watch. He worked for thirty minutes, while the onlookers stood by. They would not offer to help, nor did he expect it, for first he had to see if he could unload the engine himself. After he had worked hard at it and failed, then he asked them to give him a hand. [Chiaramonte 1970: 10]

The men who waited, watching, were not there to mock the futility of an individual's effort: To the contrary, they knew they might be needed. But when they were *asked* for help a commitment was born – a repayment was due when an opportunity arose, a repayment that might be, simply or significantly, speaking well of the helper in public. In outport Newfoundland help is not only given, often extensively, as when a house burns down, but also carefully noted. When a person's house burns a box will be put out on the counter of a merchant's store. Now that there is money in circulation, people will put money in, or notes offering furniture, clothes, and so forth, and write their name and what they gave on a list posted near the box, for all to see and to judge. Wedding presents, similarly, are brought to the reception and displayed at the festivities, with the card and the giver's name in front of the gift.

In this context bucking food for a scoff is very special, very different. But Newfoundlanders would call a fine scoff "a regular time," meaning

79

something special, different, and unusually fine, as I have just noted, and also, much more subtly, literally a regular time – not an antidote to ordinary life or a safety valve for its tensions and pressures, but a proper part of social life as it is lived.

To begin to understand scoffing in this sense of a regular time, we can look at the other occasion that is frequently called a scoff: a particularly fine meal that a family makes for itself from *its own food* – for example, a particularly good and abundant Sunday dinner, with the whole family present and not necessarily any guests.

The same kind of food would usually be served as at the party scoff: meat, or chicken, or seabird (rather than fish), vegetables, pudding, and so forth. And although a family scoff would not have the boisterous merriment of a party scoff, referring to it as a scoff implies not just an abundance of good food but also a warm and good time.

So there are two different kinds of scoffs, but one is not the opposite of the other: At bottom they are both the same. To see this identity, and then the connection between mummering and scoffing, we will look at the alliances that form and re-form in outport Newfoundland.

Mummering and both kinds of scoffing lie at the intersection of several different, but interwoven, forms of alliance within and between families. In addition to alliances of sentiment and emotion, there are alliances of kinship, of property formation and inheritance, of work and production. These different forms of alliance not only interweave but also come into conflict and contradiction with one another. They also come into conflict and contradiction with, and must adapt themselves to, the constraints imposed upon families and communities by the logic of merchant capital. The discussion of all these forms of alliance begins with the organization of the village inshore fishery during the period when the family was the unit of work for this fishery.

III

The inshore fishing season is short but intense. On the northeast coast – the most populous and productive area for the "traditional" family fishery – the summer fishery, based on the cod trap, lasts perhaps ten to twelve weeks between the spring breakup of the ice and the autumn storms and fog. During the autumn the nets are pulled out and put ashore for drying, mending, or rebuilding, and smaller crews, without the boys and older men, endure the rigors of hand lining, jigging, or gill netting for another month or so. On the south coast the season is longer, with gill nets used by smaller crews (two or perhaps three men) all during the season, and on the southwest coast there is a winter fishery, pursuing the migrating cod.

The times of our lives

The shortness of the season, the low income earned, the small size of the boats, and the self-direction of the fishermen, who do not go out on stormy days and who mix the maintenance of their equipment with socially pleasurable visiting, altogether give the "traditional" (prediesel long-liners) inshore fishery the impression if not of indolence then of a casual activity. As Thomas Lodge – perhaps the most sympathetic of the men sent out from Great Britain to govern Newfoundland after self-government collapsed in 1934 – wrote:

> In the nature of things it is not a calling which can be pursued for six days a week and fifty two weeks a year. The average fisherman can fish today and idle tomorrow if he thinks fit. He has no master to drive him to work if he happens not to wish to work. . . . It is a calling suitable enough to a people prepared to live a life of extreme simplicity with few wants outside the primitive needs of food and shelter. [Lodge 1935: 636]

Fishermen knew and acted differently – both in the intensity of their work during the season, and in the extent of the preparatory activities before and after the season. In 1972 a fisherman, referring to a time twenty to twenty-five years earlier, when he was still rowing to his fishing grounds, two or three hours each way, fishing all day, and hauling nets by hand, told me: "By the time you rowed back and pitched your fish up on the dock, some nights you were so tired you didn't recognize your own family when you walked through the door." And it is frequently painful work – wet hands in the intensely cold sea, all day long – the hands of a fisherman that can frequently be recognized from afar by the arthritic swelling of the inflamed finger joints.

In the midst of the difficulty of the work, these inshore fisher families caught a lot of fish. In 1961 – not a good year at all – the inshore fleet, using 9,400 gasoline- or diesel-powered boats, 6,700 sailing and row boats, and 8 long-liners, landed and salted 182 million pounds of codfish, slightly less than one-half of which was salted and dried, and the other half sold as "wet salt bulk" to commercial drying factories. Additionally, fresh cod for freezing and other varieties of fish accounted for a further 200 million pounds: a total of approximately 26,000 pounds per fisherman (Copes 1972: app. A; based on statistics of the crudest sort, and here only given for a general indication.)

To achieve such productivity, families had to muster sufficient labor, with a minimum and a maximum size for the work units and, particularly on the boats, a very narrow spread between the minimum and the maximum. They must also have sufficient equipment, some of which they make themselves: huge nets woven by the family, during the winter, from a spool of twine hung under the kitchen table; boats built and repaired by the men that use them, or perhaps by, or with the aid of, a village craftsman. Most

81

of the major pieces of equipment are pooled by work crews and passed on by inheritance.

James Faris, in his study of a fairly typical, small (the population in 1963–4, at the time of the study, was about 285 people) northeastern Newfoundland outport, called Cat Harbour, showed how kinship relations are used to organize the inshore fishery. There are three dimensions to this kinship organization: crew, shore crowd, and clan (Faris 1972: chap. 7; see also Firestone 1967; Nemec 1974).

The crew are the two to four men who work together on a boat. Usually these men are closely related patrikin (i.e., the links between them when, e.g., they are cousins, are usually formed through men, for reasons that have to do with shoreline possession): father and son, or sons; brothers; cousins; or occasionally uncle and nephew. The man who owns the boat, and perhaps also the cod trap, is the skipper. He may take a larger portion of the catch to reflect his costs, but he generally does not use his position as skipper to make decisions about how, where, or when to fish, nor to tell other crew members how, or how hard, to work. The ethic of egalitarian relations on board the boat is sufficiently strong that boats have been caught out in storms because no one wanted to make the decision to come back in (Faris 1972: 104).

The boat and the cod trap are each a major asset. An elderly fisherman, when retiring or at death, will often leave the trap to one son, the boat to another, and split the necessary shoreline between them. For a while the sons are likely to fish together, sharing the returns and trying to save enough for the other major piece(s) of equipment, for example, a boat, an engine or trap, perhaps a house, or some more waterfrontage, by the time their own sons are grown. At this point the crew will split from an alliance of brothers to one of father and sons, or a father and sons in one boat, a different brother in the other; and when the crew splits the shore crowd will also.

The "shore crowd" are the women kin of the boat crew – their sisters, wives, and mothers – and their children of both sexes. Usually three or four women are needed for the lengthy, technically complex, and very arduous work of properly curing the codfish.

A woman is not paid directly for this work, but her husband's or brother's or father's share of the catch depends upon her work (E. Antler 1977; 1981: chap. 4). For a fisherman to receive an equal share of the catch depends upon three contributions to the enterprise: his labor on the boat, a major piece of equipment (boat, net, motor, or shoreline), and women kin who work with the shore crowd. Although widows are sometimes fully incorporated by their husband's former crew – they pay her a full share for working with the shore crowd, and she will use half of it to hire a "shareman" to work on the boat (e.g., Firestone 1967: chap. 3) – men

rarely or never are carried. Without equipment, and usually more importantly (for equipment can sometimes not be essential), without the contribution of a kinswoman's labor to the shore crowd, a man is not a fisherman
but a shareman – a person who gets one-half the regular share of the catch.
(If there are three men in a boat, the shareman would get approximately
one-sixth of the catch, not one-third; "approximately" to allow for the
percentage taken to cover the cost of the boat, fuel, food, etc.) Sharemen
are often in a very difficult situation, unless it is a temporary situation, for
even a full share of the catch is usually a poor income. They often work
in outports that are not their home, where they will get "dieted" (room
and board) for the season – perhaps the first step in a permanent migration
from their home village, either westward in Newfoundland to rawer circumstances in newer communities, or into "town," or off the island
altogether.

There is a high degree of tension in putting together and maintaining a
fishing crew and its associated shore crowd. People are often pulled in
different directions. A man with growing sons may have to stop fishing
with his brother to accumulate (by retaining the son's earnings within the
nuclear family) enough equipment to leave to all his sons – and to earn
enough income to raise his younger children, and perhaps to acquire a
larger house. And when he leaves the shore crowd will also split. The
obligation of wives makes it clear where they will go in this split; the mother
and the unmarried sisters are, or can be, in a more complex and difficult
situation.

If the brother's sons are not yet grown when this crew splits, the brother
must take in another brother, or turn outward to a cousin or a friend – all
of whom are likely to already have fishing partners, unless this is the first
season that they are old enough to crew or their own partner left. A woman
who has been salting fish for her father and brothers leaves to get married,
perhaps before the brothers are old enough to themselves take wives,
leaving an empty space in the shore crowd. Further, the shore crowd can
also split, "rowing out," as the tensions that lead to such a break are
significantly called, requiring the crew that is associated with this crowd to
also split and re-form. Examples multiply, and the effects of several changes
each season – or more usually at the end of each season, when most
weddings and "retirements" occur – can spread widely in a small community.

These tensions and complexities are substantially increased by frequent
problems in allocating three further resources needed by an inshore fishing
family: a house on land with access to usable waterfrontage and a garden
plot. Houses are expensive to build, for lumber-quality trees are often
scarce in the vicinity of outports, and both useful waterfrontage and garden
plots are in shorter supply than might be imagined for a land so sparsely
populated. Much of the shoreline is rocky or steep, and many settlements

have developed in just such difficult locations, initially chosen either to avoid British or French naval harassment or more usually to be within rowing distance of good fishing grounds.

The "clan" – relatives of the same surname, thus kin through men – is the social unit that transmits, by inheritance or by sales to one another, access to these critical resources. As population rose relative to these available resources, in a context where the truck system inhibited or precluded expansion into a larger-boat, more distant-water fishery, and a combination of poverty, intracommunity tensions, and government unconcern inhibited the development of community wharves and piers, the tensions of allocating these scarce resources also rose. The tension stemmed from the difficulty of maintaining the fundamental equality within and between outport families when there were too few resources to pass on to sons who were founding new families or new fishing enterprises. This put pressure on some to leave and made the issue of alliances between people with access to the necessary resources more salient.

The "ideal" developmental cycle of boat crew and shore crowd – from father and sons, with mother, wife, and daughters; to brothers and wives or sisters; and then on to father, sons, wife, and daughters – was often difficult to develop and maintain. Even when generally maintained, it could often be disrupted several times for any one kin group, or not workable at all for some families. In Cat Harbour in the early 1960s, 71 percent of the crews were ideal, that is, composed of a core of patrikin; and several of these crews also had crew or sharemen who were not kin. Even when brothers fished together, there was still the issue, in large families, of *which* brothers.

The tensions that emerged in the allocation of resources and in the conjoining of crew and crowd, or even just the tensions in the daily personal interchanges of working together, could lead to decisive breaks in crews and shore crowds – or, with emigration or marriage, which for women was frequently outside the community – to a break from the community itself. Tensions routinely emerged in the work process itself: Brothers who fished together all summer long would frequently avoid each other completely in the fall, coming back together in midwinter when they jointly began to rebuild their equipment (Nemec 1974).

With frequent large families, and with village population both relatively small and often stable over long periods of time, the intimacy of working and living together included the knowledge that the continued well-being of some members of the family depended on the fact that other members of the family would not get a place in the family crew, or would have to leave the community – the men emigrating, often because there was no place nor resources for them, the women often sent out as teenagers to work for distant relatives as live-in, unpaid help, and then marrying out

84

of their home community, perhaps to cancel their claim to inherit or to be dowered with a piece of the shoreline. Intimacy and antagonistic interests came packaged together in the social relations of work and daily life, both within families – and from the effects of truck and "tal qual" (buying all the fish from a community, regardless of quality, at one price) upon these small villages of lifelong neighbors and kin – and between families. The family-dinner scoff hid within itself the same structure and the same history as the party scoff, where all the food was stolen from other fisher families: One person's well-being is another's loss, and the other – the victim – and the self are identical.

IV

The following story describes an incident that occurred in the south-coast outport of St. Jacques in the 1920s. St. Jacques was near the French islands of St. Pierre and Miquellon – remnants of the once vast French holdings on the south, west, and northwest coasts of Newfoundland – and the fishermen of nearby Newfoundland did a fair amount of smuggling to and fro. The Newfoundland government thus appointed a customs officer in several of these villages, who had to check the fishing boats before they could be unloaded.

My Uncle Isaac came into St. Jacques in his vessel and went ashore to make a customs entry report. He was told by Uncle Alex St. Croix [the customs officer] that it was a holiday, and he would have to wait until the next day to get into the customs office. Uncle Ike became indignant, stating that since he never got any holidays nobody should. Uncle Ike's temper was as bad or probably worse than Uncle Alex's so matters became worse and worse by the minute, until finally Uncle Alex roared "I'll beat up everything," and proceeded forthwith to show he wasn't bluffing. Uncle Ike had to let off steam too, so he announced, "If that's what you want I'll help you," so they smashed everything in the office to bits. Of course it resulted in a court appearance, and Uncle Ike had to pay fifty-two dollars in damages, which he said was the most enjoyable fifty-two dollars he had ever spent. The saddest aspect was that they never again spoke to one-another. [Evans 1981: 33–4]

This story is wonderful, for the two men did not beat each other, and even more tragic than wonderful, for it is a story about anger that could never be either fully expressed nor resolved and transcended. It is the *same* story as the one above about the two men waiting quietly to be asked to help by the man unloading the engine from his boat, and neither offering to help nor simply pitching in to help in a task obviously difficult to do alone. It is, in sum, a story about the distances that open up in the midst of the intimacies of village culture.

Related to these distances and springing from the same pressures is another kind of distance that opens up in village culture. In the villages (or the "tribes"; the situation is in some respects general) that produce for merchant capital, a profound difference between village culture as a whole (the "traditional" village culture that emerges in the context of integration with merchant capital) and the culture and structure of domination becomes increasingly manifest as communities of place and space become harnessed to the demands of merchant capital and its metropolitan sponsors. The "quaintness" of these villages and tribes is rarely archaic, and despite all the theories of acculturation (the homogenization of differentiation with integration), it usually increases as the noose of the "world economy" tightens. More precisely, one of the momentums of historical development of hinterland culture in the context of merchant capital is increasing local or regional particularity: There are, simultaneously, countervailing pressures and developments. We must look more closely at this.

The truck system – the form merchant capital took in its dealings with the fisher families of outport Newfoundland – "solved," or tried to solve, two general problems faced by merchant capital: (1) It attempted to deal with problems caused by major variations in amount produced and in prices. It did this through price manipulations that permitted the merchant to capture much of the profits in good years and to push off onto the fisher families much of the losses of bad years. (2) The truck system also sought to solve one of the problems faced by any system of production organized by relations of domination, hierarchy, and inequality: how to keep the people at the bottom continually within the existing system – how to keep them from developing an alternative and autonomous set of productive relations. The truck system, by substantially demonetarizing the village economy (i.e., keeping the villagers from having much access to cash, although they were in a monetary economy in other ways) prevented village fisher families from developing or sustaining an alternative and more autonomous economy. The tensions within Newfoundland village culture expressed, in part, the constraints imposed upon the village as a whole (just as the fact that American Indians were only allowed to produce diminishing resources – beaver, deer, buffalo pelts, or to sell their land or their bodies as mercenaries, etc., and were not allowed to market maize or tobacco – conditioned the social and cultural relations within and between Indian "tribes").

More than constraints, the truck system itself, and certain associated features, engendered antagonistic relations within communities. Particularly significant in this regard was the system of "tal qual" (literally, "as is") payments.

The truck system did not use cash, or not very much, but it did use prices – prices entered on the books for supplies and for fish. The prices paid – or allowed – for fish ordinarily were based not simply on the amount of fish delivered but also on their grade, with the grade based on the size of the fish and particularly on the quality of the cure. A bewildering variety of grades and systems with different numbers of grades were recognized and used. But five grades were basic – standard in name and widespread in use, but not necessarily standardized in terms of what kind of fish got placed in which category, particularly since the fish were sorted by an employee of the merchant. These grades ranged from merchantable, at the top, to West Indie or cull at the bottom, and the spread in prices allowed for the different grades was considerable.

Starting in the late nineteenth century, merchants from time to time did not grade the fish they got from a community but rather took all the fish in a community tal qual – at one average price. This price was supposedly based on the merchant's estimate of the average grade of fish produced by the community during that season. The practice of buying tal qual was not uniformly used in any one place from season to season, nor across a broad range of places in any one season; rather, it seemed to come and go from time to time and place to place. Tal qual requires a close study that it has not yet had, and that can not be done here, beyond suggesting that it was far from being what it was said to be (a way of rushing fish to market). Purchase contracts in Europe and the Caribbean were ordinarily written for specific grades of fish; the fish had to be graded, if not at the point of purchase, then before being shipped. The same merchants who complained bitterly that tal qual purchasing was destroying the quality of fish by making the shore crowd indifferent to the quality of the cure also often themselves bought fish tal qual.

One hint about the structure of tal qual lies in the scant evidence that suggests it was used by merchants in situations where the fishery was becoming sufficiently productive or remunerative to engender an outport "middle class" – fisher families with larger boats and more extensive operations. Thus tal qual buying was often encountered on the Labrador coast, in the late nineteenth century, where the catch was enormous, though these fish were slightly less desirable in Europe; on the northeast coast, following the introduction of the cod trap in the last quarter of the nineteenth century, which massively increased the size of the catch; and during World War I, when prices rose substantially and tal qual became widespread in Newfoundland: Tal qual, in sum, was perhaps more a form for perpetuating merchant domination than for payment.

Be that as it may, what is crucial here are the relations that tal qual purchasing imposed within the community, not just on the men who caught the fish and delivered them to the merchant but particularly between the women of the different family shore crowds who made the cure.

John Szwed, studying the west-coast outport he calls Ross, has pointed out that the tal-qual system penalized the women who put in the effort to cure their fish well, for the average price lumped together their good work, at much effort, with their neighbor's poorer – and easier – cure (Szwed 1966: 52). Bonnie McCay, who has done extensive fieldwork on the northeast coast, said that the bitterness over this issue was explicit, overt, and perhaps more enduring than the form of payment itself (personal communication).

The better grades of fish are not only larger, and not only require more skill and more work to cure properly, but also depend upon a certain amount of luck in having the necessary cool, dry, sunny weather for the week or so after the catch is landed. Thus the quality of the cure depends upon causes that are both within and outside people's control.

Merchants received fish throughout the late summer and early fall from the families in the outport that differed substantially in cure and thus in grade. Although fisher families would have some idea about what quality of fish was being produced in the village, and by whom, they would have no way of knowing exactly what the average cure in the village was, nor if a below-average cure was due to poor weather or poor work. When the merchant bought fish from the community at one average price he had substantial room for deceit, and this potential for deceit is also, most likely, a substantial part of the explanation for using tal qual. Fisher families could, and often did, suspect that they were being cheated by the merchant, and they could suspect that they were being cheated by their neighbors, but they could not be sure, for they would have no way of knowing who was producing what quality of fish, or why.

The structure of the party scoff – some folks are eating well and enjoying themselves from what I have done and myself made; or let us enjoy ourselves to the full from what we have taken from others – is a clear correlative of the structure of truck and tal qual. More than a simple reexpression in folk custom of social relations formed in the domain of production, the scoff may suggest – mistakenly – to its participants that they are the authors of their own antagonistic intimacies, and that their relations to each other are separate and distinct from their antagonistic (and perhaps also intimate) relations with the merchant. Scoffing and mummering implicitly claim as the village's own a culture that both is, and is not its own, but which by its very presence and particularity marks the village off from the larger structures of domination as a special, and in a collective sense private, place.

V

Mummering and scoffing are both historically specific customs, although the specificity of each is different. Mummering, in the form described in the second section of this chapter, began in the 1840s and declined to the point of disappearance in the 1950s and early 1960s: Its span is coterminous with the duration of the predominance of the family fishery. Scoffing – the party scoff – began in the 1890s, in the period just following the destruction of an emergent outport middle class and in the context of a renewed consolidation of merchant domination over almost equally impoverished fisherfolk, and it still continues, perhaps slightly diminished, in outport Newfoundland.

Each of these customs is historically specific not only in the sense that it had a specifiable point of origin and a specific duration but also in having specific connections to other forms of social relations, such as the organization of the fishery, and to each other and to other customs. A closer look at the historical specificity and particularity of these customs will serve – somewhat surprisingly – to introduce the issue of the autonomy of culture: its separateness from, as well as its ties to, social and productive organization. This topic is introduced here and is taken up at more length in the next three chapters, which consider the political entailments of folk culture on the terrain of ideology and what marxists call hegemony – the role of elite culture in securing and perpetuating domination.

The Christmas customs that Captain Cartwright observed in the 1770s among his servants (see Chapter 4) were Yule customs, widespread in the British Isles from which his servants came: the great fire, the formal drink, the cheers, and the subsequent revelry. Forty years later, as the migratory servant fishery was in the process of transition to a resident and family fishery, more particular Newfoundland customs were developing:

The ancient British custom of the *Yule*, or Christmas log or block, is universally observed by the inhabitants of Newfoundland. On Christmas-eve, at sun-set, an immense block, provided on purpose from the adjoining woods, is laid on the back of the fire-place, to be left there until it is entirely consumed; the ceremony of lighting it is announced by the firing of muskets or seal guns before the door to each dwelling house. This, among them, is the prelude to a season of joy and merriment. . . . The custom is said to be of very great antiquity and still prevalent in the north of England. . . . Christmas dinners are in general practice; so are likewise Christmas-boxes, or presents, not in coin, for this is not in common use there, but in eatables, from a turkey or a quarter of veal . . . down to a nicely smoked salmon. This custom is said to have originated with mariners. . . .

Another custom, which is said to be still observed in the North of England, prevails in some parts of Newfoundland, though not with general approbation: it is called *mumming*; men and women exchange clothes with each other, and go from house to house singing and dancing, on which occasion Christmas-boxes are expected, and generally granted previous to the performance, in order to get rid of them. The author must, in justice to the *native* inhabitants of Conception Bay, observe that frequent attempts have been made to introduce this practice among them, but they have been generally resisted, and publicly reprobated. [Anspach

1819: 475–7. Anspach lived along Conception Bay from 1802 to 1812. See also Story 1969: 169–70.]

This is the first mention of mumming, or mummering, in Newfoundland, and it depicts both forms of mummering that were to develop there. The "urban," or town, form (for details and analysis of which see Sider 1976) that occurred in the larger and more prosperous towns of Conception Bay and in St. John's became a ritual of class inversion and class challenge: a parade in which the poor often dressed in mock finery, and a semiritualized play recounting a battle, death, and resurrection among mythic heroes, which was performed in the houses of the upper class by roving groups of "working-class" mummers who more or less forced their entry. Before or after the performance they "collected," or dunned for money, which was given as much in recognition of the potential threat of their presence as from a noblesse oblige reward for the play.

In 1861 the Newfoundland legislature banned mummering by banning public masking; only these urban forms were suppressed. The village form just described continued to flourish.

This village form of mummering, in which the mummers enter as totally unknown and then must become known, seems to condense and intensify the potential for change and rearrangement that must be found in social relations for the community to continue to organize and reorganize its own relations of productive work. Central to this perspective on mummering is unmasking the unknown at the point of potential, and potentially new, reciprocities:

No adult male mummer would take a drink without first removing his mask, for if a man would take a drink without exposing his identity, he would not be able to fulfill the obligation he incurred by accepting the drink. [Chiaramonte 1969: 86. The south-coast drift-net fishery brings in smaller quantities of cod at any one time than does the cod trap, and thus the labor of women in the shore crowd is not as intense. Hence, perhaps, there is a greater focus on men's activities in mummering.]

Chiaramonte is here analyzing mummering in the "traditional" and isolated south coast outport of "Deep Harbour." He broadens and deepens this point about reciprocity and social role flexibility:

Particularly during Christmas evenings the separateness of households, the usual withdrawal of each family to its own kitchen is dramatically broken. Crowds of men tour from one household to another – singing, dancing, telling stories and drinking. Groups of mummers of all ages and descriptions are also visiting from house to house. . . . Tensions built up during the year are eased, as alienations between households and men are put aside. For this is the season of the year when the community reaffirms its sense of unity. . . .
The men who went drinking together and the various types of mummers . . . have used the Christmas season to cement and reinforce the bonds established in their workaday lives. . . . The community takes stock of its members. . . . Christmas in

Deep Harbour can be viewed, then, as an event in which the community reaffirms its identity. [Chiaramonte 1969: 81, 103]

Why is this collective stock taking important? Because while kin groups organize the social relations of work – crew and shore crowd – the community organizes the reproduction of these relations over time, and it does a substantial part of this within the domain of custom. For it is in the communitywide context of custom, which includes crucial indicators and announcements of changing status, that the communitywide implications of changing statuses and alliances can be seen, acknowledged, and begun to be taken into account in one's own plans. For example, adolescent male mummers, who work on their father's boats without getting a share, run out of the houses they visit without unmasking; young men, who crew and take a share of the catch, unmask and drink, or at least ask for one: Sometimes this request is the first specific indication that things will be different in the next season.

The scariness of mummers may come from more than costumes that conceal identity and unusually boisterous behavior. It may also come from fears for relations and alliances that cannot be formed or that will be broken, although still needed. For mummering provides, in the midst of its merriments, an opportunity for people to transfer or reaffirm their relationships – to make new alliances and leave old ones – and it also brings together on a common field a community potentially riven by the tensions of the implications of changing or reaffirmed relationships. In both ways mummering serves to reproduce the social relations of kin and village commodity production: not only the specific relations, which can be either reinforced or altered in the course of being reproduced, but also the social system that makes possible continual change and continuity in change. When the family fishery ended, and fisherfolk went to factory work (hired on trawlers, or in filleting and freezing plants), the reproduction of the social relations of work was taken from their hands, and mummering – still vividly described to me by many people in the 1970s as the most fun they ever had – came to an end.

Scoffing so clearly restates the structure of interpersonal relations that are shaped by the imposition of truck and tal qual upon family and community work processes that there is little to add to this basic observation. Yet it is more than a custom-contextualized dramatization of imposed antagonisms. Two additional factors together provide the first key to further understanding this custom.

Tal qual – the same price for all the fish in a community – is an extension and an intensification of one of the basic features of the truck system itself. Truck is more than the cashless exchange of supplies for cured fish, with credit and enforced delivery of the entire "crop" of fish. It is also, as we have seen in the context of discussing the Slade and Kelson Plan, the same prices charged to everyone in the community for supplies, and the same prices allowed to everyone in the community for different grades of fish, with the price structure set each season to permit the merchant's gains from the good fisher families to cover his losses from the poorer. Both truck and tal qual, in sum, impose upon the community an "equality" that is not conjoined with egalitarian and communal institutions of fish production "from below." There are no community mechanisms for sharing good fishing grounds, or pooling the fish catch, or doing a communitywide common cure. To the contrary, work and its rewards are privatized and enclosed within the family, or within pairs of closely related families. Thus the imposed forms of "equality" of truck and tal qual *necessarily* engender antagonisms between families, as the severe developmental and expansionary limits imposed by the truck system's demonetarization of the village economy must necessarily engender antagonisms within families.

I have suggested that there were, in outport Newfoundland during the period of the family fishery, two major structurings of the social order: one of work and daily life within the communities of place and space, and one of appropriation, creating communities of account. The structures of work – based on alliances within and between families, alliances reproduced and readjusted in part through community social and cultural processes, can be seen to be reexpressed and reproduced in the context of mummering. And the antagonisms of truck and tal qual that split and conjoin people within and between families are reexpressed and recreated in the custom of the scoff.

But it is not – not at all – the case that mummering is a custom of the community of place and space, and scoffing a custom of the community of account. For each custom, as with outport culture as a whole, conjoins both structurings of the social order.

Scoffing is not only antagonistic, it is particularly intimate: the intimacy of the party, of the family meal; the intimacy between victim and victimizer that occurs in purloining the food from an equal, or that more subtly occurs when the family sits down to eat together. The party scoff in fact defines this intimacy by carefully distinguishing "bucking" the food from stealing (Faris 1968: 117–18): Taking food from the very poor, resident "outsiders," the merchant, or the morally marginal is not bucking but stealing, as it would be if they took food from you. The party scoff in this sense is like the family scoff – a meal from one's own. We can see the intimacies upon which the party scoff rests most clearly in our knowledge that bucking food, for all the anger it creates, would create even more dangerous emotions and disastrous consequences were it to be attempted in a housing project: Among workers conjoined only by common class, it would be impossible.

And mummering is much more than social rearrangements in the midst of merriment. Merriment there is and plenty, but the mummers are scary – often very scary. The process of social reproduction, in part accomplished in the context of mummering itself, contains and creates profound threats and fundamental tensions: alliances that won't work out, or are needed and can not be formed, or that will be broken, leaving some abandoned. As scary as are the mummers, they are only the surface expression of far more profound tensions and fears that the community is largely helpless to resolve. The community may control the organization of work and the reproduction of this organization, but the organization and structure of *production* itself – the whole process of determining what will be produced, with what intensity, for what kinds of return, and under what constraints, is in large part imposed upon them.

VI

The last thing a fish would discover, Ralph Linton once perceptively observed, is water. Similarly, it seems the last thing that anthropology would discover is the peculiarity of culture. So much of our lives as anthropologists are spent immersed in its peculiarities, trying to accomplish the often intensely difficult task of describing and understanding other customs, other ways, that we hardly have time and space to ask: Why are folk cultures so "peculiar" – so different, so particular, so strange? It is usually assumed that the particularity of folk culture originated in the hazy dawn of time, and that the expansion and consolidation of supralocal institutions – state power; national, regional, or "world economies" – are now, or will soon, destroy this differentiation.

It has been, however, quite a long time for most places in the world since the neolithic revolution and the emergence both of agriculture and of far-reaching institutions of domination, conquest, and incorporation. If domination and incorporation simply destroyed differentiation, the world would be far more homogeneous than it in fact is. Clearly, incorporative structures of power *do* undermine and destroy differentiation; but they must also, simultaneously, create it.

The question of the creation of a particular, special, and different folk culture is brought to the foreground in Newfoundland, for the inhabitants are ordinary English and Irish folks, and they clearly "invented" – developed, rather – such customs as mummering and scoffing. They may have brought aspects, elements, or memories of such or similar customs with them when they came, or they may have learned about them from other places – in the contacts they had transporting fish and supplies to and from Europe, the Caribbean, the "Boston States," and Brazil. But these are customs that both emerged at particular times in Newfoundland and rapidly became widespread throughout the island: They are, in that precise way, local developments.

It is becoming increasingly clear that much of "traditional" culture is a relatively recent development and a historically specific creation. Eric Hobsbawm and T. O. Ranger, in *The Invention of Tradition* (1983), collect multiple examples of this, but most of the examples are about elites who consciously and explicitly formulate practices or customs in conjunction with domination or with political-economic or ideological manipulations. In Newfoundland we are dealing with a quite different phenomenon: developments from below – less consciously, if at all consciously, invented, and unplanned. Why then do outport Newfoundlanders mum and scoff?

Part of an answer is possible here, and it has several dimensions.

First, customs do things – they are not abstract formulations of, or searches for, meanings, although they may convey meaning. Customs are clearly connected to, and rooted in, the material and social realities of life and work, although they are not simply derivative from, or reexpressions of, these realities. Customs may provide a context in which people can do things that it would be more difficult to do directly; they may provide a context in which to coordinate and coadjust a multiplicity of emotions and interests; and especially, as the loci for intentional, forward-looking actions, they may keep the need for collective action, collective adjustment of interests, and collective expression of feelings and emotions within the terrain and the domain of the coparticipants in a custom, serving as a boundary to exclude outsiders. The multiple meanings of the word "custom" are particularly revealing on this point: Custom is both a border-defining process, the point where entrance within is regulated by those who control the "within," and also a special part of a local culture. Customs, in sum, both do things and define who can participate in the doing.

Second, the specific form that the connection takes between custom and culture on the one hand, and the material and social realities of life, work, and appropriation on the other, is crucial to understanding the autonomy and the historical dynamic of culture. I suggest that the *rootedness of culture in historically specific forms of social structure gives culture its historical specificity, and the fact that culture* – at least in the context of merchant capital – *straddles and conjoins diverse structurings of the social order* (e.g., work and daily life; appropriation) *gives culture its autonomy and its own dynamic of development.*

Such customs as mummering and scoffing not only conjoin and express diverse structurings of the social system; they also create and define the people of outport Newfoundland as a specific entity – a people with their own common ways and their own common claims. Folk culture forms or contributes to forming, in the midst of its superficially backward-looking "traditionalism," a more-or-less collective intentionality – albeit an inten-

94

tionality riven with tensions, antagonisms, and interpersonal distances, and also with ambiguities, paradoxes, ambivalence, and contradictions.

This self-creation of a people as a separate and special people, situated in relation to a perhaps vague, mythical, and mystical past and to an also vague and often illusory but equally significant future, is, I think, a key aspect of the creation of an autonomous and special folk culture. The special claims upon the future that "traditional" cultures can make, or not make, define and delineate its special and current presence in the larger social world: It was, for example, ultimately the people of outport Newfoundland who took the extraordinary step, in 1948, of voting to terminate the autonomy and independence of their country and to confederate with Canada. And the same people, fifteen years later, found themselves incapable of organizing to resist the largest forced relocation scheme ever imposed on a populace, outside of a situation of war, by a modern "democratic" state. It is to the political terrain on which folk culture also exists – takes shape and finds, or fails to find, its voice – that we now turn.

Deep Harbour. One of the safest harbors on the south coast. In stormy weather, deep-sea trawlers from Newfoundland, Canada, Portugal, Spain, and France make for this shelter. The cliffs are 500 feet above the village, and there is still no road to the village – local people can travel to neighboring villages only in their own small boats, or on the "government steamer" that stops once or twice a week on its route along the south coast.

Houses in Deep Harbour, Ash Wednesday, 1966. On Ash Wednesday the village is largely deserted, as people go to the top of the cliffs to go "sliding." At the left some people can be seen returning. The foreground buildings across the harbor are "stages" for storing coal, fishing gear, and baited trawl. They were later replaced by a communal storehouse, built as a government works project, which fell into disuse and was converted into a social hall – what the people had in mind when the communal stage was built.

Interior of a shop. This shop is owned by a merchant who lives on a nearby island, owning a shop and a fish plant (for frozen filets) there. The merchant's schooner brings ice and supplies, daily in season, and takes the fish away. The closing of such shops, a frequent occurrence since the early mid twentieth century, often forces people to abandon their community.

In this photograph are the shopkeeper and his wife, a fisherman and his daughter. The fisherman works from a row dory, which is less expensive to use than a motor dory, and he fishes by himself, rowing "cross-handed" [a style of rowing explained in Chapter 10] the mile-and-a-half-long reach out of the harbor and back "every day of his life"; that is, when it is not too stormy to fish. A big, powerful man in his sixties, he still walks the streets of the village in the afternoons holding hands with his wife, a woman renowned for her crocheting skills and her pattern designs, to whom other women come for advice.

(facing) *Unloading fish at the merchant's stage*. At the rear is the shop whose interior is shown above. On the right is the craftsman who is building the boat in a subsequent photograph. His daughter, who works in the shop, has come to the stage to get a fish for dinner. The man with the pitchfork works for the merchant, unloading fish and taking care of the hardware department of the store, for which he is paid somewhat less than a fisherman. He is a reader, borrowing books from relatives and the schoolteacher, and a man known in the community as someone to talk to about history or to visit, as he works on the wharf, for interpretations of world news – the "radio news."

Boatbuilding. A fisherman who is also one of the craftsmen of the community, building a boat for his nephew with the help of his sons. These dories must be over 28 feet long to qualify for the "bounty" – a subsidy of $8 a foot from the government. The craftsman agreed to build the boat for $65, making a dory that would sell on the mainland, with an engine, for around $2,000.

After this photograph was taken, the craftman went into the woods with his sons to hunt, and his nephew tried to continue the work. The day was too cold, and some of the planking boards split. The craftsman was furious, and he refused to finish the boat or to accept any pay for the work he had done. A year later the uncle and nephew were fishing together from the nephew's boat, finished by someone else, but with the nephew, who as the boat owner should have been called captain, calling his uncle "skipper."

(facing) Fishermen. The brotner of the mummer, and his son – one of eleven children. This fisherman spends about half of each year away from home, working on a "dragger" that fishes the ocean banks from a Nova Scotia port. His son is sixteen and dropped out of school to fish with his father.

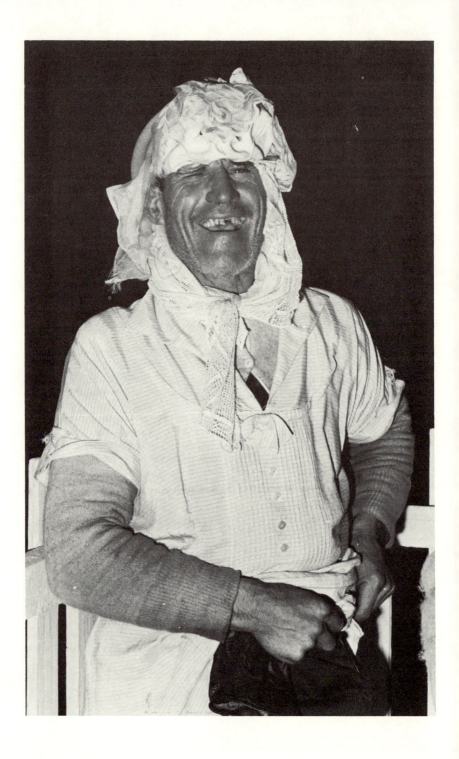

Mummer with woman and her sons. This is the same man as on the facing page. When he entered the house, with three other mummers, the woman "goosed" him good and hard to find out what anthropologists would call the "gender" of the masked visitor. They are now posing for the camera.

(facing) *A Newfoundland mummer between house visits.* A village fisherman, much sought after in the community as a man to go mummering and drinking with, who is famous for the number of songs he knows. In a woods camp, on a hunting trip with some other men in the community, he sang for four successive nights without any repetition. When folklorists come to record him, he always leaves a verse or two out of each song, for the songs are his, and a part of who he is. He is a good fisherman, an exceptional hunter, and an extraordinary master of local wisdom, who husbands his skills carefully, choosing whom to take hunting and how he uses his knowledge.

Mummer accepting a drink. The host has come close to guessing who the mummer is and has been teasing the mummer, who still refuses to take off his mask. The mummer reciprocated for the drink with a song.

All photographs are by Louis Chiaramonte, professor of anthropology, Memorial University of Newfoundland, who also provided details for the captions. All were taken during 1962–3 in the south-coast outport village he calls "Deep Harbour."

PART THREE

The politics of subsistence production

Hegemony at work in a collapsing state

I

In 1932, just before the Newfoundland state collapsed and relinquished self-government, Sir Percy Thompson, the senior British financial advisor to Newfoundland, said: "No elected government [in Newfoundland] can really govern successfully; it is much too closely in touch with the governed" (Noel 1971: 205–6). He was not at all likely to have been referring to an identity of interests or a set of common values, for both interests and values often have bitterly divided the populace from the government. Nor, at this point, was the government capable of meeting the minimal needs of a substantial part of its populace: seventy thousand people – one-fourth of the people – were then on "able-bodied relief," which was being paid at the semistarvation rate of six cents a person a day and at that rate was taking 15 percent of all the government's revenues. A further 65 percent of the revenues were being spent to service the national debt; the government could do no more.

Sir Percy was much more likely to have been referring to one of the most salient features of the Newfoundland state: the total absence of any local government outside the capital city, St. John's – a situation that persisted past the mid twentieth century. The national government was thus also the local government, such as it was. There were no town governments and no county organization. There were only electoral districts, and the member of the Newfoundland House of Assembly for each district, both of necessity and under public pressure, was invariably directly involved in the allocation and delivery of a wide range of local level goods and services – for example, roads, community wharves, bait-storage depots, and the associated employment opportunities. Under public pressure and the threat of not being reelected, it was often claimed that the member-sponsored government expenditures were neither appropriate nor properly

99

constrained and that both waste and corruption were rampant. The visible signs of government largesse in most outports were, however, rather scarce.

Whether or not this direct connection between the government and the people was the source of the problem, Newfoundland governments, from their inception, did have substantial difficulties governing. There were a series of major constitutional crises that began immediately following Britain's first grant of Representative Government in Newfoundland in 1832 and continued throughout the nineteenth and twentieth centuries, including, in one instance, the prime minister seconding the motion of no confidence in his own government (in which more was involved than an impending change of parties). The crises culminated in 1933 with the voluntary suspension of the constitution and of independent Dominion status by the Newfoundland Legislature – dissolving not just the government in power but the state itself, in favor of resumption of direct colonial administration by Great Britain. After thirteen years of administrative government by Crown-appointed civil servants, without any parliament or elected representation from Newfoundland, Newfoundland was offered a return to self-government. The populace voted instead to renounce independence and join Canada, and on 1 April 1949 Newfoundland became a Canadian province. (More precisely, the actual union occurred just before midnight on 31 March, so as not to take place on April Fool's Day, but the ceremonies occurred on the first [Gwyn 1972: 120].)

Throughout its career as an independent state, and continuing after Confederation with Canada, explicit and persistent attempts were made to create an economic, social, and ideological basis for a governable state. There has been a wide range of such attempts, but two were fundamental. Although both failed to provide a secure basis for the state, each had a profound impact on daily life and the political process. The first was a state-sponsored religious sectarianism that split Catholic from Protestant and one Protestant denomination from another. The second was a series of state-sponsored attempts to force economic growth – which failed in every instance and culminated both in a massive population-relocation scheme designed to transfer labor out of the inshore fishery to factory work and also in the largest bankruptcies in North America.

The chapters in Part Three are not a political history of Newfoundland; quite good ones already exist (e.g., Reeves 1793, Prowse 1896, McLintock 1940, Hiller 1971, Noel 1971, Gwyn 1972, K. Matthews 1973, Neary 1973, Gunn 1977, Hiller and Neary 1980). Rather, the focus here is on political culture: those aspects of outport culture and custom that bear significantly upon the political process, and those aspects of the political process that most powerfully have shaped outport culture. In this context, we shall pay some attention to the historical record of the causes of, and the attempts to cope with, the fragility of the Newfoundland state, and with certain other features of Newfoundland such as the suppression of private property in land. Moreover, in looking to outport culture, we shall pay particular attention not simply to the content of folk culture but also to its logic; in particular, to the contradictions of folk culture.

II

In 1971, at the age of seventy-four, Victor Butler – still a fisherman and a former fish dealer (as a merchant's agent), and a former boat builder and schooner captain (as a merchant's employee) – began to write his recollections of his life in Harbour Buffet, an outport village on an island within Placentia Bay, on the south coast of Newfoundland (Butler 1975, 1977, 1982). His autobiographical stories, focusing on the period when independent government collapsed, are particularly compelling.

In November 1934, in the midst of the Great Depression, impoverished and worried that his family would not have enough to eat if forced onto the poor-relief dole (still 6¢ per person per day), Victor Butler decided to try winter-fishing from his open row dory, working out of, and living in, a shed six miles across the bay from his home. His eldest son was still too young to work on the boat, and his neighbors were unwilling – perhaps to take the risk both of bodily harm and of losing their nets in the winter storms.

Butler did find one man to go with him: Billy Dicks, a giant of strength and endurance, only barely able to talk understandably due to childhood diphtheria, and at this point again ill, incontinent, and passing blood in his urine. An orphan from early childhood, and though married and childless, Billy Dicks had no kin to fish with or help him.

So they fished together, from November to February. They cut firewood for their families on days too stormy to fish, rowing the wood back across the bay at night, so they could fish all day. They salted cod and packed herring in barrels to be delivered to their merchant in Harbour Buffet, who gave them, together, $55 credit for a winter's food for themselves and their families.

While they fished and lived together in the shed, Butler cared for his companion as best as he could, making tea in the morning while Billy Dicks dried the clothes he wet in his sleep, tending him in bed when he passed out, worrying about his suffering while they fished, cold and wet, and sitting up holding Billy's hand the last few nights before Billy died. (Butler 1977: 9–15; from the title story of the book, *Sposin' I Dies in D' Dory*. These were the words of Billy Dicks when he agreed to winter-fish with Victor Butler: "By Dod I will, Vit, sposin I dies in d' dory." "Sposin" (supposing) means both "even if" – a sign of some hope in the opposite outcome – and "although I will.")

101

The politics of subsistence production

Victor Butler was clearly a decent man – working to the limits of his strength, proud, as is common, of his strength, his endurance, and his capacity to work, caring about others, and involved with his covillagers. It is, however, part of a rather strange pattern of caring and involvement. To begin, and this perhaps is the most personal of the factors, it is self-centered: We must ask why Butler did not insist that his companion go home; he was clearly too sick to winter-fish; yet fishing alone would have been extremely difficult, if possible at all for Butler, who could find no one else to go with. Putting this aside, what Butler did do is part of a pattern of caring and coinvolvement that is more episodic than sustained. At one point in the depression, when Butler was making eleven cents an hour working for the merchant, with three cents deducted toward his past bills, he bought a plug of tobacco for a very old man who was smoking used, dried tea leaves – but at the same time he observed, without comment, that this old man would walk, every other day, a round trip of six to eight miles through the snow to cut and haul out firewood for his wife and himself, and no one in the village seems to have helped (Butler 1977: 60–2).

In fact, the general lack of mutual helpfulness among village fisher families is strikingly poignant. In the fall of 1940 Butler's wife, two daughters, and mother were all stricken with diphtheria. The infant daughter died; his wife, mother, and elder daughter were completely helpless, needing to be spoon-fed broth. Butler and his young son tended to them as best they could, while still having to fish. After two months of tending his very ill family much of the night and fishing all day, Butler was so exhausted that his legs failed, and he described having to go up the stairs to their rooms on his hands and knees – and no one in the village helped at all, just some women from another village who sent over bottles of soup with the visiting nurse.

This lack of help cannot be explained simply by fear of contagion, though this was strong. A few years earlier, Butler's youngest son became ill and got rapidly worse. I quote Butler, who simply wanted to borrow a motor boat:

I had to get the boy to hospital by some means. There was a constable stationed [here]...and a clergyman as well. My associates owned boats but none raised a helping hand to try and save a young boy's life. I borrowed an open boat from John Collett, a man operating a small business in the northwest of the harbour. He was a very sympathetic man. He only charged me 50 cents for gas. [Butler 1977: 74]

So he went, in a storm, with his sick young son and his elder son to help, to the hospital across the bay. That night, unable to return because of the storm, he found that the boatmen anchored in the harbor would

102

only begrudgingly let his older son sleep out of the rain in their decked boat, offering him neither shelter nor food.

He returned a week later, with a cousin and a coffin he made himself, to fetch the body of his young son back from the hospital:

No one will ever know the effect the death of my boy had on me. Besides mourning the boy's death I felt bad about the way he died without my being in a position to get medical aid in time to give him a chance to live, for want of twenty dollars to hire a boat. . . . I always kept my troubles to myself and never let my emotions show. I became morose and I just about lost confidence in human nature, especially my associates and the clergy particularly as I did not get any help from anyone in time of need. All this caused me to have a different outlook on life. From this experience, I learned a lesson I will never forget – *if a man is not self-sufficient, what help he will get from others will be damn small.* . . . Ever since that time I have tried to help neighbors with sick or dying children, or in any distress and unable to help themselves. [Butler 1977: 76–7; emphasis added]

This conjunction of experience and "agency" (as it is called in contemporary British social history) – raising experience to the realm of knowledge, with a commitment to change – is a complex matter. If many people had learned a similar lesson from such experiences, perhaps more help would have been forthcoming. Or if a lack of helpfulness was a pervasive feature of such villages, then perhaps Butler would not have expected anything. To comprehend the structure of this experience, and the transformation of experience to agency, we must look to what was known about social relations, as well as learned in such situations, and how social relations were known, and why they were thought to be as they were. In doing this we should pay particular attention to the contradictions of culture: "If a man is not self-sufficient, what help he will get from others will be damn small" – and remember, all the while, the appalling magnitude of human suffering at stake for the people in this process of grasping experience and shaping agency.

It is of particular importance that in his description of the circumstances of his son's death Butler focuses on his "associates" and the clergy (especially in the full description in his book, from which the excerpts just quoted were drawn) and does not blame either the state, except for a passing reference to the constable, or the merchant. The same wireless telegraph that enabled the hospital to notify Butler of his son's death could have been used in reverse to request aid, but the state-supported "cottage hospital" did not have a motor dory, even though it served communities all around the bay, few of which had any access to the hospital by road. Even more noticeably, Butler does not mention "his" merchant, for whom he had worked for the past several years not only as a fisherman but also as a craftsman, building boats, rebuilding wrecks, and repairing engines. Butler not only worked for the fish merchant, one of the largest in the bay, he served him.

The politics of subsistence production

In 1925 the fish merchant, W. W. Wareham, bought a store and dock facilities on nearby Merasheen Island. Butler, who earlier had met and married his wife on Merasheen, moved there to manage the place for Wareham. It was a usual merchant's operation, run on the truck system, with credit given in the spring for supplies and again in the fall, after the fish were delivered, for winter supply.

With a poor catch in the summer of 1930, and the onset of the depression, Butler's agency was in trouble. I quote Butler again (from the printed record of a tape transcript), serving his merchant's interests:

Now [Wareham] told me to fit out all the fishermen [with production and consumption supplies, in the spring of 1930] at as limited amount as I could, you know, not try to run too heavy into it. Now 'tis a bad fishery . . . so I seen now [toward the end of the summer] I was going to have a job to get paid all the debts [at the end of the season]. So I came down [to Wareham's office], I talked to him. I said, "Look, best thing we can do is move out of Merasheen the coming fall." I said, "I'll get out what I can [i.e., get the fishermen to pay as much of their spring bill as possible with their fish, and then close up shop and leave before giving any winter supply]. We might be out perhaps five or six hundred dollars, I don't know. If I stays there the winter, they're going to be looking for credit all the winter." I said, "In the spring of the [next] year you're going to have a big bill before you [i.e., they] starts fishing." "Well," he said, "that's a good plan. That's what we will do." [Butler 1975: 37; from the taped autobiographical introduction recorded by Professor W. Wareham]

Almost since a government was formed in Newfoundland in 1832, merchants had been trying to pass the costs of winter supply on to the government. One has only to recall the Slade and Kelson Plan, discussed in Chapter 5, to realize that what was being proposed here is abandonment, supposedly to the government dole but actually to a dole payable in commodities, not cash, and thus difficult to draw upon without a merchant in the community. The state could never adequately cope with this task, for it required diversification from the fishery; a diversification long desired by various governments but politically impossible to achieve, in substantial part due to merchant opposition. The merchants were pushing on to the state a task they knew it could not do; the protests of the fishermen were largely ineffective.

In 1933 Britain sent out a commission to enquire into the impending collapse of the Newfoundland state, whose fiscal problems were regarded as in part originating in the low level of returns in the fishery. Their report notes drily:

The merchants, instead of being looked on as friend whose cooperation is necessary if the [fishing] industry is to prosper, are apt to be regarded as enemies whose sole object is to exploit the fishermen for personal gain. In the absence of mutual confidence between producer [fisher families] and exporter [merchant], the industry crests on a basis of distrust and suspicion. [CMND 4480; quoted by Overton 1976]

The politics of subsistence production

Fisher families had complex relations with merchants – relations mixing dependency, subservience, deference, and rage. But however angry fisher families may have been at merchants and their agents, I do not think that it is likely that Victor Butler's isolation at times of extreme need was simply due to – that is, a retaliation for – his service to and association with the fish merchant. Such service is probably not irrelevant (Rex Clark has made an important argument on this point; 1984: 42–3); and any full explanation of Butler's situation would have to take into account the personal dimension of his social relations. But although Butler has a particularly poignant personal history, colored by a variety of social and specific factors, he is far from unique: In 1973 several people relocated from south-coast communities to a Newfoundland factory town were interviewed about the advantages and drawbacks of their situation after relocation, and one man was asked about medical care:

> *Q:* What about being close to a doctor, and a road, and that sort of thing?
> *A:* Well, that's one thing, I suppose. If you got a car its alright. But if you don't have a car it'd be bad. You'd probably have to fool around getting a taxi, and half the time you can't get them. *But if you got a car of your own, and somebody's sick belong to you* you can go right on with them, you know. [MUN-FLA, F1319, 73–144; Collector CBC; emphasis added]

These words were spoken more than forty years after the incident Butler described by a man who grew up nearly one hundred miles from Butler, and they are nearly identical to what Butler said about his situation: There is no mention of help from friends and relatives; the focus is on services that were hirable, if available at all, and on the assertion that one should take care of those that "belong to you": a narrow net. (A very strong caution must be entered here: The story of Butler is designed to bring out for discussion one aspect of outport life, and is not at all intended to characterize the full range of social relations. The same people have frequently risked their lives on the smallest chance of helping people in shipwrecks, or those in trouble on the sea; and Newfoundland outport people speak to each other, in general, with a warmth and intimacy I have seen nowhere else: One man, for example, will hold another man's hand while he is singing a ballad at a social gathering; singing is something people are intensely pressured to do, and do with both pleasure and anxiety. See Wareham (1982) for very rich descriptions of such intimacies, and remember this is a description of the same community that Victor Butler lived in.)

Outport Newfoundland is far from unique in having an ambiguous mixture of warm alliance and cold distance, or antagonistic alliance and easy reserve; their conjoining does seem particularly intense. In any case, the "individualism" – one term that has been used for an aspect of the issue here – has been noted and commented upon by Newfoundlanders themselves.

105

The politics of subsistence production

Joseph Smallwood, who led Newfoundland into Confederation with Canada and was the provincial premier from 1949 to 1972, spent the years from 1934 to 1937 trying to organize fishing cooperatives on the northeast coast. Failing in that endeavor, he wrote:

Perhaps the very nature of our struggle, of our methods of wresting a living from nature, has helped to unfit us for constructive and creative effort.

It is a fact that for centuries we have lived by killing cod and other fish; by killing seals in the water and on the ice, and animals on land; by cutting down trees. Has all this developed in us a trait of destructiveness, or narcotized what ought naturally to be an instinct for creativeness? Is it not true that we have been intensely, bitterly individualistic, each of us preferring to paddle his own canoe and turn his back on the other fellow? [cited in Gwyn 1972: 48–9]

Killing fish and seals however, is not likely to be a major part of an explanation for such social relations: Inuit ("Eskimo") people, for example, have no trouble with cooperation or, as is well known, with sharing.

How characteristic are Victor Butler's experiences? How relevant are these stories, which focus on illness and emergency, to times of health and ordinary activity? If they are characteristic, what kind of social system do they represent? Such questions cannot be answered by counting similar or countervailing cases but rather by situating Victor Butler within a larger field of social relations. Rather than claiming that Butler's situation was the result of his association with the merchant, or his and his community's killing fish and cutting down trees, we must look for deeper structural causes. These causes, which turn out to also be part of the explanation of the fragility of the Newfoundland state, begin in the history of property in Newfoundland.

7

The memorial of the merchants of Poole

Victor Butler, describing the early years of the depression on the islands in Placentia Bay:

On the fifteenth of July, Alberto [Wareham, his merchant] called me to his office and said, "I want you to go trading for me this summer as I want to keep my good dealers around the Bay supplied with goods and I have a lot of dried fish to collect in and I wish to buy all the dried fish I can get. As you have been skipper of trading schooners before, I want you to fit up the *Lillian and Mary*." . . .

Trading was a busy job. We had to work long hours when the weather was fine enough for handling dried codfish. Around fifteen percent of the fishermen in the harbours on the eastern side of Placentia Bay who were operating fishing boats from Cape St. Mary's and Golden Bay made a fair living through the Depression years. Some men who had dealings with merchants at Buffett [this is Victor Butler's community; the two Wareham brothers, each with his own company, were the principal merchants] were gradually falling into debt and, before the Depression ended, some had to turn in their boats to the merchants.

On the island of Iona, the fishermen fished in open fishing boats around the year 1930. A few years earlier they discontinued the use of Cape boats [a large boat of 15–30 tons – rigged fore and aft, carrying three dories and a crew of seven men (DNE)]. These fishermen were struck hard by the Depression. The majority of them dealt with Alberto Wareham. They would fish all the summer. I would collect their fish, the value of which would be credited to their account.

I was given strict orders, before leaving on a trip collecting fish from the merchant's dealers, to advance the fishermen five dollars worth of food after collecting their fish. When the fishing season was finished, they had nothing in the shape of food stuffs prepared for winter months.

This was a bad situation, living on a small barren island with a low supply of food on hand, seven miles from the nearest merchant. Sometimes in winter when the bay was packed with ice, they would go two months without having their dole orders filled. It is surprising how these people survived. Root vegetables could not be grown on the island as the soil was not suitable. Therefore, they did not grow any vegetables with the exception of cabbage.

The politics of subsistence production

Those people suffered unbelievable hardships and privations through the years. If it had not been for the seabirds they shot, they would have starved completely. I know this to be a fact as I visited Iona many times through the summer and fall months for years. [Butler 1977: 39–40]

***

We did a good business for Mr. Wareham that fall at Flat Islands. With the fish we collected in the harbours on the east side of the Bay and the large amount of provisions we sold, Mr. Wareham must have made a good profit form the business we did in the *Lillian Mary*. The wages he paid us did not reduce his profits much. . . .

After making our last trip to Flat Island for the fall we had to make one more trip to the eastern side of the Bay. We visited Iona first. It was nearing Christmas and the weather was very stormy. The purpose of this late trip was to collect fish from some inshore fishermen who still owed bills to Alberto.

This late trip did not appeal to me. None of these men could pay their bills in full. *This left my good friends with nothing to see them through the winter months. I had plenty of food on board the trader.*

We proceeded to Long Harbour. . . . On Christmas Eve the wind freshened from the southeast . . . Both anchors dragged and just at nightfall the boat drifted ashore, stern first. . . . The boat began to tip headlong and lie on her side. . . .

All that night we could not light a fire in the forecastle. The night was bitterly cold and blowing a gale. We were soaking wet and hungry and could not leave the boat to go to any houses nearby. We were in a bad way to usher in Christmas Day.

Christmas morning . . . we . . . hove her off to an anchor, cooked breakfast, and rolled in our bunks for some badly needed sleep.

That was how we celebrated Christmas that year. We finished the trip; came home; cleared out the boat; and tied her up for the Winter.

Through the Depression years we could not stay home for a holiday. We had to keep working in order to earn every dollar possible, just to exist. . . . [Butler 1977: 57–8; emphasis added]

The formation of capital, in any of its shapes including merchant capital, must *not* be regarded as primarily about the formation of specific material and productive goods: ships, warehouses, factories, and so forth. Capital formation is, rather, the formation of certain kinds of social relations – different with each kind of capital. Whatever these relations are, they invariably entail the *deformation* of other kinds of social relations. Victor Butler not only had what marxists would call his "surplus labor" appropriated from him, but his Christmas's as well. He knew this; it is less clear that he sensed the complex ambiguity of what was being appropriated from him when he called the fishermen of Iona – for whom he would leave five dollars worth of food for the winter, and about whom he was clearly upset – his "good friends."

In Part Two we saw the connection between the development of merchant capital and of "traditional" folk culture in Newfoundland. We must now deal with the distance and the confrontations between them, particularly as this relationship of creation and destruction, intimacy and antagonism, becomes politicized. The name that has been given to one aspect of this

108

confrontation – the asserted dominance of elite values – is *hegemony*; it is a concept that will require reevaluation by placing it in a broader context than the clash of values.

II

As the depression intensified and the Newfoundland state collapsed, the fisherfolk had neither a market for their fish that would meet the cost of fishing nor much in the way of property – and almost none that was salable – nor even a developed subsistence agriculture to fall back upon. The absence of landed property and of agriculture cannot be simply explained by noting that these are fishing communities: That fact itself, as well as the characteristics of property and the small-scale gardens, which only supplemented the needed food supplies, all together originated in policies designed to secure the domination – or, more broadly speaking, the hegemony – of fishing interests over the settlers. The success of these policies was not only a substantial factor in the desperate situation of the fisher families during the depression; it was also a major cause of the failure of the state. The success of these policies also undermined the capacity of the people to resist state domination – including their capacity to resist the largest peacetime forced-relocation project in a "democratic" country, a project that caused a very great deal of suffering while bringing very few benefits. The question of why the absence of both agriculture and property (particularly substantial property in land) should undermine people's capacity to resist domination – a key topic of this and the next two chapters – entails an interpretation of Newfoundland's political, social, and cultural history that is best begun by first reconsidering the anthropological concept of culture.

The most widespread of the contemporary anthropological concepts of culture is that of "shared values" or a "system of values, beliefs, ideas, and worldview, and the rituals and practices that convey these values." Whatever the utility of this concept for understanding hunting and gathering bands or relatively egalitarian village-based social systems, it is not very effective for understanding class-based societies. In situations of class conflict, the notion of shared values provides little help – other than as a starting point for a more specific concept – in understanding either how upper-class cultural hegemony is imposed on a populace or how oppositional cultures are formed and asserted.

The English language suggests a concept of culture that may be more useful (following the perceptive work of Raymond Williams 1976; 1977: chap. 1). Several words that are critical cultural referents in class societies are, linguistically at least, linked to the material world in general, forms of property in particular, and implicitly to oppositional and antagonistic social relations: propriety and property, appropriate (in the sense of socially correct behavior) and appropriate (in the sense of taking something from nature or from other people and making it one's own), culture and agriculture. I doubt that the linkages suggested by the language are fortuitous or accidental. Rather, they suggest that what is vaguely referred to as culture, in the current anthropological sense of shared values and patterns of meaning, is in fact linked to class phenomena in specifiable ways.

The suggestions raised by these linked terms are useful not only to point toward a materialist and social-relational concept of culture but also, simultaneously, to a more culturally embedded analysis of the material world. Property, for example, is not so much a "thing" – an acre or hectare of land with a fence – as it is, fundamentally, the material crystalization of a set of social relationships: "A hectare of land cannot be sued at law, nor is a boundary dispute a dispute with a boundary" (Davis 1973: 73). And when we understand property as a "bundle of rights," of different kinds and combinations – now almost a commonplace perspective – these rights are, primarily, social connections: "We are not dealing with the rights of a person over a material object, but rather with the rights between persons to a material object. A man without social relationships is a man without property" (Goody 1962: 287).

"Property," in other words, is one form that social relations take. "Culture," I shall argue, is another. The two domains, in class societies, are linked. To find out what these linkages might be, and so to begin to formulate a more useful and specific concept of culture, we will look to a situation where this linkage was purposely broken by denying private property in land and discouraging agriculture.

III

Between 1610 and 1637 England tried to sustain *both* a seasonal migratory fishery and regular, chartered, year-round settlement on Newfoundland. In 1610 King James I chartered the London and Bristol Company to settle in Newfoundland, granting that this company

Maie cause to be made a coine to passe current betweene the people inhabitinge in these territories for the more ease [of] traffique and bargaining between and amongst them. . . .
And further to nominate by such names or styles as shall seeme good to them . . . all governours, officers, and ministers, and to make lawes, formes, and ceremonies of government and magistratie. . . . [The full charter is given in Prowse 1895: 122ff.]

Every one of the rights granted to this company of settlers, including the right to settle and hold property, was soon denied to these and any

110

other settlers. The early settlements collapsed, but for reasons that had little to do with their rights. They could not compete financially with the migratory fishery (Cell 1981: 57–9); simultaneously, the English merchant sponsors of the migratory fishery felt that their own position would be undermined by settlement, and pressured for the withdrawal of rights and the removal of settlers.

Between the mid 1600s and the late 1700s, very little year-round settlement was officially permitted. Yet all during this period the number of settlers was rising, very slowly until the mid 1700s, increasingly rapidly thereafter (Ryan 1980). And although these settlers were from time to time burnt out or chased from their coastal settlements by British naval patrol boats, they were also tolerated – so long as they could be kept under the domination of the migratory fishery, for which they provided additional labor, winter workers, bait, and additional salt fish to carry back.

This domination over the settlers (and over their own migratory labor force) was established in two related areas: government and the organization of the economy.

First, no local judiciary was permitted until 1791, and no representative government in Newfoundland until 1832. Until then Newfoundland was ruled by a succession of naval governors sent out from England. These governors were only summer visitors until 1817, when the first governor was directed to winter over on the island. The governors' rule was supported by patrol boats that, like the governor, were only present during the fishing season. In the fall they went back with, and to protect, the merchant fleet, leaving the settlers to their own devices.

The judicial system was most unique. The captain of the first English fishing ship to arrive in any harbor for the season was to be the "fishing admiral" of that harbor for the season, and to hear and judge all court cases among the migratory fishermen and the settlers, and between the migratory fishermen and the settlers – despite the fact that this captain was sometimes both the judge and one of the parties to the dispute. This system of justice and government was established by a series of Star Chamber and Board of Trade rulings in the 1600s, and consolidated by the Act of 10/11 William III, c. 25, in 1698. (The complete act, with comments, is in Reeves 1793: app., pp. i–xv. Reeves was the first chief justice of Newfoundland. The earlier rulings are surveyed in S. Antler 1975.)

Empowering ship captains to sit as magistrates had the explicit advantage of keeping control over the fishery in the hands of the English fish merchants, but the disadvantage of inefficiency. When needed, the fishing admirals might be out fishing, too busy to bother, or to have gone back to England. Moreover, as major cases had to be remanded to England, it sometimes happened that people who committed serious crimes went unpunished while "a petty thief was often severely flogged." (On the unique-

111

ness of early Newfoundland and the organization of the judiciary, see McLintock 1941: chap. 3; p. 57. The floggings were severe even by British standards of the day, as Prowse, McLintock, and others make clear through copious citations.)

To remedy the shambles caused both by blatant self-interest (particularly in cases between different captains in the migratory fishery) and by inefficiency, by the mid 1700s officers of the British naval patrol, acting as surrogates of the governor, became a "local" court of appeal. Contrary to the intent of parliament, and thus illegally, they also functioned as a court of first instance.

After 1791 a local judicature was created, replacing a series of quasi-legal ad hoc practices that collapsed when challenged by a case appealed to England in 1787 (K. Matthews 1973: 199–208). And as the local fish merchants in the larger settlements became the justices, the system changed little over the next few decades:

The courts soon won a reputation for unconventional and disorderly procedure. It was not uncommon for the judge and clerk of the court to bring forward the necessary evidence and to draw up the indictment. Moreover, owing to the lack of lawyers at St. John's – the direct outcome of the naval governor's refusal to countenance them – persons unacquainted with the rules and usages of a court of law were permitted to plead. Consequently scenes of uproar and indecorum, far beyond the power of the court to restrain, were the inevitable outcome of a farcical system. [McLintock 1941: 132, citing CO 194/ 44, 55, Sir Erasmus Gower's Report, 18 July 1805, and Keats/Bathurst, Annual Report, 29 Dec. 1814]

McLintock was writing primarily about St. John's; the situation in the market-town outport courts was probably worse. In the late eighteenth and early nineteenth centuries fishing admirals persisted in dispensing their often rough justice while subsequent forms of judicature were developing, and they actively sought to undermine any other authority. As a "theater of power" it may have been farce, but the floggings and the seizures of property, fishing rooms, and fishing equipment by both the fishing admirals and the naval surrogates were, as we shall soon see, not a light matter.

The second element of English merchant domination over the increasing number of settlers lay in denying settlers both landed property and the possibility of agriculture. The domination established on this basis, however, proved difficult to sustain even though it made the settlers materially more dependent upon their merchant suppliers.

The denial of property took two forms. First, no ownership whatsoever was to be allowed of land not used in the fishery, and second, the settlers would be allowed to have land used in the fishery only if it did not interfere with the fishing rooms traditionally used by the migratory fishery. This denial of property outside the fishery was specifically designed to keep everyone fishing (or manning the garrisons that were thought to protect the fishery from the French); the possession of landed property gave an independence from the fishery that could not be tolerated.

In 1769 Hugh Palliser, naval governor of Newfoundland, wrote:

The indulgence that has formerly been allowed to the officers and soldiers of the Garrison of this place, to make gardens and potato grounds and to build houses on the vacant grounds about the fort, has heretofore been greatly abused, by the practice of afterward pretending to sell the same as property in payment of debts contracted for liquor, and other scandalous dealings, by which means the fort has been surrounded with buildings and enclosures . . . [and] thereby rendered defenseless, besides causing a great increase of poor idle disorderly people to stay in the Country to inhabit such houses, who neither belong to the fishery nor to the Garrison, who live mostly by sheltering Rogues, Thieves and Murderers, and by selling strong liquors, and entertaining Soldiers, Fishermen and Seamen in idleness, drunkeness and all kinds of debaucheries and excesses, as well during the fishing season as during the Winter . . . to the exceeding great loss of all concerned in the fisheries. . . . [CO 194/ 162]

Palliser, in his rage against property, insisted that all such buildings and enclosures must be torn down, at least in the vicinity of the fort. He would have totally eliminated all private landed property in Newfoundland in his concern to defend the interests of the migratory fishery – a source of well-trained sailors for the British navy as well as a source of wealth for British merchants – but he found he had to permit some landed property to be held, particularly for soldiers and fishermen to have potato grounds "for better subsisting their families in this dear and severe climate."

The main concern therefore was to prevent any economic independence by not allowing people to own land useful for either farming, or for fishing apart from, or in competition with, the migratory fishery. The land claims of year-round settlers threatened the migratory fishery in two basic ways: The settlers could occupy the most useful places from year to year, thus diminishing the good shoreline available to the boats arriving in the spring, and settlers used up the timber necessary for stages, flakes, sheds, fuel, and boat repair for their own fuel and structures, or simply by clearing land near the coast for farming.

By the late 1700s "quiet possession" of property was, in some places, well developed; property was rented and sold, and there were a number of absentee landlords, residing in England, who held property – particularly privatized ships' rooms and shore facilities – in St. John's and the larger market towns of Conception Bay. But ownership of property was not fully legal (until 1824!), and there were episodic attacks on private property, some of which seem random and some seemingly more focused and purposive. Property ownership came under attack – albeit increasingly ineffectively throughout the late eighteenth century – not only to constrain interference with and independence from the migratory fishery (and thus to help shape the terms of appropriation from the settlers) but also, and significantly, to prevent the settlers from developing economic ties to each other. In 1793 Admiral Milbank, the naval governor, ordered:

As to Alexander Long's house, which has been built contrary to His Majesty's express commands . . . it must and shall come down. The pretense now set up, of its being intended for a craft house [a building for the fishery], serves rather to aggravate than extenuate the offense; for by . . . [his] confession . . . no such use was to be made of it, as he said it was intended only as a covering to his potato cellar, though there is a compleat chimney, if not two in it, and lodgings for at least six or eight dieters [fishing servants]. I shall embrace this opportunity of warning you against making an improper use of any other part of (what you are pleased to call) your ground . . . (except such buildings and erections as shall be actually on purpose for the curing . . . and husbanding of fish . . .) . . . . And it may not be amiss . . . to inform you . . . I am also directed not to allow any possession as private property . . . in any land whatever which is not actually employed in the fishery. . . . Therefore it behooves you . . . to employ the whole of the ground which you lay claim to, in the fishery, lest others should profit by your neglect. . . . [McLintock 1941: 204–5, quoting 3d report, Commons committee, 1793, app. 11, letter to George Hutchings]

Without legal property in land outside the fishery, agriculture was nearly impossible, and the absence of a commercial agriculture was probably the major factor keeping Newfoundland residents from developing extensive ties to one another. "Gardens" – very small-scale plots for producing foodstuffs for one's own table – were both encouraged and widespread; agriculture – crops or animals raised primarily for sale or exchange – was not.

A long succession of government officials, from the early naval governors to the architects of and apologists for the post-Confederation population-relocation scheme, have claimed that the chief obstacles to agriculture are "poor climate and indifferent soil" (e.g., Copes 1972; Copes was the major planner of resettlement). Although Newfoundland is not Iowa, these are far from the crucial reasons, as both the profusion of small vegetable gardens and the relative prosperity of those people who managed to develop even small farms testifies. (See Bonnycastle 1842; Prowse 1895: 395–9; Lodge 1939: 165; and Newfoundland and Labrador, Province of, 1955. Lodge, one of the three administrators sent out from England in 1934 to govern Newfoundland, pointed out that the per-acre potato yield in Newfoundland was "better than the average in England.")

Governor (and Admiral) Buchanen, in 1786, showed that what was really at stake in the suppression of agriculture, but not gardens, was the continuation of the fishery with laborers who had to fish yet could fish for lower wages (as servants) if they were feeding themselves:

Few spots . . . can be improved without injuring the woods, which the Act [10/11 William III, c. 25] . . . reserved for the use of the fishery . . . but potatoes and vegetables contribute so much to the health of the people and the cheapness of living that it must be of advantage to the fishery that small pieces of ground be permitted to be improved for the purpose of raising them. . . . It is in some measure owing to the assistance which the poorer sort of people have derived from their potato-gardens that they have not given up the fishery and retired from the island. [Buchanen 1785]

When Representative Government came to Newfoundland in 1832, the House of Assembly sought to encourage agriculture and to build roads, essential to the development of land-based commerce. These efforts were blocked by the governor and the appointed Legislative Council; after several years of conflict over these issues, the Assembly stated:

The policy heretofore pursued by the parent government . . . at first to forbid residence, anon to deny agriculture; in fine to fetter the resources and cramp the energies and blast the prospects of the people, has produced the natural result. *Native gentry there is none; a resident landed proprietary there does not exist, and consequently society is reduced to two classes.* . . . The native inhabitants of Newfoundland are sighing for the promotion of agriculture. . . . The merchant sees in the accomplishment of their wishes the grave of his monopoly. [JHA 1838, cited by Innis 1954: 388; emphasis added]

IV

In 1821 – the same year that he forcibly shipped a large number of women and children back to Ireland, and ordered others to Prince Edward Island to help meet the demand there for winter labor (McLintock 1941: 29) – Newfoundland's governor, Sir Charles Hamilton, wrote to the earl of Bathurst, secretary of state for war and the colonies:

My Lord,
I have been requested by a large but not a general meeting of the inhabitants of St. John's to transmit the accompanying Petition which, as it is their wish should be presented to his Majesty through the proper channel, I have considered it my duty to forward to your Lordship, though I can neither approve the statements or co-incide in the conclusions.

Hamilton

To the King's Most Excellent Majesty . . .
In the neighboring colonies in North America and in all the British West Indies, the Judgment seat is filled by Gentlemen of professional education and previous distinction at the bar. In the British possessions in the east, the persons who preside in the courts are selected from the upright and cultivated ranks of Westminster Hall, . . .
But in Newfoundland, composed as it is of Natives of Great Britain and Ireland or their immediate descendants, and more closely connected with the parent state by proximity of situation and frequency of intercourse than any other colony, the administration of justice is confided to the hands of Captains, Lieutenants, and even Masters of the Navy. . . .

[Here were several cases of people losing property through ignorance or malfeasance of judges; small boats being taxed for support of hospital, etc.]

115

The politics of subsistence production

But it is not of the ignorant or willful misconstruction of the law as it may affect our Properties of which we complain to Your Majesty so much as it is the flagrant and unlawful violations of our persons.

We humbly beg to be permitted to lay before Your Majesty two cases which occurred in the present year, exactly as they were developed in the Supreme Court of the Island, and in order to save Your Majesty trouble, we will briefly state the outline of one of them. James Landergan, a native of this Island and a respectable Planter at Cubits in the District of Conception Bay happened in the fishing season of one thousand eight hundred and eighteen to fall in debt for Supplies, to the inconsiderable amount of £12. It is not usual with the Suppliers for the fisheries in this island to distress the Planters who may chance to be in arrears to them at the Fall of the year, and more especially when they are possessed of fishing rooms as security for the debt – but the sum due from Landergan to his supplier was immediately put in suit in the Surrogate Court at Harbour Grace, and judgment passed against him by default shortly after which his fishing room was sold and the Clerk of his suppliers became the purchaser for the amount of the debt – He had personal property at the time, fully equal to satisfy the judgment, and his room was estimated at £150. in value – When the Sheriff's Officer went to deliver possession of the room Landergan was absent, and some uncourteous language passed between his Wife and the Officer, which was interpreted into a resistance of his authority and made the subject of complaint to the court – accordingly when Capt Buchan of Your Majesty's Brig Grasshopper and the Revd John Leigh the Episcopal Missionary at Harbour Grace, held a Surrogate court at Port de Grave, Landergan was summoned to appear before them, and being found in the act of hauling a little fish for the present use of his family, he apologized for not being in a situation just then to attend court and said he would do so the following morning. On being told by the Officer that a party of Marines would be sent to bring him he simply replied "I wish you and the Marines a good time of it." – The Officer reported what had passed to the Court, and for this offense if offense it can be called the unhappy man was seized in his Bed at night and conveyed on board the Grasshopper where he was confined until the following morning; he was then brought before the Court . . . [and] adjudged to be guilty of a high contempt of Court and sentenced to receive thirty six lashes on his bare back. This infamous sentence was immediately carried into execution by the Boatswains mate of the Grasshopper and Landergan was tied up and flogged until he fainted under the severity of his punishment – He was then taken down and removed to the Court House where at the first symptom of returning life he was required to yield up possession of his room, as the condition upon which the remainder of the punishment should be remitted; and in a few hours after the unfortunate man, together with his wife and four infant children became outcasts upon the world – Such is the manner in which the Surrogates hold plea of civil suits in Newfoundland. . . .

An opinion has gone abroad, and it is not without its abettors in this Island, that Newfoundland is regarded by the parent country mostly as a Nursery of Seamen, and with this view, that it is the policy of government to discourage settlement in the island. Supposing this to be the case, it may be sufficient to explain how it has happened that this Island . . . should remain in the same state as when it was originally discovered *without cultivation and without roads*, the first requisite of civilized society.

Upon which Hamilton comments:

116

The memorial of the merchants of Poole

... It is highly to their honor [the Naval Officers, functioning as Surrogates] that no charge of injustice has ever been brought against them – that very few of their decisions have been appealed against (and of those some have been unjustly reversed) and except from persons who have deservedly suffered under their unbiased decisions, none have complained, and indeed considering the sad ignorance of this population, generally their power has been exerted with more lenity than might have been done by others less acquainted with the dispositions of the lower orders of mankind living like wild Indians half the year. [CO 194/ 64 Hamilton to Bathurst]

When Hamilton said that the fisherfolk of Newfoundland were living "like wild Indians half the year," it is difficult to tell if he meant the migratory fishermen who were largely outside the bounds of Great Britain's governmental and judicial institutions while in Newfoundland or, a bit more likely, the residents who were left to their own devices during the winter. The issue, in either case, was the absence of what both Newfoundlanders and their seasonal overlords called "civilized society." And in both cases, at the center of this charge or this complaint was the absence of roads and agriculture, and with these a local gentry or squirearchy.

"They are making roads in Newfoundland," testified Peter Ougier, English fish merchant, protesting the idea of granting self-government to Newfoundland, "next thing they will be having carriages and driving about" (Prowse 1895: 428). It was the same complaint, with the opposite intention, made by the petitioners while stirring up the agitation that contributed to granting self-government: They decried a Newfoundland "without cultivation and without roads, the first requisites of civilized society," and they called for a judiciary, as elsewhere in the colonies, of the "upright and cultivated."

The undeveloped agriculture and the paucity of roads necessary for a land-based economy to emerge created a society in the early nineteenth century composed of a mass of relatively – and almost uniformly – impoverished fisherfolk on the one hand, and merchants on the other, with few intermediate positions. Although the nineteenth century would see both the emergence and destruction of an outport middle class of schooner owners and artisans, in the first part of the century, while Newfoundland struggled toward representative government, this intermediate class was not yet significant. At the point when Representative Government was granted, S. J. R. Noel found social classes in Newfoundland the most "sharply polarized" in North America (1972: 8).

The absence of a gentry, and the weakly developed middle class, even at midcentury, were simultaneously a source of political turmoil (as we shall see) and of cultural and ideological strength for the fisherfolk:

From many causes the people generally are much altered in temper and bearing from the class in England to which they belong. They have not the benefit of living near, and depending upon, persons of higher birth, wealth, and education. The

117

three or four persons of superior position and education in the principal settlements are there *in consequence* of the presence of the fisherman upon the shore, and expressly for his purposes; and he well knows, for no concealment of the fact is or need be made, that they are there only for the sake of salary or fees, and would greatly prefer to live elsewhere. It is to be expected, then, that the fisherman will be largely possessed with a feeling of his own importance. Indeed, he regards these persons as directly or indirectly maintained by himself. [Moreton 1863: 23–4; emphasis in original]

The incidents that Moreton recounts have more of an edge:

A man, asked whether he could read and write, replied "No, I'm thankful to say I can't else I should be as big a rogue as those who can." Another man, witness to a marriage, whom I asked to sign the register, replied, "No, I can't write, I must trust others, like most poor men. But I suppose there will always be some well taught enough to live by their neighbors." [p. 26]

And the more indirect assertions of the fisherfolk show a self-assurance that Moreton came to understand (correctly, in the context of what was happening) as confrontational:

A poor, very untaught young woman had been guilty of an offense for which it was needful that I should rebuke her. Long time passed before I got the opportunity to do so, and she lived among persons who would, I feared, only lead her to think lightly of her fault. At last I did speak to her, and she met my rebuke in a manner which was at once touching from its artless simplicity, and such as to disarm me: dropping a short curtsey, she said, "Yes, sir, bad thing I was to do it, sir, wasn't I?"

There was a man in my flock, whose general conduct was unsatisfactory and often needing rebuke, and who, though most respectful in manner, seemed in no way corrected by any admonition. I was standing by him at his work and speaking upon some common subject when one of his customary oaths escaped him. Instantly he forestalled the expected rebuke by shaking his head remorsefully, and striking it a revengeful thump with his fist; at the same time interspersing his discourse to me with words of self-reproach, "Bad man, Bill (thump)! What did you say that bad word for (thump)? Bad man!" [pp. 52–3]

Whereas Moreton had remarked, concerning the more direct statements his parishioners made against the elite, that "Happily most men of my flock did not think with these," the problem Moreton faced was a general issue; to introduce this issue, we should return to, restate, and finish the point in which Moreton poses the confrontation in its most general form:

Having complete command of their time, these people are of a strange imperturbable habit. Unaccustomed to move at other men's bidding, they are hardly to be excited to action unless impelled by their own perception of need. "When I see my own time" is a phrase continually in their mouths. Their very look betrays this feeling; and unless when for the moment they are eager after some advantage, their gait and every action seems possessed with a dignity, which would be ludicrous if it were not the token of so hurtful a temper. *This is a chief obstacle to the missionary's work amongst them. Nothing is more painfully imprinted in my re-*

118

membrance than the long-continued effort it cost me to surmount this, before the accomplishment of any work for their own good. [26–7; emphasis added]

V

We have entered the terrain that marxists, particularly those under the persuasive influence of Antonio Gramsci, call hegemony: the dominance of one particular class in the domain of culture. More precisely, we have entered the terrain of struggle to secure and maintain this dominance on the one hand, and to carve out an assertive and more autonomous life on the other.

Gramsci's writings on hegemony are scattered throughout his corpus and, written with one eye on the censor, are elliptical. (See esp. Gramsci 1971: 3–23, 175–84; Cammett 1967: 204–12. On the notion of *civil society,* which is an integral part of this concept of hegemony, see Marx 1963 [1844], 1976 [1859].) The clearest brief summary and critical interpretation of Gramsci's perspective is by Raymond Williams (1977: 108–14), and we will start with this.

Gramsci distinguished between *rule* "expressed in directly political forms and in times of crises by direct physical coercion" and "the more normal situation [which] is a complex interlocking of political, social and cultural forces. Hegemony [for Gramsci] is either this whole interlocked package, or just the social and cultural forces."

Williams asserts that the concept of hegemony goes beyond both the concept of culture and the concept of ideology. It is more specific than culture in that it relates whole social processes, in which people "define and shape their lives," to "specific distributions of power and influence." It is more broadly based than ideology, for "what is decisive is not only the conscious system of ideas and beliefs, but the whole lived social process as . . . organized by dominant meanings and values" (Williams 1977: 108–9).

Hegemony is a complex concept: important and useful, because it brings culture into the domain of understanding class power and the problems of stability, resistance, and change. But it is a problematic concept, in much the same way that the anthropological concept of culture is problematic: derivative and thus static, however fascinating and intellectually enriching to contemplate it might be.

Hegemony, as understood by Gramsci, has a material base: It is the cultural dominance of a particular class as expressed in, and through, the specific institutions of "civil society": churches, schools, newspapers, public buildings and spaces, systems of status symbols, and so forth. The relative underdevelopment of this *particular* material base in Newfoundland, in the context of a fairly intense struggle over hegemony, serves to clarify – to announce more forcefully – the entrance of culture into the political process. And it calls to the receiving line, for this entrance, a number of specific questions, questions that made their own appearance in somewhat different guise when the concept of culture was introduced: Is hegemony simply a derivative of the political-economic power base of the dominant class, or is it more autonomous? If it is more autonomous, where does the autonomy come from? Not, certainly, from the association of all cultural practices with what is loosely called tradition: We have seen just how historically specific and volatile cultural "traditions" are. Further, is hegemony totalizing, as "culture" is thought to be, pervading people's consciousness "to the level of common sense?" If it is not totalizing, what is the basis of its partialness: Where do alternative hegemonies and attempts to counter or oppose existing hegemonies come from? The answer given to this last question in the marxist literature on the topic is fairly straightforward, and not wrong but inadequate: Historically emerging classes bring with them new hegemonic cultures as, for example, did the emerging bourgeoisie in its struggles and alliances with the old landed aristocracy. But this returns us to a derivative concept of culture, where it simply serves the interests of a class, and it invokes a more sharply and narrowly defined notion of class that does not stand up to the complexities of class systems.

The answers to these questions begin with our more specific concept of culture and can be developed first by elaborating the role of culture in the conjunction of production and appropriation and then, in the next chapter, by examining the role of the state in this conjunction.

I have suggested a way of conceptualizing culture that goes beyond the question of the *content* of culture (values, beliefs, symbols and rituals, etc.) and addresses the connection between culture and social relations. To summarize so far, as a basis for further development of this approach: The core of culture is the form and manner in which people perceive, define, articulate, and express their mutual relations. In class societies this form of social perception and this mode of behavior mediate between, on the one hand, the relatively egalitarian aspects of work and daily life and the collectively self-determined aspects of reproducing this domain over time, and, on the other, the primarily unequal domain of the appropriation of the product and the reproduction of appropriation. The marxist concept of *production* unifies both the organization of work and the appropriation of the product of work. Indeed, in capitalism, the very organization of work reproduces forms of ownership and control. But even here this connection, though intimate and very solid, is not total. And in precapitalist forms of social and productive organization, particularly in situations that we have grouped under the general heading of merchant capitalism, where communities are the locale of work organization, the conjunction between work and appropriation is made through multiple and diverse connections that well repay close consideration.

Hegemony, as I define the term, is that aspect of culture that, usually in the face of struggle – or simple noncompliance – most directly seeks to unify work and appropriation, and to extend appropriation beyond work into neighborhood, family, forms of consumption; in sum, into daily life.

A particularly succinct illustration of this concept of hegemony can be found in two Sumerian proverbs of the early second millennium B.C.: "Into the plague-stricken city one must drive him [the peasant, the underling] like a pack-ass." The hegemony here consists not in the assertion of power for an (implied) specific productive end, nor in the degrading insult to the less powerful, but precisely in both together. "Not all the families of the poor are equally submissive," comments another Sumerian proverb, with its usual pithy candor: suggesting, especially when considered with the first proverb, that the conjunction of force and meaning in the service of appropriation, when faced by resistance, must be extended into daily life.

The jump from Newfoundland to Sumer and back is rather large, but two important issues are at stake in making it. First, it brings us to the notion that hegemony is a general problem in societies where appropriation is unequally organized. Second, seeing hegemony as a general and pervasive issue requires us to look more closely for the origins of its specific characteristics in a particular society; to look, in particular, at the specificity of work and appropriation.

Hegemonic cultural assertions are, of course, not the only way that production and appropriation are conjoined. Force is another method. Production can itself be organized so as to conjoin it with appropriation: This is the characteristic feature of capitalist production. But if, even under capitalism, every act of production were also and simultaneously fully an act of appropriation, there would be neither need nor social logic for the hegemony of the ruling classes, nor any need for the producers to oppose existing forms of hegemony or to assert the hegemony of their own ways in order to rise.

The private ownership of, for example, machines and factories, and the purchase of labor power in a form where the whole product of labor is taken in exchange for wages, brings appropriation within production. But it is crucial to point out that even here production is not *unified* with appropriation. Even Marx, who forcefully pointed out that the *reproduction*, over time, of capitalist social relations of production depends on the conjunction of production and appropriation (1967a [1867]: 571) referred elsewhere to the "duty" of workers to "respect the product of [their] own labour, and [their] own labour itself, as values belonging to others" (1971 [1857–8]: 104–5). Countless thousands of strikes and job actions testify to the fact that this duty is not automatically engendered in the workplace but has to be constantly recreated and reinforced, and this is ordinarily attempted by a combination of political, economic, and cultural pressures. *It is this combination, and not the cultural pressures alone, that provides the characteristic structure of hegemony.*

Hegemony is thus not an abstract but a purposive assertion of elite styles and claims. Assertions of hegemony are rooted in the social organization of appropriation and elite status, and they enhance their effectiveness by mixing and merging cultural expressions with more direct claims to the product of labor. This mixing of abstract cultural symbols and specific claims ordinarily occurs within civil society; the diminished presence of the usual institutions of civil society in Newfoundland will let us see the mixture of culture and claims more clearly. It also lets us see more clearly how an opposition to elite hegemony is structured.

Hegemony, I suggest, is not opposed by protesting elite values in the abstract – simply as values – but by opposing the conjunction of these values with appropriation. The point is obvious but crucial: Merchants may sponsor missionaries, but people can make religion their own, at least under certain circumstances. These circumstances can be brought more sharply into focus by noting that the opposition to elite cultural hegemony hardly occurs in the simple act of suggesting alternative values, or spinning oppositional value systems out of bitter critique and thin air. Teasing Reverend Moreton, however pleasurable, does little to counter the hegemony he represents and expresses. Rather, opposition to hegemonic domination advances values that are, or become, rooted in the ties people have to one another in daily life and in production. The fragmentation of these ties in Newfoundland shaped both the hegemonic assertions and the capacity of the fisherfolk to resist.

With this conceptual framework, we can return to the struggle to impose and resist domination in the Newfoundland fishery.

VI

As early as 1715, the brutal and obviously interested justice dispensed by the fishing admirals was interfering with the efficient prosecution of the fishery, as the ship captains infringed on each other's fishing rooms, stole timbers, raided each other's half-cured stacks of fish (in part to sell to Boston), terrorized the inhabitants who provided bait and guarded the ships' rooms from season to season, and then, sitting as "admirals," decided cases in their own favor: "Their tyranny and oppression in the harbours, where there are none of his majesty's ships, is not to be reckoned amongst the least causes of the decay of the fishery" (Reeves 1793: 78, citing Commodore Scott's letter, 16 Nov. 1718).

The memorial of the merchants of Poole

A century later, in the Landergan petition, the inhabitants were blaming the naval officers for many of the problems of justice, and the attendant disorder; this petition was one of a series of letters and representations to the Board of Trade, where the populace blamed the naval officers for the unhappy state of affairs in Newfoundland, and the naval and military officers blamed the fishing admirals, while concurring in the observation of the "sad state of the populace." In remedy, the Board of Trade was urged – apparently by one of the English fish merchants, who were not oblivious to the problems – to impose

civil government . . . persons appointed to administer justice in the most populous and frequented places, that they [the inhabitants and fishermen] may be governed as Britons, and not live like a banditti or forsaken people, without law or gospel, having no means of religion, there being but one clergyman in all the country. (Reeves 1793: 90, quoting Mr. Cuming's representation, Feb. 1714–15)

Merchant appeals for civil government were rare in the eighteenth century: In general, during this period merchants were more opposed to civil government than to settlement (see K. Matthews 1973: 32; 1977). But this conjunction of law and gospel is a characteristic feature of hegemonic assertions, along with the derogation of the populace – forsaken, banditti – in terms that are somewhat more appropriate as descriptions of their overlords, the fishing admirals. The same conjunctions were used by the West Country merchants, sponsors of the fishing admirals, in their resistance to civil government.

John Reeves, writing shortly after he had been appointed the first chief justice of Newfoundland (1791), summarized the merchants' argument against civil government, which was part of their plea that they be given greater power – over the fishery and the fishermen – to put Newfoundland in order. Reeves quotes the "memorial from the merchants of Poole, in answer to a letter from the board [of trade], 3d December 1715," and adds the important note: "Another, word for word the same, came from Weymouth." Reeves reviews the twin memorials:

They complain of the great quantities of liquor and tobacco, which had paid no duty, and were imported by the New England-men, whereby the fishermen were debauched, and the fishery greatly hindered; . . .

They prayed, that all store-houses, &c., built by planters since 1685, in front of fishing ships rooms, towards the water, should be declared by act of parliament to belong to the ship to which the fishing room belonged – this to be enforced by forfeitures, to be levied by the fishing admirals. . . .

They propose some strict regulations, to prevent aliens and strangers sending out ships as English owned . . .

And then they turn to the heart of the matter: their relations to the fishermen:

In order that the poor labouring fishermen might not suffer oppression and disturbance from any military, or public officer, soldier, they desired, that no military person, on any pretense whatsoever, should intermeddle with the fishery or fishermen, inhabitants, or others; nor should let the soldiers out to hire, nor keep suttling houses [places where food and drink, by implication skimmed from military stores, were sold], nor have, for their own private use, any house out of the lines of fortification, or any gardens that have served, or may serve, for fishing rooms, according to the judgment of the fishing admirals of the harbour.

And because the commodores of late years have taken upon them to keep courts, and send warrants to several remote harbours, for commanders of fishing ships, in the height of the season, upon frivolous complaints of idle and debauched men, and others, without the complaint being first heard by the fishing admirals, according to the act of parliament, to the great prejudice of the fishery – they prayed, that the commodore might not in the future be permitted to do the like; that all complaints might be decided by the fishing admirals, and that no commodore should presume to intermeddle with debts between merchants, masters, planters and fishermen, as they had lately done, to the great prejudice of the merchants. . . .

They pray, that none should retail liquors to fishermen, or persons concerned in the fishery, but only to their own servants; . . .

They pray, that fishermen [who at this point were fishing on servant contracts] should be obliged to fish till the last day of August, if required by their masters. The usual day had been the 20th of August, but the fish now came later. That fishing admirals should have the power to give corporal punishment to all persons, of what degree soever, who profaned the Lord's-day, and all common drunkards, swearers, and lewd persons; that a sufficient number of ministers should be sent to the principal harbours, to instruct the inhabitants; and that they might be paid from England, the country being very poor. [Reeves 1793: 90–5]

Although dripping with – and perhaps undermined by – blatant self-interest, this is a key document for clarifying hegemonic assertions and the sorts of confrontations that occur over hegemony. Let us approach the issue indirectly, through the eyes of Sir Ralph Williams, KCMG, who two centuries later, in 1909, was sent out to be governor of Newfoundland. "One of the early matters which struck me," he wrote in his memoirs, "was the neglect to raise their hats to the governor on the part of so many of the people." His explanation of this is so charmingly idiotic that it serves to clarify what is really at issue with hegemonic confrontations:

At first I was inclined to ascribe this to purposeful rudeness, but I learnt better later. The Newfoundlander of the humbler classes is self-contained, undemonstrative, and shy, and he does not readily transform his goodwill into demonstrative action. [Ralph Williams 1913: 406. Before coming to Newfoundland, Williams was British agent in the Transvaal, resident commissioner of the Bechuanaland Protectorate, and governor-in-chief of the Windward Isles; a man accustomed to deference, whose comments on the lack of it in Newfoundland make delightful and thought-provoking reading.]

Not tipping hats may well be a struggle over deference, which is one manifestation of hegemonic conflicts, but in and of itself it is not a claim against – or for – hegemony. The merchants' memorial just cited is, and what makes it so, as I see it, is the combination of claims packaged together: extending the fishing season, flogging folks who profane the Lord's Day,

124

getting ministers, and retaining control over the supply of food, rum, labor, and justice.

Toward this end, the merchants were well tied together, as witnessed by the duplicate memorials from Poole and Weymouth. The problem the merchants had was *not* convincing the Board of Trade – for quite some time they continued to get much of what they wanted – but in their *lack of the kind of real, day-to-day connections with the populace* that would ease the enforcement of their hegemonic assertions. Compared to what was available to the gentry of England – where, for example, the absence of lawyers in felony trials enhanced the decorum of the courts, as the defendants came to rely on gentry intercession and pardons (see Hay 1975) – these connections were largely missing in Newfoundland, both in the domain of direct involvement in the daily affairs of people and in the domain of display and the recurring "theater of power" (cf. Thompson 1974).

The difficulty that this lack of direct involvement created for the assertion of elite hegemony is succinctly expressed by another incident that befell Governor Williams:

Once when out with my wife and her niece for a drive we called at a little house where the people were drying their fish, and on leaving, the good woman of the house turned to the ladies of my party, giving them four eggs, and saying, "There, my dears, take them home and eat them with your tea to-night." [Ralph Williams 1913: 407–8]

Several interpretations of this, which is not an isolated instance, are possible. I think it is most likely that the good woman of the fishery meant no insult. Rather, she gave what to her seemed a good and generous gift, part of a pattern of friendliness that would not let important guests leave empty-handed. Governor Williams, however, described the gift with mocking condescension. After centuries of appropriation by an absent elite, after a domination that had to be secured by constant tampering with the organization of production – keeping people fishing for the merchants by denying them agriculture, roads, and the local gentry that ordinarily comes with such connections – the problem was that this good woman did not have the slightest idea how the elite really lived. There were no manor houses at which she, or one of her neighbors, could have served, no – to return to the charter of the Bristol Company, cited in Chapter 7, Section III, and never a reality in the outports – "forms and ceremonies of government and magistratie" that could, in their own way, teach this good woman what she really ought to give, which was both less and more: less of a gift and more of a curtsy.

What permitted elite hegemony – imposed more in the domain of structure than of symbolic culture – to work, to secure the base of the merchants in the village fishery, if not to develop this base very far, was the absence of the kind of ties between fisher families that would provide the basis for an increasing development of counterhegemonic strategies: of a culture of confrontation and claim. This situation will be discussed more fully in the next chapter; a preliminary point of clarification is required here.

I do not want to imply that there were only minimal counterhegemonic strategies asserted by the fisher families of outport Newfoundland. They were in fact pervasive, but they are often difficult to see and to specify except in the occasional spectacular upheaval, such as the fishermen's co-operative and political movement (the Fishermen's Protective Union) that emerged in northeastern Newfoundland at almost the same time as Governor Williams. In the smaller, more ordinary domain of daily life there were also counterhegemonic assertions, but they primarily occurred not in the relatively obvious realm of symbolic action, such as refusing to tip one's hat or asking for a drink of water, but in the more concealed realm of social structure. Just as elite hegemony in Newfoundland was, after the collapse of the servant fishery, asserted more in structure than in symbol, so too were the counterhegemonic pressures. Consider the following two instances:

The first is again from Governor Williams. He is here discussing the sorry state of Newfoundland's political affairs, which he regarded as being caused by the clamor for services from the fisher families of the outports to their parliamentary representatives (who, Williams thought, had to satisfy too many claims in order to be reelected):

It is a fact that some years ago a prime minister of Newfoundland, in asking [his parliament] for money to relieve distress, which he painted as acute almost to starvation in a certain district, read out a letter from a clergyman, who wrote that if relief did not soon come, the people would be compelled to draw out this money from the savings bank in order to support themselves. [Ralph Williams 1913: 413. The outport fishermen could obtain some cash from fall wood cutting for pulp companies and from the spring seal fishery. Characteristically, this was very eagerly sought, even though the returns were exceedingly small in recompense for the hardships and dangers endured.]

The picture implied here – a self-centered, grasping, and childlike populace, with money in the bank while they came near to starving – is far from unique. In 1933, with Newfoundland at the point of collapse, Britain sent out a commission of investigation. Their report paints an identical picture, wondering what there is in the "childish" nature of the Newfoundland fishermen that makes them continue to bind themselves to the merchants with chains of credit, or appeal to the government for aid, when they have cash in the bank (CMND 4480).

The second illustration is from Thomas Lodge, one of the three commissioners sent out to govern Newfoundland the next year. He saw the

126

other side – and the issue before us, the organization of confrontations in the domain of social structure:

The codfishery . . . is almost unique as an industry in that the class which owns the capital employed in it has managed, somehow or other, to throw the whole risks, or very nearly the whole risks, which capital normally takes, and on which it bases its abstract claim for reward, onto the shoulders of the working classes. Moreover, it is a striking example of an industry in which the real capitalist has gone very far towards making a profit the first charge on the proceeds of the sale of the manufactured article, taking precedence even over a bare subsistence for the primary producer.

 . . . the sanctity of cash balances in the banks of Newfoundland, something almost incredible to an English mind . . . a bank deposit is something which cannot be touched except in the direst extremity. . . . Behind this is something, maybe irrational, but nevertheless explicable. It is the fisherman's instinctive method of throwing back on to the capitalist class the real capital risk. Whatever may have been the consequences to the individual fisherman – and they clearly have been, in most cases, very unpleasant – it has to be recognized that, as between classes, the method has been successful in transferring the ultimate consequences of this risk to the shoulders which, perhaps, might always to have borne them. [Lodge 1939: 49–50]

The notion that profits ought to have "first charge on the proceeds of the sale of the manufactured article" runs very deep among the dominant groups in Newfoundland. In 1942, for example, the administration appointed a labor-arbitration board to consider the wage claims of shop clerks in St. John's. After this board determined an absolute minimum living standard, which included setting a late age for when shop clerks ought to get married, taking into account when and how frequently shop clerks ought to have children (later and fewer than people in fact did, of course) and also considering how many single women might share the same rented room, the board ascertained a "minimum" necessary wage, called this wage "fair," and stated: *"The only justification for paying less than a fair living wage is that profits would fall below seven and one-half percent"* (Emergency Powers [Defense] Act, 1940 [emphasis added]).

For this period in capitalist countries and their colonies, there is probably nothing unique about either the primacy of profits or what we might call the easyhanded attempt to shape working-class lives to fit elitist conceptions. Fisherfolk had certain special options in response, rooted in the complex intermixture of their individuality and their community. Thus, for example, the fisher families, by forcing merchants to overextend their credit lines against the real cost the merchant of the supplies advanced to him, could occasionally bankrupt merchants (approximately once a decade, and sometimes more frequently, at least in southeastern Newfoundland), if not control merchants' ordinary, appalling, and at times immensely profitable predations. This is what I mean by social-structurally based, rather than symbolic counterhegemonic strategies.

When hegemony is understood not as the simple expression of the culture of the dominant class through the institutions of civil society but rather as the particular way elite culture is conjoined with the organization of appropriation; when the opposition to hegemony is understood as entailing not just alternative values but rather the structuring of these values into social relations and the continual production of alternative values from autonomous domains of folk social relations; *then* we have reached the point where the organization and operation of government can be seen as playing a crucial role in the confrontations and conjunctions of producers and appropriators. These confrontations and conjunctions will run the gamut from economic organization to the culture of daily life. And they will, as we shall see, necessarily become politicized due to the role government plays in social reproduction. The inability of the Newfoundland government not only to reproduce itself but also to reproduce the social relations of the fishery, or to break them and provide an alternative, highlights this whole process.

8

A political holiday

On 28 November 1933, on the occasion of the House of Assembly voting to dissolve itself in favor of direct colonial administration by Great Britain, Prime Minister Alderdice rose in the Assembly to state:

Yesterday . . . I went back in mind to the year 1855 and visualized the members of this House on that day sitting in this chamber and congratulating themselves upon having at last attained the privilege of Responsible Government [a step further than the representative government granted in 1832], and I wondered . . . if they would have been as gratified [now] at the result to the country of seventy-eight years of Responsible Government. It seems to me that if we had been in their place we would not consider that we had any cause to congratulate ourselves on having obtained the privilege of Self Government, and if they were here today they would, I think, concur in the view that what we need now is a political holiday. [quoted in Neary 1973: 41]

It was, as we have seen, a poor holiday indeed for the fisherfolk, and even for many outport merchants, hardly enriched by Alderdice's sanctimoniousness. On the surface at least, the collapse of the state was fiscal. Newfoundland simply ran out of money to pay its debts and bills and could get no further credit; England, presumably scared of the spreading effects of default, decided to both bail Newfoundland out and put the government in order. Lord Amulree's Commission of Investigation in its 1933 Report (CMND 4480; a very interesting and important document) laid a major part of the blame for the situation upon the fiscal irresponsibility of Newfoundland politicians; upon this, Clement Atlee (secretary of state for the dominions), visiting Newfoundland nine years later, commented, "I doubt if Newfoundland politicians were worse than those of Canada or Australia, but they had a narrower margin to work on" (Neary 1984: 106).

More to the point are the structural causes of this "fiscal" collapse. Four interpretations have been widely argued.

The politics of subsistence production

1. There were not enough fish and too many people.
2. The merchants were too individualistic and competitive to develop joint marketing or other innovative approaches to the fishery. Rather, they simply sucked the populace dry, leaving the people too poor to tax effectively and, at least in the winter, too desperate for the government to ignore.
3. The political system was ineffective, inefficient, and corrupt, dispersing its funds more for patronage than long-run social needs.
4. An impoverished country, with a dispersed population increasingly expensive for the government to service with what became regarded as basic amenities (schools, mail delivery, medical care, etc.), producing a low-valued product – "food for the poorer Catholic countries and Negroes," as Atlee put it – simply could not generate enough revenue for a modern state.

Related to the fourth interpretation is the notion that Newfoundland is "naturally poor"; a view that has always been widespread in Newfoundland itself but one that remains startling when we consider the immensity of the resources that are present in, and have been removed from, this country. Be that as it may, the bulk of the revenues of the state, while it lasted, came from import duties on supplies and consumption goods used in the fishery and by fisher families; when the fishery failed and the need for governmental aid was greatest, revenues were lowest.

All these perspectives on the fiscal problems of the Newfoundland state have some validity; all take the general situation of Newfoundland from, say, the early nineteenth to the mid twentieth centuries as a given, and describe the problematic features of this given. If, however, we look to the development of some aspects of this situation, and the obstacles that were encountered with the remedies attempted, a different and more general set of structural problems emerges.

A schematic chronology and overview of the early governmental crises will orient the subsequent discussion. Representative Government was granted in 1832. The same year, the Reform Act was passed in Great Britain; but it was not an auspicious time for Newfoundland. After a period of particularly high prices and good returns to the fishery during the Napoleonic Wars (1796–1815), with a very substantial increase in population (to 40,000 by 1815), Newfoundland underwent fifteen disastrously bad years in the fishery. By the early 1830s, the potential and actual tensions between fisherfolk and merchants were on the rise (K. Matthews 1977).

The constitution that Newfoundland was given created an elected House of Assembly and an appointed Legislative Council: a form of government that had been granted in several other British colonies and that worked, if not well, then at least passably. In Newfoundland this form of governmental organization was particularly problematic, for it was practically impossible to use the franchise to adjust participation in the representative House in ways that would make it even partly amenable to cooperation with the interests of the Council. With a mass of impoverished fisherfolk on the one hand, and a few relatively wealthy and certainly very powerful merchants and merchant agents on the other, property qualifications were impossible to use to select an electorate likely to see their interests in accord with the elite. Either almost everyone would vote, or almost no one would. The franchise chosen for Newfoundland had no property qualification and required only one year's residence to vote, two to serve. The Legislative Council and the power of the governor would be the effective check upon popular democracy – creating, at the outset, an antagonism between them and the Assembly; an antagonism that intensified over time, with tensions that were further heightened, as we shall soon see, by the absence of a secret ballot.

The election of the first House of Assembly, in 1832, was rather quiet, and the turnout in general was low. Merchants and their spokesmen predominated in the Assembly; "reformers" – who represented fisherfolk's interests – had only two vocal representatives among the fifteen members. By 1836 the parties represented in this first legislature would officially be called Conservative and Liberal; the shape of future antagonisms was prefigured, as the party system took shape, by their popular labels: "merchants party" and "priests party."

The first substantial action of the Assembly was to reject the governor's plea that it merge – "amalgamate," as it was called – with the appointed Legislative Council. Although at this early point what was at stake was the autonomy of the elected representatives, and the powers of representative government, the tensions would shortly be transformed into merchants versus fishermen.

The issues that most saliently shaped this split were poor relief, road building, education, and control over or influence in the colonial administration via Assembly control of salaries and disbursements. Poor relief was directly linked to road building (and indirectly to the promotion of agriculture) by proposals to employ the poor in road-construction projects – and to build party patronage in the process; the issue of education was the desire of the Liberal and Catholic members of the Assembly to keep the Bible out of state-supported schools, for if it were introduced Council would make it the Protestant Bible and most of the Catholic children would have been withdrawn from the schools. Taken together, these issues not only split the Assembly from the Council – the Assembly constantly proposing and the Council as constantly rejecting – but also increasingly associated the fisherfolk's interests with the Catholic hierarchy (the priests and the bishop), even though half the fisherfolk were Protestant. Democracy, from the Conservative perspective, required intensifying the conjunction of Liberals and Catholics to split the Protestant fishermen's support from the Liberal Party.

131

The politics of subsistence production

As tensions increased, the first election under Representative Government, in 1836, was won decisively by the Liberals, marked by riots and accusations of fraud, and annulled by the governor. In the subsequent election the Liberals swept the field, but the Assembly still confronted implacable opposition from the Council. An address from the House of Assembly to the queen conveys, in a few brief excerpts, the bite and flavor of the developing impasse:

Most Gracious Sovereign . . .
    . . . In fine, of the 32 Bills which passed this Branch of the Legislature, among which were a Bill for the establishment of an Academy, a Bill for securing education for the poor, &c., &c., owing to the influence of this Hon. Individual in the Legislative Council [Chief Justice Boulton], only TEN have passed into laws, and the Country remains subject to a system universally complained of.
    Your Majesty's faithful Commons of Newfoundland, in the present Session of Assembly, learning through reiterated statements laid before the House by order of His Excellency the Governor that the failure of the fishery was unexampled, and that the autumn and the winter threatened the people with all the horrors of starvation, were deeply solicitous to expend as much money as the resources of the Country could possibly admit, in the making and repairing of Roads, in order to afford the poor the opportunity of procuring relief and support in the remuneration of their labor, and in reward of their industry rather than by alms, while at the same time . . . facilitating the communication from settlement to settlement, promoting agriculture and permanently improving the Country.
    In this spirit this House introduced and passed a Bill in which they granted to her Majesty the sum of £16,801 for that purpose, but it was through the same influence twice rejected by her Majesty's Council, on the most frivolous pretenses;
    . . . the House of Assembly . . . adopted the course . . . of making the grants for Roads form a part of the general Bill of Supply, but in its being intimated to them that if it were sent up again detached from that Bill, it would be carried in opposition to the Judge, they at once complied and sent it up accordingly, being a FOURTH TIME, and It was only by these means it was carried in the Council. . . . Upon the Supply Bill going up to the Council, it was rejected, first on the ground that the Road Bill formed a part of it. . . .

In 1841 the governor dissolved the Legislature and suspended Representative Government. In 1842 a new constitution was imposed, with the Amalgamated Legislature that had been the desire of the governors of Newfoundland since Representative Government was announced – a desire that intensified as it became clear that the Liberals would win most of the elections for membership in the House of Assembly. The new constitution lasted from 1842 to 1848, when the original constitution was restored.

By 1854 the Legislature had again reached an impasse, and in 1855 another new constitution granted Responsible Government. The Legislative Council was still an appointed body, but its power to obstruct the House of Assembly was substantially diminished – although not made trivial until the Legislature Act of 1917. From 1855 on, the House of

132

Assembly was the locus of power; and the prime minister, along with his cabinet, dominated *normal* processes of government.

But as the Australians were to find out a little more than a century later, British-appointed governors can have a real aversion to liberals in power, and they can also hold notions about their own powers that the natives of colonies like Newfoundland and Australia can find rather surprising: In 1861 the governor of Newfoundland dismissed the Liberals from office while they held a strong majority (just as the Australian Labour Party was dismissed in 1975, like errant schoolboys), and amid the most intense turmoil and rioting (the Australians took it rather more quietly), the Conservatives won the majority of occupied seats in the legislature. It was a slim majority, based on annulling the election returns for three Liberal victories and vacating the seats, but a secure majority nonetheless.

Having been given the government, the Conservatives now had to figure out how to keep it. They did this, in large part, by a new form of legislative "amalgamation" of religious differences.

During the first three decades of semiautonomous government in Newfoundland, the long struggle between Liberals and Conservatives reflected, in broad outline, two social antagonisms: between fisherfolk and merchants, and increasingly both as a metaphor for this antagonism and as a vehicle for transforming it, between Catholics and Protestants. Fisherfolk were both Catholic and Protestant; merchants were almost entirely Protestant. Protestant religious "unity" had become an increasingly important part of the electoral appeal of the pro-merchant Conservative Party. And the Conservatives now figured out how to give religious unity a new and different importance to Catholics, while using it to keep themselves in power. In 1865 the Conservative prime minister brought into his cabinet several Catholic, pro-fishermen Liberals, who were as much representatives of the Catholics as of the fishermen; which is to say that these representatives seemed more pro-fisherman and pro-Catholic than anti-merchant. Without the anti-merchant bite to legislation, their pro-fishermen pronouncements were reduced to bark.

With the Catholic representatives in place in this new order, the legislators began to refer to the House of Assembly as the "Amalgamated Legislature." This phrase meant something entirely different than it had before: It did not mean the amalgamation of the House of Assembly and the Legislative Council; these were still two distinct bodies. It now meant the amalgamation of Catholics and Protestants within the Assembly. The effect, however, was the same: The Conservatives were in power, and they would stay there for quite a while. The Conservatives were scrupulous about dividing the benefits and spoils of government: Civil service and patronage positions were proportioned almost exactly according to the proportion of each religious orientation in the population (roughly one-third Catholic, one-third Church of England, and one-third Dissenter). Peace and Conservative predominance were secured, but not the stability of government.

II

Prior to the establishment of Representative Government, relations between Protestants and Catholics, both in the outharbors and among town dwellers, had been an ambivalent mixture of mutual support and hostility. Until the Catholic Emancipation Act of Great Britain in 1829, Catholics could not hold positions in the Newfoundland civil establishment – as magistrates, customs collectors, and so forth – and this was a source of some tension. In addition, there were some partly imported conflicts, such as the planned United Irish rising of 1830 in the garrison and the streets of St. John's – but these plans were foiled by information provided by a priest. Yet there were some strongly positive connections:

It was the practice for the labouring people, and all the servants of the different establishments, to turn out and give the Roman Catholic Bishop a hall of wood, as it was termed; that is, they went into the forests, cut wood, loaded their sledges with it . . . and presented it to the Roman Catholic Bishop, and in this all the people, Protestant and Catholic, joined without distinction. After two or three weeks had elapsed, the Roman Catholics generally did the same thing as a compliment to the Protestant Rector. [Great Britain 1841: testimony of Thomas H. Brooking]

Thomas Brooking, who had been a merchant in the Newfoundland trade for forty-three years, twenty-four in residence, went on to testify that when the Catholic bishop died in 1830, he had three Protestant and three Catholic pallbearers – which would have been unthinkable when Brooking testified in 1841. By 1837, Brooking complained, the Catholics were calling Protestants, himself included, "mad dogs."

Brooking may have been overstating, at least somewhat, the extent of Catholic–Protestant amity before and hostility after the advent of Representative Government: Merchants had a long-standing aversion to self-government; during the whole period of Representative Government, 1832–55, they took frequent opportunity to point out that it would not work in Newfoundland. At the center of the merchants' charges were two phenomena: the conflict between the House of Assembly and the Council, and the riots and violence that frequently occurred during elections.

Catholics, constantly charged with sole responsibility for rioting at elections, did not have a monopoly on violence but only predominated in one of the forms that violence, particularly in the outports, took. Newfoundland did not have a secret ballot until 1889. Before then voting was public, and the polls moved from place to place across a district over a period of several days, or a week or two, so that it was possible to see how any particular candidate was doing while there was still time (to put the matter abstractly) to alter the circumstances that led people to decide how they would cast their vote – in front of the audience, or audiences, that were watching the vote and the voters. Catholic fisherfolk had clubs and sticks; merchants had threats that were at least as frightful: For example, Thomas Holdsworth Brooking is being interrogated, in Great Britain, about the role of his merchant house in the election of 1837 – the same Brooking we encountered earlier, commenting on the wonderful effects of drawing the noose of credit tighter:

> *Question:* Your establishment set up one candidate?
> *THB:* Yes, there were two large establishments in that place [Trinity, Trinity Bay] , . . . Mssrs. Slade and my own; and there was a man by the name of Graham, who it was understood was to be elected, but a dispute took place between our agent and the agent of Slades' house and in consequence of that dispute this fellow Moore slipped in. . . .
> *Question:* Your agent and the agent of the other house could not agree on the nominee?
> *THB:* They had agreed, I believe, but there was some trifling difference . . . it was a most ridiculous thing. . . .
> *Question:* If the wealthy merchants of the place had combined, they might have got Graham in, but owing to their disunion Moore [the fishermen's candidate] got in?
> *THB:* Yes, and if they had sent up word to those places [the outharbors of Trinity Bay, which they supplied] that Mr. Graham was the more respectable man of the two, he would have been returned. . . .
> *Question:* Suppose you and other gentlemen like yourself were to shut up your establishments, what would be the effect on the constituency?
> *THB:* If many large establishments were to be closed in the course of the year, without ample notice, it would completely pauperize a great portion of the population.

The last question was prompted by an earlier exchange concerning the victory of Moore in this election:

> *Question:* Do you think him a fair specimen of what the representatives of the different districts would be like in ordinary times?
> *THB:* No, certainly not; for if it were so I would rather shut up my shop than suffer to be represented by a fellow such as that. [Great Britain 1841: testimony of Thomas H. Brooking]

Brooking might not have been telling quite the whole truth: Gunn argues that the merchants may in fact have sponsored outrageous candidates to discredit the Assembly (1977: 36–7). More to the point, merchants had a subtler and less self-punitive set of possibilities than simply closing up shop: They could close out specific people. The crowds of cudgel-carrying fisherfolk, following the polls from place to place, or trying desperately to get the merchants' candidate to withdraw his nomination before the election started, must be seen in this perspective.

135

The politics of subsistence production

To a substantial extent, but not completely, the Catholic position was anti-merchant, not anti-Protestant. Brooking was asked if an attack from the bishop's pulpit on Chief Justice Boulton – the nemesis of the Assembly in its early days – was motivated by religious considerations. "No," replied Brooking, "his wife was a Catholic. It was political. He gave a judgment from the Bench that seemed to be very hard on the working man. It gave the merchant a power he never had before, of seizing the fishermen's nets and tackle for debts." But the Catholic fishermen were becoming anti-Protestant: Their clergy were Irish, their political leaders often involved with the Irish struggles against England as well as Newfoundland affairs, and the Protestants were, increasingly, being coerced, led, or encouraged to take anti-Catholic stands, for it was largely on the basis of an anti-Catholic appeal that Protestant fishermen could be encouraged to side with the merchants. This was not an easy task, as shown by the election of 1855. That election, the first for Responsible Government, was organized by redrawn districts designed to give a small numerical edge in representation to the Protestants. But in the critical district of Burin, Methodists, separating themselves from their Church of England fellow-Protestants, sided with the Catholics to elect two Liberal representatives – and were publicly attacked as traitors to Christianity for so doing.

In 1866 Ambrose Shea, a leading Catholic Liberal member of the House of Assembly, was invited to join the ruling Conservative cabinet. Accepting the invitation, he stated: "Sectarianism has been tried and found wanting" (Noel 72: 25; "sectarian" and "denominational" are used interchangeably in Newfoundland to refer to Protestant-Catholic splits, and also to splits between Protestant denominations). To the contrary, sectarianism was still very much on the rise, and increasingly useful, although both its political shape and social basis were massively changing.

Starting in 1865, the Conservatives denominationally proportioned not only their cabinet but also all other civil-service and patronage positions. In conjunction with the school system, which was given completely to the churches, Newfoundland was split and rejoined from bottom to top on denominational lines – with the very top reserved for Protestant merchants and their allies. As S. J. R. Noel, author of perhaps the most conceptually cautious and thorough survey of Newfoundland's twentieth-century political history, put it:

Denominational segregation ... [became] an unwritten law of social organization. ... There was now scarcely an area of social life into which organized religious sectarianism did not intrude, sustained and reinforced by a system of education that was totally church-controlled. [1971: 21]

Church control of education was instituted in 1856, with the advent of Responsible Government. All education in Newfoundland (save now for

136

the university and technical colleges) is financed by government grants to the religious denominations, proportioned according to population. The churches used these funds (or, especially in the nineteenth century, a portion of them) to build and run schools for their adherents in the outports – outports that became, with Protestant–Catholic population shifts in the late nineteenth century and, for Protestants, with changing church membership, increasingly denominationally homogeneous. This increasing local homogeneity was due in part to the system of education and in part to increasing religious tensions and prejudices. It was reinforced by a context where much of the organized social life of the outports takes place in church halls, if not organized by the church. All this increasingly consolidated the social centrality and political presence of denominational hierarchies, although not apparently having much effect on the religiosity of the people. The system of religious segregation and control of education was considered so important that special arrangements were made for it to continue after Confederation with Canada, and the recent fiscal pressures for consolidated schools has only slightly eroded this arrangement.

III

Antedating and developing alongside this increasingly entrenched sectarianism in the last half of the nineteenth century were two related developments that altered its social basis: increasing merchant power, and the increasing transfer of the locus of economic activity and control to St. John's.

In the mid nineteenth century, when sectarianism was politically and socially institutionalized in Newfoundland, it was not simply an act of politically inspired mystification of the realities of power and well-being; it also had a new social basis, but a basis that would erode and disappear almost as soon as sectarianism was consolidated. The early mid nineteenth century was the high point, until the recent post-Confederation period, of the development of social-class differentiation in the outports; the sectarian claims for place and position were in part rooted in this differentiation.

On the south coast, an outport-based ocean-bank fishery was flourishing. On the west coast, salmon were bringing higher returns than cod, and lobster-canning factories were proliferating. And on the northeast coast – by far the most densely populated area outside the St. John's region – a productive and profitable seal fishery was being prosecuted from locally built and owned schooners that sailed to the Labrador coast for the summer cod fishery after the sealing season ended. All together, the Newfoundland fishery then provided an array of jobs in shipbuilding, sail making, coopering, and work aboard the boats; mostly with local employers, and much of it substantially independent of direct merchant domination. The greater autonomy from merchant domination that such diversification provided during this period was sufficiently substantial to effect the physical placement of communities: Patricia Thornton has shown, for the advent of a multifaceted family-based fishery during the early nineteenth century along the west coast Strait of Belle Isle (which for reasons particular to the west coast was more autonomous than elsewhere), that the "change in status from servant to self-employed fisherman was reflected by a move away from the headlands and islands where cod-fishing establishments were located, to the river-banks and then to the heads of bays . . . [for] shelter and easier access to wood, fur, salmon and seals" (1977: 171, 173); this process was reversed later in the century.

Each of the religious denominations saw, emerging within its midst in the outports, people of modest prosperity and seemingly brighter futures, to whom other members of the community were connected by bonds of kinship, church membership, close residence, and employment outside the merchant-dominated truck system.

The new denominational amalgamation in the House of Assembly was rooted in this emerging social reality. The Assembly's sectarian allocation of positions and patronage offered employment and prestige to the emerging local elites and their children – as schoolteachers, magistrates, and in a variety of government-paid positions – and it brought some of these people into the government itself. But no sooner was it established than its social base began to collapse, with the collapse of outport economic activities apart from the codfishery, with the tightening hold of merchants, and with the increasingly common and widespread immiserization of the outport populace.

In the summer of 1846 a disastrous fire leveled most of St. John's, destroying not only much of the inhabitants' housing but also most of the merchants' stores and warehouses. A large sum of money was raised, particularly in England, to alleviate the distress caused by the fire; shortly thereafter, the governor decided to use a substantial portion of the funds raised to rebuild the Anglican cathedral – "an expense," he said, "which must otherwise be borne by the shopkeepers of St. John's" (Gunn 1977: 105). In the fall of the year the potato blight struck, and most of the remaining funds were used to provision villagers – formerly a responsibility of the merchants, who had been clamoring for years to pass this obligation on to the government.

The rising power of the merchants seems also to have been expressed in the changing form of urban mummering. For a decade or more before 1846, the mummering in St. John's centered on a parade that was both a procession of costumed mummers and the movement of a large and unruly crowd through the central streets of the capital, the whole ensemble hov-

138

ering on the edge of melee and violence between Catholic and Protestant, the crowd and the elite. Costuming for the parade involved some sexual reversals – men dressing as ladies – but the emphasis was very much on the reversal of social class: the costumed "fools" who appeared bedecked with ribbons and male finery and who were particularly violent, with a violence that was part mock and part mocking. After the fire, perhaps as a concomitant to the increasingly total power of the large-scale St. John's supply merchants (a codevelopment with the early growth of autonomous outport economic activities), the fools disappeared, and their place in the parade, until the whole parade was put down in 1861, was taken by an urban form of mummers, dressing as ladies and calling at the houses of the elite in a much gentler – if still provocative and somewhat confrontational – performance.

The increasing political and economic power of both large St. John's merchants, and many of the outport fish merchants, in the mid nineteenth century was further consolidated, in a particularly perverse way, by the building of railroads in Europe. These railroads made it possible to bring Norwegian codfish to Naples in a few days, compared with the several months needed to collect and deliver Newfoundland fish (K. Matthews, personal communication). Although the Newfoundland climate produced a very high-quality cure, the longer time it took to deliver the fish lowered its condition at delivery. The price for Newfoundland fish and its share of the market declined. This lowered income for all concerned, and it put a large number of outport businesses with fewer resources than the St. John's firms "belly up in the harbour."

The sudden advent of steam-powered sealing boats almost completely destroyed the interlinked range of relatively autonomous economic activities flourishing on the northeast and northern coasts:

By 1827 there were 290 ships and 5,418 men engaged in the [sealing] industry; in 1857 these figures reached a peak of 370 and 13,600. The average size of the sealing vessels also increased. After 1863, when steam vessels participated in the seal fishery for the first time, the number of sailing vessels declined. By 1882 the steam fleet had increased to twenty-five while only twenty to thirty small sailing vessels were involved. By that year the number of men employed had declined to about 5,000. The introduction of steamers required a larger capital expenditure and allowed St. John's to monopolize the industry for the first time. Only Harbour Grace of all the outports was able to remain active in the seal fishery and even there the decline was drastic: 53 ships and 2,825 men in 1870; 17 ships and 1,515 in 1880, and, at a time of general decline in the industry, 3 ships (steamers) and 600 men in 1890. . . . The whole Newfoundland economy was affected by this change [which included the declining harvest of seals] but the Conception Bay outport economy most of all. In this area prosperity had been built on the interaction of the sealing and Labrador enterprises. [Ryan 1980: 45]

With the outport economy undermined to the point where fishing for the merchant was about the only thing left to do other than working for the government, and with the increasingly desperate situation of the populace in the winter (a trend that is impossible to measure, but this is my impression from my reading of nineteenth-century data), the process of government became focused on access to government funds, which the Amulree commission, investigating the collapse of Newfoundland in 1933, called "political spoils" and saw as substantially due to a combination of patronage and sectarianism:

The spoils system has for years been in full force in Newfoundland . . . [and] it is natural that in the minds of many people politics should be regarded simply as job-farming. It has been the practice for each incoming Government to side-track or sweep away all Government employees who were appointed by or were suspected of any connection . . . with their predecessors, and to replace them with their own nominees, irrespective of the qualifications. . . .

Post-election changes are commonly of a sweeping character with effects which manifest themselves in every corner of the Island. . . . Post Office and Railway employees, Customs Officials, Relieving Officers, Fishery and Timber Inspectors and Wardens [etc.] . . . all are liable to sudden dismissal, however competent their work. . . .

It has been shown . . . that up to 1861 sectarian rivalry was a marked feature of the political life of the Island; that it was the practice for each general election to be fought in an atmosphere of denominational jealousy and bitterness; and that the riots of 1861 finally led to an agreement that "all religious parties should be fairly represented in the arrangement of an administration and in the distribution of offices." This understanding has been faithfully observed since that date. The constituencies of the Island, now numbering 27, are divided equally into those which return candidates from the Church of England, the Roman Catholic Church, and the United Church of Canada [i.e., Methodists and Dissenters], respectively. Similarly, the Executive Council, or "Cabinet," with a membership of 12, is composed of four members representing the Church of England, four representing the Catholic Church, and four representing the United Church. This arrangement, while doubtless achieving the salutary object of avoiding overt rivalry between the Churches, must necessarily be a handicap to good administration. . . . Thus, if a member of one denomination obtains a contract from the government, the members of the other main denominations must be selected for some compensating favour. . . . The denominational divisions, of which the people are daily reminded, so far from exercising a beneficent influence in the direction of cleaner politics, have failed to check, if indeed they have not contributed to, the general demoralization. . . .

It is safe to say that under no other system would it have been possible for the budget to remain unbalanced for twelve successive years and for a public debt to be amassed the interest charges on which, without provision for a sinking fund [for paying the debt], amount to over 50 per cent. of the average annual revenue of the country. We have good reason to think that by 1928 it was appreciated . . . that the country was rapidly approaching insolvency. Yet there was no modification of policy. . . .

This continuous process of misgovernment has increased the burden on the fisherman and on the poorer members of the community until it is now insupportable. . . . no less than 75 per cent. of the revenue of the country is derived from customs duties. As expenditure increased . . . customs duties were therefore raised. . . . When the depression set in and revenue fell . . . customs duties were once more raised. Previously it had been the practice to admit free of duty certain of the goods, such as petrol for fishing boats, salt and flour, which might be said to form the raw material of the fisherman. . . . These were now taxed . . . there appears to be reason to believe that the duties are now so high that the law of diminishing returns has begun to operate. [CMND 4480: 87–90]

IV

The fragility of the Newfoundland state, temporarily concealed by denominational alliances, once more had reemerged on center stage, and once more seemed irresolvable without drastic constitutional change. The crisis now seemed fiscal: Presumably irresponsible politicians, having pushed the bulk of the fisher families to the wall as they fought for places at the trough for themselves and their allies, had no further source of supply for their bucket. Atlee, however, made an important point: Newfoundland politicians were probably not much more corrupt, shortsighted, or inefficient than those in British colonies elsewhere; they just had a narrower margin to work on. Why was this so – why were there no other sources of revenue?

In 1855 the House of Assembly, faced with a decline in catch and cod prices, another failure of the potato crop, and widespread poverty and dearth, undertook an investigation into "pauperism," questioning "prominent persons in the outports" about its extent and causes (JHA 1855: app., pp. 255–90 publishes excerpts from the replies).

A wide range of replies was received, but several themes were particularly salient. Apart from attributing much of the specific difficulty of the year to the failure of the potato crop, these themes centered on the organization of the fishery, and in particular on the fact that poverty was far worse in places where people could do little but fish and depend upon the merchant for winter supply. When winter supply functioned effectively,

it gave the operative population of the country great contentment and security . . . but, in my opinion, the cost of that absence of Pauperism, owing to the system I have just described [winter supply], is a population incapable of expansion – a neglect of every other employment save the system of the fishery; and by and by, when the system ceases to operate, the subjecting [of] the present population to the same trials and hardships . . . and also the same incapacity on the part of the population . . . to resist its disastrous results. [p. 259]

It was not, however, simple neglect that kept people from alternative employments:

Pauperism exists to a great extent in Fogo District, particularly among fishermen with large families, who have no credit with nor employment from the merchants – these men are willing to go into the Bays to cut timber if they had the necessaries to go with – these Bays afford great facilities for employing the poor; . . . the great curtailment of the usual supplies to the fishermen is one cause of their destitution;

141

the catch of codfish has fallen off; but not to that degree in itself that would involve the people in poverty.... There is no soil of any kind in Fogo proper, worth speaking about; but ... there would be no destitution in the District, if people had the means afforded them to enable them to proceed into the Bays for the purpose of felling timber, &c.... [p. 267]

[From Placentia:] The felling of timber, making staves, oars, laths, &c., &c., is employment that is not in the power of Paupers to accomplish for want of support to labour at said work, and should their labour prove remunerative, which we have every reason to believe that it would not, they would find no person that would supply them at work of this description. [p. 272]

Although some were prospering, during the mid nineteenth century, with the development of larger-scale, outport-owned forms of fishing, and with agriculture – "the Agricultural produce on this shore [Placentia Bay], for the most part, is the growth of live stock, which appears to be daily increasing.... There are families on this shore that have nothing to do with the fishery that live comfortable and happy" (p. 269) – many were still rooted in the merchant-sponsored fishery. Their increasing impoverishment was affecting their productivity: "The classification of Paupers in this District [St. Mary's] is as follows, viz.: Widows with young families, orphans, aged and sick persons, and men fishing in small craft (punts and skiffs) ... " (p. 275). Similarly, P. W. Carter, stipendiary magistrate and chairman of the board of commissioners for the poor, attributed "the failure of the Fishery, in some respects, to the substitution of small boats for larger ones; the small boats not able to keep on the [fishing] ground when the large craft could ... (p. 263).

Although prosperity and poverty coexisted in the outports during the mid nineteenth century, the balance was decisively shifting, and except perhaps in some of the larger market towns of Conception Bay, poverty became increasingly common. As the nineteenth century drew to a close, this poverty became an increasing pressure on government resources, contributing to the failure of the banks in 1894 and introducing another decade of governmental crises and turmoil. Canadian banks came in, bailing the government out and changing Newfoundland to Canadian currency. Although the attempt to diversify the economy by a massive commitment of state revenue to railroad building was also a major factor in the collapse of the economy, diversification of necessity became a central item on the state agenda, where it has remained throughout the twentieth century.

But not only did the state fail to sponsor either growth or diversification into a productive and successful nonfishing economy; it could not or did not even create a form of diversification that would be both fishery-based and village-based. The Fishermen's Protective Union, a cooperative and political movement that emerged in the first two decades of the twentieth century, which at its height comprised half the fishermen of Newfoundland, fought long and hard to have the state organize and rationalize the production and marketing of fish. Save for a few ineffective concessions, it lost (McDonald 1980; forthcoming). Compounding this was the further failure of either merchants or the state to develop local uses for fish by-products or, in many places, to develop the processing and marketing of varieties of fish other than cod. Even with the addition of salmon, lobster, and herring, this leaves a number of commercially important species to be thrown back dead into the sea. The Norwegian example already cited, where the waste from cod is purchased to feed mink (at the same price paid for fish in Newfoundland), underscores the problem. Indeed, the relative prosperity of village fisher families in Norway and Iceland constitutes the strongest indictment of the failures of government and the merchants in Newfoundland.

What Newfoundland did do for and with the fishery was to sponsor the development of frozen-fish-fillet production by privately owned factories that had their own oceangoing trawlers. This not only created a number of very arduous and low-paying jobs, it also substantially worsened the plight of the remaining inshore fishermen. Romeo LeBlanc, Canadian minister of fisheries in a Trudeau government, described the structure of this situation in the 1970s: Factories hire the labor for their boats as "co-adventurers" – which means that they are paid with a share of the catch, rather than a wage. The factories then purchase fish from their own boats at a low price, taking a tax loss on the catching operations, as the ship's half of the catch does not cover the costs of fishing. This not only keeps wages down on the trawler; it also depresses the price paid to "independent" small-boat fishermen, who nowadays mostly deliver their fish, un-cured, to freezing plants, rather than salt the fish themselves (R. Matthews 1980).

One of the basic reasons for the drastic decline of the inshore fishery since World War II is that few fish are left near the shore – in large part as the result of political-economic decisions by the provincial and federal governments. The immense factory trawlers of a dozen different nations (including some Newfoundland-based boats) that drag the bottom of the ocean banks with huge nets, and also at times come close to shore (because Canada until the mid 1970s did not put very much effort into enforcing its modest territorial sea rights), have systematically overfished the stocks. Since Confederation, the provincial government has been subsidizing the local construction and ownership of larger boats – long-liners forty to sixty feet in length that fish the "near-shore" grounds between the inshore village fishermen with their smaller boats and the offshore ocean trawlers. These long-liners can also fish longer seasons, which supported the developing frozen-fish factories' demand for a more regular annual supply. But they have had a strong impact on the inshore fishery:

The politics of subsistence production

The summer of 1973 on Fogo Island is an instructive example. . . . the longliner fleet was forced off the middle distance grounds through gear loss and harassment by trawlers as well as diminished stocks in waters fished out by these vessels; the longliners moved into the inshore grounds and the inshore fishery – already suffering decreased catches due to intensified offshore efforts, suffered an immediate and drastic decline in catch. [E. Antler 1974]

Community-based long-liners, superficially similar to the "traditional" inshore fishery, in fact establish substantially different social relations of work and production. Rather than one man or family owning a boat, others the gear, and fishing together, the tendency is for one man to assume a loan for boat and gear and to hire crew. Although the crew may work on shares, the shares are small and the skipper is under the kind of economic pressure that requires novel demands on the crew. The skipper becomes, in a very real sense, a boss whose success in organizing the labor of his crew will increase the difference in material well-being between himself and his crew. But in the late 1960s some fishing communities still retained enough cohesiveness – or if cohesiveness is too strong a word, at least enough of a common orientation – to force a return to smaller boats by refusing to crew for the larger boats that not only sailed longer season but were also away from home several days at a time (Stiles 1973).

In the five years from 1967 onward, while Newfoundland was in the midst of its forced-relocation program (closing 143 communities with 16,114 people between 1965 and 1970), the trawler fishery was permitted to intensify. The inshore annual cod catch dropped from 270,000 quintals (112 lb. per quintal) to 108,000. But in 1974 Canada imposed a 200-mile claim to its ocean resources (as much or more for the oil potential as for the fish), and allocated half the remaining total allowable catch to the inshore fishery, which doubled the size of its catch in the next four years. A little more life was given to fishing communities that could not be completely destroyed because there was nothing else for the people to do, in the wake of the transparent and nearly complete failure of forced growth and diversification policies.

V

Merchants did not substantially diversify the range of economic activities in "their" outports; indeed, they probably could not have done so and maintained control over the fishery and the necessary labor force. Beginning in the late nineteenth century, the state tried hard to foster diversification. But despite giving away a very large portion of Newfoundland's natural resources, it failed to do so – failed in the prime areas of generating an alternative financial basis for the Newfoundland state and of providing

144

secure and decently paid employment outside the fishery (and the government's payroll) for a substantial segment of its population.

Two theoretical points need to be stated and developed to understand the failure of the state to force economic growth through policy and practice:

1. a sharpened concept of capital formation, which focuses *not* on the establishment of factories, mines, and mills, or on the required material infrastructure (e.g., transport and electricity), but rather on how the social relations essential to the continuity of existing forms of capital and to the formation of new capital are developed and sustained
2. a concept of the role of the state in what is loosely called the *political economy* – a concept that while nowhere near a full analysis of, or perspective on, the issue of the state and the political economy, at least calls to the foreground the role of the state in creating and reproducing those forms of inequality that are, or are regarded as, essential to the functioning of the economy and that the economy itself cannot generate.

The second point sounds more complicated in the abstract than it is: Think, for concrete illustration, of giving the fishermen in the eighteenth century first lien on the proceeds of the catch, and then taking this right away in the early nineteenth; each action participated in creating a different kind of labor force, with a different relationship to the planter and merchant masters of the fishery.

From this perspective we can ask: Are the social relations necessary to form new kinds of capital (e.g., mines, mills, and factories) incompatible with the social relations necessary to maintain existing forms of capital? If so, the core problem becomes not just the fiscal costs of capital formation but also the fundamental social disjunctions of development; disjunctions whose powers are measured, unfortunately, not by the misery of the populace but by the structural impasses development schemes meet and cannot cross. From this perspective, crises of the state that on the surface seem to be "fiscal" can be seen as rooted in the structural inability of the state either to effectively organize social reproduction (including both the reproduction of the old and the development of the new), or to account for its failures or for the ensuing further impoverishment of substantial sectors of the populace. Nor can the state convincingly delineate, institutionally or ideologically, at any point in this process of repeated failure, the prospects for the future.

The entire period during which Newfoundland had its own state and a "representative" or "responsible" government approximately coincided with the duration of the family fishery and the truck system of payment. The state could not, as we shall see, either play the role required of it to sustain the social relations of merchant-capital production, or develop an alternative.

The problems the state encountered throughout this period, and in par-

145

ticular during its early decades, did not originate, as the early governors often claimed, simply in the extent of the franchise, which created an Assembly that until sectarian amalgamation (and episodically thereafter) was opposed to many of the merchants' desires and needs. The other half of the story of continual crises is rooted in the *necessary* reliance of merchant capital on the assistance of the state – an assistance that the state could not provide whether it wanted to or not.

The forms and methods through which merchant capital has sought to control its labor force have been many and varied. Ordinarily, however, merchant capital must have a politically privileged position to continue: monopolistic control of the market for some factors of production, or for the commodity itself, or some direct or indirect assistance in constraining producers' alternatives to doing business with merchant capital (including in some places, such as the Amazon basin, direct brutality). In some few instances, such as Italian silk production, merchants owned the tools and the raw materials, and thus had somewhat different political needs vis-à-vis their workers. European linen production, using inexpensive raw materials worked with low-cost tools, often called forth monopolistic structurings of the productive process in order to secure and exercise control over the labor force.

Newfoundland merchants using the truck system faced problems similar to those of European merchant capitalists using the putting-out system of cottage production (particularly textile production), but they were incapable of resolving similar problems in a similar fashion. In both the truck and putting-out systems merchants advanced the raw materials of production (in Newfoundland essential foods were often also given) and laid claim to the total product of labor at the point when supplies were advanced. This claim was backed by a complex array of factors, including the producers' need for further supplies, which encouraged compliance, and by laws that specifically supported the merchants' claims. In both systems the producers characteristically bore the costs of acquiring and maintaining their productive equipment; merchant claims to the product were not usually based on the ownership of the equipment of production.

Merchants in such systems came under various kinds of pressure. They faced continual problems of "leakage" in the production cycle: The producers would sell to someone other than their supplier a portion of the product they made with the supplies advanced – which was often called "embezzlement" in European and North American textile production, and "trespass" (by the purchaser) in Newfoundland. Merchants in both systems also characteristically faced problems of labor supply – either of getting more labor when demand surged, which was more a European problem, or of dumping labor when demand fell, which was very much a problem in Newfoundland, where there was neither an agricultural sector nor concurrent crop raising and commodity production to at least feed the people who were dropped.

In rural Europe and mainland North America, merchants, although invoking state power (viz., laws against embezzlement), could over the long run "resolve" the difficulties of securing labor and of controlling the productive process more tightly by acquiring ownership of the implements of production and by centralizing the work. Further, they could often lower the unit costs of production by doing this. Thus an "economic" problem could be dealt with by solutions within the economic domain. And in the short run they could dump labor back upon its own small-farming resources (at least in the rural areas of cottage production) without creating short-run drastic problems of starvation, and still have this labor available to be called back into commodity production. In Newfoundland, particularly until the advent of refrigeration on trawlers, the long-run economic solution was not possible. It was impossible to lower the unit costs of production by centralized merchant ownership of the small boats and nets, which were constructed and maintained by dint of much labor from the fishing families. It was also impossible to centralize and more intensely capitalize the production process; larger boats, fishing further offshore, and returning to land less frequently produced a poorer grade of cured fish, and used much more salt to do so. Without an economic solution to their problems, and with the drastic implications of even temporary declines in the demand for labor, the Newfoundland merchants were forced to turn to the state for political solutions to problems of control over labor and to deal with unwanted labor – as well as to lower their costs, particularly during times of poor prices, by having the state take on the costs of winter supply. This situation pitted the state against the fisher families – who had been called into the political process by the breadth of the franchise and forced to act directly by the absence of the secret ballot. Moreover, some of the structural problems of the fishery remained irresolvable even with state intervention.

The impoverishment of fisher families did not permit any substantial accumulation of their goods by their creditors; and as the state's revenues came almost completely from import duties on goods used by fisher families, it was particularly difficult for the state to fund assistance in times of need. Partly to keep fisher families fishing, which required keeping them continually in need of credit for food and clothes, partly to be able to market the codfish in low-income areas of southern Europe, the Caribbean, and Brazil, and partly to inhibit the development of alternative economic activities in the outports, merchants had to pay a low price (or allow a low return) for fish. But unlike farmers, whose land can be taken when they fall too far in debt, the impoverishment of the producers was of no benefit of no benefit to the merchants; it allowed the merchants very little slack in the system to press further against the producers when, say, fish prices fell in Europe. All they could do in such instances was deny winter supply, leaving the government to deal with the debris of their practices. In the fishery crises of 1847, 1860, 1884–94, 1930–9, and 1947, approximately one-third of the population of Newfoundland was on relief, and relief payments, however minuscule, often rose to over 25 percent of government revenues. Poor relief – its costs, and controversy over its extent and management – figured prominently in every major crisis of the Newfoundland state.

The most famous phrase Joey Smallwood ever uttered in his long political career – and he was a very colorful speaker while leading Newfoundland into Confederation with Canada in 1949 and as premier of Newfoundland from 1949–72 – was "Burn your boats, boys, there will soon be two jobs for every man." He now denies he ever said it, but the phrase still reverberates throughout Newfoundland. A recent popular book, for example, was entitled *Now That We've Burned Our Boats* (Newfoundland and Labrador Federation of Labour, 1978).

Smallwood stands in a long line of Newfoundland political leaders (long because before him they changed so often) intensely committed to developing an economy apart from the inshore fishery. From the first – Prime Minister Whiteway's railroad-building program in the 1880s – these projects all failed to do what was expected: open the economy and provide a substantial number of jobs. Nor have they ever contributed significantly to tax revenues. Smallwood was distinguished only by the magnitude of his efforts, which included the largest construction project in Canadian history (Churchill Falls hydroelectricity, from which the Province of Quebec takes all the profit); the magnitude of his failures, which included the largest bankruptcy in Canadian history (the Come-By-Chance oil refinery, in which Newfoundland heavily invested); and by the consistent failure of his development projects, every single one of which failed or was continued by massive government subsidy (Canada, Economic Council of, 1980; Newfoundland and Labrador, Province of, 1980). Smallwood was also distinguished by his capacity to stay in office in the midst of this havoc for almost twenty-three unbroken years – on the basis of his popular appeal.

The enormity of the concessions made to foreign capital – the amount given away for little or no return – even when judged by contemporary colonial standards, is one of the most prominent features of Newfoundland "economic development." Joseph Chamberlain, Britain's colonial secretary, wrote to the governor of Newfoundland that he did not have the responsibility to refuse assent to the Railway Contract of 1898, between the government and R. G. Reid, a Canadian developer, although

148

under this contract, and the earlier one of 1893, for the construction of the railway, practically all the Crown lands of any value become, with full rights to all minerals, the freehold property of a single individual: the whole of the railways are transferred to him, the telegraphs, the postal service, and the local sea communications, as well as property in the dock in St John's. *Such an abdication by a Government of some of its most important functions is without parallel.*

The colony is divested for ever of any control over or power of influencing its own development, and of any direct interest in or direct benefit from that development. . . .

That they [the Legislature] have acted thus in what they believe to be the best interests of the colony I have no reason to doubt; but whether or not it is the case, as they allege, that the intolerable burden of the Public Debt, and the position in which the colony was left by the contract of 1893, rendered this sacrifice inevitable, the fact that the colony, after more than forty years of self-government, should have to resort to such a step is greatly to be regretted. [CMD 8867, 23 March 1898; emphasis added. See also Chadwick 1967, chaps. 7, 5]

Although the government bought back – at substantial cost – several provisions of this contract, indirectly admitting its mistake (for the politics of this contract see Hiller 1980), three basic features of the negotiations for, and establishment of, the railway express a pattern of so-called development that has persisted throughout the twentieth century:

1. The enormity of the concessions made to foreign capital turn out, on close inspection, to be based as much or more on political need as economic factors, and the concessions made it impossible, in the long run, to satisfy the political needs which impelled them.
2. The government could not resolve the tension between providing alternative employment and maintaining the fishery.
3. The government, in offering to provide alternative employment in response to public clamor, raised ideological issues that it could not resolve.

It is ordinarily claimed that the economic difficulties of Newfoundland arise from the "natural poverty" of the country. In the fishery this has meant too many people and not enough fish – an interpretation from which I have already distanced myself. Outside the fishery this has meant that to attract capital to such a far-off place for such ordinary resources as wood, ores, and hydroelectric power, Newfoundland would have to practically give them away.

The resources of Newfoundland are, in fact, not at all paltry, and the enterprises that extract these resources are – considering the extent of poverty among so small a population – surprisingly large. In the twentieth century Newfoundland has had the largest iron mine and one of the largest pulp and paper firms in the British Commonwealth and the second-largest lead mine and largest zinc mine in North America. The people remain the poorest in Canada, making the lowest average wage for workers, paying the highest percentage of their income in taxes, and having the lowest level of public services: the product of a century of gifts to capital. The govern-

The politics of subsistence production

Table 1. *Projected revenue sources 1980–1*

Source	Amount in millions $Can.
Retail sales tax	254.3
Personal income tax	169.5
Gasoline tax	45.7
Corporate income tax	45.5
Liquor corporation	44.0
Tobacco tax	24.0
Mining tax and royalties	21.7
Vehicles and driver's licenses	16.0

Source: Newfoundland and Labrador, Province of, 1980: 32.

ment itself – either when independent or as a province – collects scant revenues from any of its projects; so scant that in 1975, after substantial protest within the Provincial Legislature, the tax laws were drastically revised to shift more of the burden onto the large corporations. Five years after this revision, with the new tax structure firmly in place, the projected provincial revenues were as shown in Table 1.

A wide variety of motives on the part of the government ministers who arranged this situation brought Newfoundland to this point. The literature on this is replete with accusations both of personal gain, particularly in the early years of the century, and of shortsightedness – as well as of invocations of necessity. Yet the consistency of the pattern calls for a different kind of explanation. In the 1960s the provincial government agreed to supply electricity at 2.5 mills (¼¢) per kilowatt-hour in order to attract a phosphorous-refining plant to Newfoundland. The amount of electricity involved was enormous – about 10 percent of all the power on the island – and the price was substantially below the cost to the government. When the magnitude of the giveaway became known (by measuring projected costs against the most favorable projections of direct and indirect returns, and by ignoring such secondary and incidental costs as the fact that the toxic wastes from the plant at one point killed all the fish in the area and required closing a large area of Placentia Bay to commercial fishing), Premier Smallwood "realized" and publicly admitted his mistake. But he entered into a contract for the development of an oil refinery that agreed to supply electricity to the refinery at the same price (Crabb 1974). It could not be shortsightedness; for all the attacks on Smallwood, no one has ever even hinted at personal gain. And if it was necessity, what necessity drove Newfoundland to continually make such losing deals?

150

A political holiday

Two factors seem continually crucial: (1) the government's need to raise revenue for itself, even if in a losing deal in the long run – a factor more significant in the late nineteenth and early twentieth centuries; and (2) the government's need to provide employment and to deliver on its perpetual promise to create jobs outside the fishery. Poor relief, and the fiscal crises of the state that became associated with poor relief and unemployment, were part of both needs. The railway, for example, was begun in fits and starts in the early 1880s; it was essentially completed in 1896. The infamous railway contract had nothing to do with building the railroad. Its main purpose was to raise cash for the government to help avoid bankruptcy and impending turmoil; the giveaways to which Secretary Chamberlain referred were made in return for one million dollars, and for operating services that the government could ill afford, not for building the railroad.

The need to provide employment is more complex than it might seem at first, for the issue was not simply making jobs other than fishing available. John Kent, acting colonial secretary during the 1855 investigation of "pauperism" by the House of Assembly, testified that the effect of the truck and credit system "was to direct the attention of the people solely and entirely to the prosecution of the fisheries." The problem for the state, which had to answer to merchant as well as popular interests, was to provide jobs without letting this attention wander. When William Whiteway was elected prime minister in the fall of 1889, promising the unemployed and destitute to restart construction on the railroad as soon as he took office, a constitutional crisis was provoked, for the governor kept the losing Conservatives in power until the end of December (Mitchell 1958). Whatever the governor's real reasons, the effect was clear to everyone: Fisher families were forced to find winter supply, if they could, by binding themselves to a merchant, on the merchant's terms, for another year of the fishery.

Elections throughout the past century have almost always had, as one of their central themes, the promise of jobs and "development" – "opening the country," as it was called. The jobs that were provided, for the most part, were either short-term construction jobs getting the new projects built (the one return of any substance from the recent "development" schemes) or else provided mostly seasonal employment. Most woods workers for the two very large pulp mills on the island until recently cut wood in the fall and winter and fished in the summer; the mines often used men on six-month stints so they could also fish (the south-coast men fishing in the winter); and in recent years men have gone by themselves to construction work in Labrador or elsewhere in Newfoundland, leaving their families, their boats, and an open door behind: In the recession of 1973 the number of fishermen doubled. The jobs that were provided in this context were inadequate in every respect – low paid, temporary, and under very harsh conditions; and the government itself gained little or nothing.

151

The politics of subsistence production

John Crosbie, Progressive Conservative minister of finance in a Newfoundland provincial, and then in the Canadian federal, government – and the
eldest son of one of the wealthiest fish-merchant families in Newfoundland
– summed up the situation:

It would really turn your stomach to see what American Smelting [and Refining
Co.] took out of Buchans in the years they have operated there, and Price [Com-
pany], without paying anything in taxes and employing people there at miserable
wages and miserable conditions in a company town with miserable housing. [It]
would really cause you to become a savage – you know, marxist. [*Financial Post*,
12 June 1976; quoted by Overton 1976]

VI

The political basis of Newfoundland poverty, particularly in the fishery,
also has had an ideological component. "In my own experience," wrote
Thomas Lodge, one of the three commissioners sent out to govern Newfoundland in 1933, and the one most active in trying to develop the economy, "dried codfish is one of the easiest things in the world to do without"
(Lodge 1935: 644). Lodge's disdain for Newfoundland's staple product was
shared by the Newfoundland elite – it was taken as, and it was in fact, a
sign of poverty when Smallwood, before becoming premier, served codfish to guests (Gwyn 1972: 50). But for southern Europe, the Caribbean,
and Brazil, where salt cod is one of the least expensive sources of protein,
Lodge was wrong.

More to the point is the disdain not for the fish but for the fisher families.
What particularly dismayed the elite were the shortness of the fishing season
and the self-direction of the fisher families:

In the nature of things it is not a calling which can be pursued for six days a week
and fifty-two weeks a year. The average fisherman can fish today and idle tomorrow
if he thinks fit. He has no master to drive him to work if he happens not to wish
to work.... It is a calling suitable enough for a people prepared to live a life of
extreme simplicity with few wants outside the primitive needs of food and shelter.
...[Lodge 1935: 636]

Or consider Smallwood's statement, at the opening of the Marystown
shipyard in 1967:

One-third of Newfoundlanders cannot make a decent living. They have nothing to
do except for a few weeks when they catch fish or lobster, or pick berries or work
on the roads. What are we going to do with them? [Gwyn 1972: 317]

Or Jay Parker, president of the Newfoundland Board of Trade:

We have got to persuade these [extra 120,000] people to move [out of Newfound-
land] for their own sakes.... How can anyone live decently by working 95 to 100
days a year? [Gwyn 1972: 317. This was in 1970.]

152

A political holiday

Fisher families may *fish* 95 to 100 days a year, but as is well-known in Newfoundland, they *worked* at the fishery very much longer than that, building and repairing boats and engines, knitting nets, making their lobster traps, and so forth. Moreover, the inshore fishery has always been more productive, per unit of labor or of capital, than the offshore fishery (Antler and Faris 1979).

This *ideological* put-down of the inshore fishery, which at its most sympathetic took the form of dismay at the impoverished condition of fisher families, reached its pinnacle in the allocation of cabinet posts in the Newfoundland government. Since the mid nineteenth century the minister of fisheries has only very rarely been a member of the cabinet, although the bulk of the island's export earnings and its income, until well into the twentieth century, came from the fisheries.

To assert that we have entered the domain of ideology is to seek to make that concept useful – to map the terrain of the term in ways that help us further the analysis and keep us out of the thickets of controversy over what the term means. Ideology is not, I think, most usefully conceptualized as a "thing" – a set of symbols and values made relevant to politics by expressing "interests" or "strains" (a critique formulated by Geertz 1973). Drawing more specific boundaries around the concept permits us a more dynamic and processual formulation.

Ideologies, by definition here, have four characteristic features:

1. They are about inequality. It makes no sense to talk about a traditional Inuit ("Eskimo"), San ("Bushman"), or Australian Aborigine ideology, because these people had no fundamental structural inequalities.
2. Ideologies situate inequality in time. Each offers explanations of the "historical" causes of inequality, and presents a vision of the future where things will either be very different or more intensely the same.
3. Ideologies present these temporal explanations and visions of the future in the context of a consciously and explicitly recognized opposition – potential or actual – to the position taken.
4. Ideologies explicitly or implicitly invite people to take sides on the issue of inequality – to participate in the process of social reproduction and social transformation.

Ideologies become part of the political process as they participate in the reproduction and transformation of inequality. This participation cannot be defined abstractly; it varies from case to case.

There are, clearly, ideologies "from above" and "from below." But it would destroy the utility of the concept to mechanically reduce either sort of ideology to the simple material interests of a class. And it would be another kind of travesty to abandon the attempt to connect ideological processes to processes of class formation and transformation by retreating, as is popular, into a focus on symbolic "meanings."

153

The politics of subsistence production

The issue before us now is to show that ideology does not simply reflect class structures but also operates in the process of social reproduction at least partly autonomously. That is, it operates in ways that both arise from, and potentially reshape, the experiences of people and the understandings people form from their experiences. This is the historical dynamic of ideology, which we must try to recover. To do this requires us to situate ideology in the context of culture, and in particular, in the context of the contradictions of culture.

In 1932 when an angry crowd of unemployed people in St. John's began pounding on the locked doors of the House of Assembly, they were stopped by a government band that came out and began to play "God Save the King." The crowd stood at attention for the duration of the song, and when it ended they broke into, and ransacked, the building (Gwyn 1972: 44).

This is *not* what could most usefully be termed a "cultural contradiction" – nor are discordant values. Rather, this is just part of the ambivalent and ambiguous richness of culture.

In the introduction to Part Three, it was stated that Victor Butler's phrase "If a man is not self-sufficient, what help he will get from others will be damn small" pointed us toward a cultural contradiction. This contradiction is not expressed by the illogicality of the statement (self-sufficient people do not need help) but rather *is* expressed by the protest against sustaining the two divergent sorts of social ties underlying this statement: the fragmented and isolated ties generated in the context of the fishery but pervading village and family daily life, and the closer and more cooperative ties experienced within some aspects of family, of customary occasions, and in some work situations, and thus potentially expandable beyond these domains.

The cultural contradictions of outport Newfoundland are not "realized" – either analytically or in the historical unfolding of the society – by placing one value or set of values against another, but rather by the tensions, disjunctions, and contradictions between the social ties these values express and help to recreate.

The political process enters into the development of these contradictions in two ways: (1) through the pressure such cultural tensions can create, within local communities, to turn outward to the state for resolution (a point I shall take up again in the next chapter); (2) by the capacity of ideologies to penetrate, clarify, and seemingly resolve, or offer to resolve, such cultural contradictions.

I think that the power of ideology to do this comes from the fact that in the sense of cultural contradiction proposed here, ideologies have no contradictions. Ideologies of course ordinarily contain inconsistent state-

154

ments, are illogical, wrong, and so forth, but until they are embedded in daily life and work, and reemerge in the domain of "common sense" – unless and until, that is, they become "culture" – they lack contradictions, for contradictions emerge from the complex array of social ties to which culture is connected. What ideologies have are not contradictions but opponents. And if we listen closely to Victor Butler, agonizing over the lack of help from his associates or the clergy while his son lay dying, and not or hardly mentioning the merchant or constable, it is possible to claim that, at least at times, opponents, however powerful, are easier to deal with than contradictions.

Ideology thus may derive both its force and limitations not only from the political powers it serves or opposes but also from the cultural contradictions in which it is rooted.

When the Fishermen's Protective Union was organized in 1908, it adopted as its symbol for parades and demonstrations the fisherman's wool jersey. Worn "in town" this jersey had been a stigma – a badge of membership in the bottom of the social order. The FPU proclaimed it their symbol – a symbol that derived its power partly from the facts of common work experience and partly by converting to ideology the visible marker of their denigration. They were claiming, in symbol and in speech, to be both the source and the victims of the country's wealth. A less contradictory cultural symbol would have been less ideologically powerful.

The instance is far from unique, in Newfoundland or elsewhere. In 1959 the loggers of Newfoundland's two large mills struck. The most bitter and intense strike in Newfoundland history, it was not simply for wages but was equally focused on the inhuman living conditions in the winter woods camps – extremely bad housing and poor and scant food. Smallwood used all the power of the state to break the strike and to make the loggers seem the despicable enemies of "progress"; his radio speeches against the loggers have subsequently been used in a textbook on propaganda. At the outset of the strike H. Landon Ladd, the president of District Two of the union, spoke to a meeting of the loggers. Afterward a retired logger said: "What you say is right, and what you are trying to do is right. But you will never get it. We are only loggers." That phrase, "We are only loggers," became their slogan for the duration of the strike (Gwyn 1972: chap. 18).

Such slogans, with their roots in profound cultural contradictions, may make for emotionally powerful ideologies; but are they as politically effective in mobilizing people on behalf of their claims as they are emotionally powerful? The power the state brought to bear against the loggers, who were regarded as standing in the way of further "development," was so immense and pervasive that it is more difficult to see what the weaknesses might have been on the loggers' side than if the battle had been more equal. Thus it must suffice to suggest that cultural contradictions may not only generate but also limit ideologies; both the ideologies that come from within, and that are imposed upon and confront, a culture.

Mr. B, a man now in his early sixties, lived and fished in Harbour Buffet – the same community as Victor Butler. He told me two stories, one immediately following the other, which bear upon this point. The first (cited in Chapter 5, Section III, but worth repeating in context) told of the physical difficulties of the fishery, describing how he would, at times, row two or three miles to get to his "grounds" and haul weighted nets from thirty or forty fathoms by hand. He concluded: "By the time you rowed back and pitched your fish up in the dock, some nights you were so tired you didn't recognize your own family when you walked in the door." (Note the use of the generalizing and inclusive "you.") He next told me that one day Pat Canning, the member of the House of Assembly for his district and a strong advocate of development, came to Harbour Buffet to campaign for reelection. "I was standing there in the gathering when Pat Canning said, 'If you're a fisherman you're a disgrace to Newfoundland.' " "What did you do?" I asked. "Nothing. I just walked away." Canning lost, not that, but the next election.

These two stories, told together, fit together. Had the work not have been so hard, so much a source of physical pain, as well as a source of a sense of accomplishment, of belonging to a community, I think Mr. B would have laughed or thrown something back at Canning. To walk away, a characteristic response we shall soon see again – to limit, not confront, such ideological assaults – is to return himself, Canning, and us to the contradictions of outport culture and to the sufferings and accomplishments, the doubt and pride, that reside in the work process and daily life.

Both the periodic crises of the Newfoundland state and the failure of sustained, substantial mutual aid and concerted action within the villages express the *partial* collapse of processes of social reproduction. On the one hand, the villagers could not bear the costs of both state and merchant appropriation – either the fiscal costs or the attendant social fragmentation – and continue to be a viable base for the political economy. On the other hand, neither the villagers nor the state nor the merchants could muster the forces for constructive change.

The production and reproduction of capital in Newfoundland took two forms, one rooted in the fishery and coordinated by the merchant, and one rooted in the state, which sought to develop an alternative form of capital while the fishery withered, but without confronting and transforming this fishery (as was, e.g., done in Iceland, by state-sponsored cooperatives that have created a viable and rewarding village fishery).

Both forms of appropriation in Newfoundland were incomplete. Merchants could not penetrate and transform the village organization of work. They could shape it – keeping the boats small by continued impoverishment – and they could harness it to their own interests, but they could only accumulate wealth and not possess, transform, and develop the means of production. The state, which turned outward for development capital, could not in fact develop the economy; for, as is characteristic in underdeveloped areas, each project and each sector of the economy had few forward or backward linkages to other sectors.

The fact that merchant and state appropriation, however severe, was not total – that the fisher families kept their own equipment and the capacity to organize, within family, kin group and community, their own social relations of work rather than becoming a mass of propertyless laborers – provided one basis for the continual existence and strength, however limited, of village culture.

But even while the village fishery lasted, the existence and the strength of village culture were being undermined. To see this requires expanding the notion of appropriation.

In the act of appropriation from the village fishery, the merchants and the state took far more than the economic "surplus." By appropriating a large portion of the product of the fishery, they took into their control part of the social relations, the community social life, that went into generating fish and fisherfolk: For almost every Christmas during the depression Victor Butler was away from home, working for the merchant. To repeat: Capital formation is, of necessity, the deformation of prior culture, which is simultaneously created and destroyed in the context of the formation of different kinds of capital.

In Part Two it was suggested that culture is a central part of the mediations between daily life and appropriation. More specifically now, we can perhaps begin to see that folk culture can be part of a battleground between classes and between divergent ideologies – a locus both of appropriation and of resistance to appropriation. The contradictions of a culture express the processes that make folk culture – including presumably "archaic" and "traditional" folk cultures – both highly adaptive to specific historical contexts and a central terrain for the struggle over the meaning and future of historical development.

9

We must live in hopes

There was a proverb more often used than any other, of which I must either believe it spoilt by misquotation or else confess myself too dull to perceive its force: "We must live in hopes, supposing we die in despair."

The Reverend Julian Moreton,
Church of England Missionary to Bonavista Bay, 1850–63

I

Elizabeth Goudie was born in 1902, at Mud Lake, Labrador, the daughter of a woods worker and a trapper. She lived most of her life as the wife of a trapper. In 1963, shortly after the death of her husband, she wrote down the story of her life. Her story has been edited and published (Goudie 1973); the following quotations, focusing on the early years of her marriage, come directly from the notebooks in which she wrote (Goudie n.d.).

... there where 5 Villages along the shore as far as Pearl River the averiage size of a Village where from 3 to 5 families the to teachrs on an averiage traveled about 60 miles on dog team they spent about to & a half mounths at a place I had the prevalage of going to school to winters...

I enjoyed life along the way it ment a great deal to me so as I grew older the war came and I had to go out and earn my own bread so to speak and I never was home very much after the age of 14. the wages where verry low I went to work for 2 dollars a mounth if the families where Very Poor you only got your food or may be the makings of a new dress and this work werent easy you had to do every thing by hand scrub warsh bring wood and water and help to cook and mend clothing we never had a dul moment life in Labrador where a life of hard work but we had Peace of mind and contented hearts and I think this was what made life worth while

our Parents where concrrened about our sprituill life as our physical lives the Bible where red daily in the Homes. that where the last thing where done at night the Sundays were kept ... the folks folowed up the comandments of Moses though shalt not so to speak I think they went to the extreme a little yet I think a lot of theore rouls along these lines helped us along the way our parents where always

158

reminding us of being Honest and Truthful and kind to others so I think these where some of the things that help us to be contented with one another and with what we had and what we had werent not verry much compared with what we have today . . .

people had to always keep working at some thing to make the to ends meet so to speek the daily Diet where made up of fresh meat & fish peas & beans   Morning meal generily where rol oats or fish we did not have milk milk were only used for eny one sick or Christmas or Easter Mollases where used for tea and on your porage i till you we where glad to see Christmas & Easter . . .

. . . so this was the sutation and we could not expect eny more so 1917 I went to work for the Grienfield Mission [the Grenfell Mission had a cottage hospital and provided medical care to the people on the northern coast of Newfoundland and the Labrador] and I got 4 dollars a mounth there and 10 dollars a summer of used clothing this was what the mission gave their girls at that time I served as an ade on the womens ward we where out of bed 5 in the morning and on our feet until seven in the evenings we got one after noon of a week and we where let of to go to church on sunday this was where I met my first boy friend [whom she married]. . . .

so we got ingaged in Feb when he was going in the country [to trap] in 1920 and when he came out the first of april we set the date for our maraige the 21 of april so I learned when he came out of the country he almost lost his life it was a bad rapied in the river open water and verry narow ice to walk on and there was another man with him and as they where trying to get there sleds around the rappid the sled sliped of in the rappid and puled him in to he drove down the rappid about a half mils in 30 belo zero so the other man got him out after a wile they where about a half mile from there cabon he had to walk a half a mile in his frozen close he was almost persihed [perished] when he got there so I was so glad it didend happen I would not be writing this story

so he stayed that night for a reast the second of apirl he started for North West River he had to travel 40 miles on snowshoe and Hall his load before he got to north W. River [to sell his furs] and then he had to walk 25 Miles more up the Gross Water Bay to the Hamilton River to get my father and mother consent before we could get married I was to the head of Grand Lake so he Hired a dog team and send up for me so I arived in North West River the 18 of apirl I only had 4 days to get ready for the wedding I had to make some of my wedding cloes. I bought my dress form Mrs Paddon it cost me 5 dollars it was a white dress with a little blue strip in it it is 43 years now since I was married and I still have my dress

so the 20 of apirl I was 18 years old and the 21 of apirl we got married we where married at a dubble wedding to cupils stood the one time the Grendfield Mission nurse made our wedding cakes we had quite a lot of people we seves a supper for every one and we dance untill 3 oclock in the morning My husband brother played the violin his right arm was cut of about 6 inces belo his elbo they tied the bo on to the stump of his arm and he played for our wedding dance he had a T.B. arm and he had to have it cut of he could play the violin well   so we stayed to his Home for 2 weeks and we moved to our own house . . . when I got married I did not have much money of my own I saved a nough to bye my self a warsh board I worked for 2 dollars a mounth from the local people and from the Grenfield Missom 4 dollars a month . . .

so now I was starting all on my own so I had to do my best I looked forward to a family of my own so I had 2 years be fore I starded a family so in them to years

159

The politics of subsistence production

I injoyed my self with Jim that was his name we used to go hunting and fishing I
learned to shot with the gun we injoyed our selves out in the quite country I used
to be left a lone when he was a way in country the most dreadful thing being a
tapers wife as you would not here from them from the time they would go a way
until they would return again there where no way to get mail the trappers would
not come from the traping grounds until a period of 3 mounths we use to stand on
the shore and watch them leave in their canoes only about 6 in. above the water . . .

the first year I was married there was a woman expecting a baby and there was
no midwife there   there was one about twenty miles from there and they family
was going to get her about 2 weeks before the baby was due and a cold snap of
weather come a partly froze up and they could not get the midwife it was in nov.
and the baby came and I had to ack as midwife I got a long all right with the help
of an old man was there I was so afraid I would lose the mother or they baby I
was sick in bed for 3 days after but the mother lived and her son it was a little boy
things like these where they things we had to go through to live and get along in
Labrador this was in the first year of my marriage so as time move on and I recovered
from the shock after the oice completed froze over I went to catch trout for my
winter I walked 4 miles and carried my food for a week and I catched trout I
catched about 5 Hundred . . .

the custom for tappers wifes are to have something cooked for when they come
home we use to have pie and cake and then they would rest up for a week so we
went to North West River to sale his furs after he had a rest so I put on my
snowshoes and went to so we had 2 or 3 days there and then we went back home
he rested up for a mounth and went back in the country again . . .

it is sunmer now and we are planing a boat trip 90 miles down the Hamilton in
to Rigolet there where more people down there it was the salmon fishing tome
where all the people went for the summer so we went down there just to spend
the sumer among them we realy had nothing to do so we started of in a 14 foot
boat we had rails on her and we would row when it was calm and there were lots
of places to explore on the way it was a nice trip nice land and little rivers . . .

we catched our fish for the winter and dried them by the time we got that finished
it was a bout the the middle of Agaust so we all went to Rigolet for the big round
up for the year the custom of the fishermen when the fishing season was over they
always had a big dance in rigolet its the oldest H.B. Bay post on Labrador so we
spend to or 3 nights dancing and every one broke up for another year so everyone
went to there winter Homes and started preapering for winter . . .

now it was the 1 september so we had just a month to get everything for the
winter Jim was bessy about getting his wood home and sawing it up for the winter
and I went about making boots and close for him we had to make 2 shefting [sets]
of close and everything mits socks and boot we always prepared extra things for
fare of axcedent such as getting lose in fire on loosing their canoe in the river so
the trapers wifes took a mounth to get their Husbands ready and this was my first
year we dident have much time for fun we worked early and late so the day came
for him to leave that was a very sad day for a trapers wife . . .

his wife would spend a more lonely time she was always at Home but there was
some thing about that life is hard to put in words it is a life not ful of people or
what people could offer you would rise in the morning no people around you but
every day had something to make you happy we were satisfied . . . we always said
if God wants us to live he will povied for us poveding we do our part and we were
content with that thought . . .

my second year looked briter there was a baby on the way so when Jim left for

160

his tapping ground he left me in care of my mother so as the winter rolled on and apirl came a round Jim came back from the country and I moved to North West River my baby was due in the month of may there was a doctor there Jim thought I better be near the Dr. but when the time came I never went in the Hospital the was a medwife there so I stayed there so the day came on 14. day of May 1922. I had my first son he was 8 lbs 1/2 he was just like his Dady he was dark complected and I was proud of him when he was 17 days old I had to take him to the Doctor he had sore eyes and the Doctor ask me his name and I dident have a name then so the Doctor looked at him and he was Hairy about his shoulders and neck so he said he would call him Esau so His Name is in the Hospital Book at North West River as Esau but later I named him Horace

The precision of the name the doctor gave to her son and the son of the man she so clearly loved – Esau the elder, the hairy, the hunter, and the disinherited; all of which Elizabeth Goudie knew – expresses with almost overwhelming power the subtle and manifold cruelties of domination. And throughout her text, but crystalized especially in the quietness and self-containment of her response – the same response Mr. B made to an ideological assault upon his way of life – we can see the whole strength and the whole tragedy of folk culture: the marriage of dignity and hurt, ability and powerlessness, hope and history and, bringing it all together, the extraordinary mixture of sociability and encapsulation – a closing in upon neighbors, kin, family, and self that goes along with a very strong sense of connectedness to others, to custom, and to culture (e.g., what other trappers' wives do; her future husband walking to her parents house to ask for her hand) in the midst of, and transcending, an intensely felt physical isolation. It is to this strength and this tragedy – hope and history within culture – that we now turn.

II

The importance of the proverb that we quoted from the Reverend Julian Moreton in the epigraph to this chapter – "We must live in hopes, supposing we die in despair" – lies not only in the claim to the future in the midst of experiences that lead people to realize, very concretely, the possibility of an anguished ending, but also, and perhaps especially, in the plural form: "hopes," not "hope." The use of the plural for a general noun is not now, and from my reading of nineteenth-century texts was not then, a usual or common linguistic form; it must be read, in this occurrence, as specific and intentional. It will take the whole of this chapter, and a detour through several different but related issues, before we can come back to this point. The detour starts with a consideration of the conscious presence of history in one particular custom.

In outports along the northeast coast of Newfoundland, men, mostly, tell each other a kind of story they call a "cuffer." (Faris 1968, 1972 has the

161

fullest description of these stories in print.) Cuffers are told at informal gatherings – in the sheds where men gather in the afternoon or the evening to mend equipment and pass the time together, or at night in the early winter woods, after a day cutting firewood for their homes. A cuffer starts out like any other story that turns on, or recalls for discussion or illustration, a remembrance of the past. "Remember the fall of 1948, when Sam Jones lost his boat to the ice?" – so a cuffer might begin. Only it was not 1948 but 1949, and it was not Sam but his brother John, and it was not a boat but a cod trap that was lost: A cuffer is untrue from beginning to end. As the cuffer is being told, as with any other story, some of the men listening will be agreeing with and encouraging the story teller – "Yes, yes bye" ("bye" means, approximately, "buddy") – and others will be starting to disagree, to correct the story teller. The disagreements can become, or are provoked into becoming, fairly intense: Men shout, occasionally shove, make bets, and even threaten one another. And it is impossible to tell if these disagreements are sham – pretense from beginning to end – unless someone goes too far and gets really angry. Those who do not cross this line might have been taken in by the cuffer, at least for a while, or they might just be disagreeing for the sport of it; and the same for those that agree with the storyteller. But when people get really angry they get very angry – either from the cuffer itself, the provocative or genuine arguments, or from having been "taken."

A cuffer, on the surface, is a lie about history – a history of the village that everyone "knows," or almost knows, and almost everyone present has lived through. As a lie, and a mock, cuffers are antagonistic; but they are also extraordinarily intimate.

The intimacy of the cuffer is made necessary and called forth by the logic of the event. If, for example, a cuffer would be attempted by a man in his late seventies, about events sixty years ago, to an audience of men in their thirties and forties, it would likely fall flat, as the audience would have little or no way of knowing whether what was said was true or not, unless it were about an event so major that people could be expected to have heard it recounted. And as cuffers are ordinarily told about events that were, once at least, of substantial import in the community – people losing boats or nets, having affairs with other's spouses, fires or storms and their consequences; or on the positive side, a particularly bounteous catch of seals or fish: events that test the social ties within a community, revealing and perhaps changing what relations mean and will mean – it would be impossible or extremely difficult to tell a cuffer about an event that happened last month or last year. Cuffers are told at the boundary between the known and the forgotten, the known and the partly known, and thus they demand, in the midst of their antagonisms, a profoundly intimate knowledge of the audience, and of the history of the village as this history lives, increasingly hidden, within the present.

For all the tensions cuffers cause, they are encouraged: "Tell us a cuffer, George," one man asked another (Faris 1972: 148). The audience is also intimate with, and antagonistic to, the storyteller. This shared mixture of intimacy and antagonism changes our understanding of the connection between cuffers and history.

Cuffers, I might suggest, recreate history by keeping alive and clarifying events and relationships that were receding into the past. This is a plausible explanation of one aspect of cuffers, but it is shallow and probably mostly wrong – for it assumes that the history of the village consists of a sequence of events and relationships, from past to present, whose content changes while little else does. I think it is much more analytically advantageous in trying to understand village history to argue that cuffers are one of the customs that *introduce* history, history as an ongoing process, into current village life by creating, in the here and now, a profound tension between what was and what is: For history in the village, no less than in nation-states, is not simply the passage of time and events but also springs from, and resides in, the tensions, disjunctions, and contradictions that become increasingly unsupportable. Cuffers, by both the content of their stories and the fact of their existence as an informal village custom – a custom that in its very enactment re-presents the mixture of intimacy and antag-onism that is so much the product of the village fishery – confront people not just with their dim and receding knowledge of the past and their relations in the present but also with their intentions for the future and with the rough-cut fit between past, present, and future.

Cuffers, partly believable, show to the people present what they have forgotten, or only half remember, about the events described – the storms, the losses at sea, the affairs, the bounteous catches of fish and seals. These were, for the most part, events in which people at the time they occurred took stock of one another, privately and in public discussion, finding in the help that was given or withheld and in the comments made to them at the time, new dimensions to their social relations, dimensions that could be gains or losses. It seems unlikely that people could hear a story about events that were once so socially significant in a context that reminds them of how much has changed, in their knowledge of each other and in their social relations, since what was learned then, without also considering what this augers for the future. This is a speculation, not an interpretation; the data are not yet available. What supports this speculation – an admittedly fragile, but still a thought-provoking support – is a further consideration of the logic of the cuffer.

I think that in a very subtle way cuffers teach another lesson about lived history: There are two histories present, one "real" – real in the sense of what actually happened; whether it was Joe or Sam that lost a boat or a net to the storm or the ice – and one contingent upon what people can, or are willing, to remember. Social relations emerge from the cuffer as *simultaneously* real (concrete, specific) and contingent. What I said earlier about scoffs (Chapter 6, sections II and IV) – that they teach people, wrongly, that they are the authors of their own antagonistic intimacies – now can be seen as only an introduction to a much more complex process.

The scoff and cuffer are clearly related phenomena. Both express, in fairly dramatic form, the mixture of intimacy and antagonism that characterizes much of outport culture and social organization. But the cuffer, more clearly and forcefully than the scoff, mocks not just the victims but also the very intimacy and antagonism that it expresses. Thus it perhaps suggests a different future, a future more in control of the people who sustain the custom. I think this is why cuffers, in this form, seem to be primarily a northeast coast phenomena, for the northeast coast has been the most affluent, politically expressive, and assertive of the outport regions of Newfoundland – the center of the Fisherman's Protective Union, for example. And I think this is why, at bottom, people are made so angry by cuffers: They become angry not simply because they are mocked, for people are frequently teased in outport Newfoundland, but also because their social relations, and perhaps their futures, are shown to be more contingent upon their own actions and beliefs than may be comfortable to contemplate.

III

With the cuffer, we have returned to the point raised in the beginning of Chapter 1: Cuffers, taken as a whole – including the presentation of the story and the reactions to it – create a form of knowledge that both grows out of and becomes somewhat distanced from, and yet is situated within, the concrete and specific material and social realities of daily life. The problem before us now is: How does that matter, if at all? Is this part of the formation of a political culture: a culture capable of reincorporating experience into social structure in ways that create openings for change?

The cuffer and scoff are, as noted, related customs. But whereas cuffers subtly introduce history into outport social relations, scoffs in large part deny it. To explore and explain this point, we must contrast scoffs with gift exchanges and look at certain other nuances of outport social relations concerning reciprocity.

The reciprocities of village life are a matter of rather intense concern – a concern that focuses on the balance of give and take. The gift, though central to the process of give and take, is only one small part of the search for balance. The following three incidents will introduce some other dimensions of reciprocity in outport Newfoundland.

The first incident occurred in a Conception Bay outport town in the 1930s:

My uncle, who was a merchant, had an odd sense of humor. In the depression days he would play the meanest tricks on the poorest people. I was always one of his gang after I became an acceptable age. The town had the usual two or three beggars who were supposedly sick or crippled. One night during the Christmas holidays he was in the mood for mischief. He looked me up and we decided we would play some sort of trick on Bobby Smith. Bobby had been on government relief for a lifetime. On the day of the night in question my uncle, through the Orangemen [the Protestant Loyal Orange Association] had collected two loads of firewood for Bobby along with some food and Xmas gifts. When we arrived at the Smith place that night the first thing we noticed was the firewood piled against a wall which was about four feet outside the house. We decided to founder the works [knock over the pile of wood] against the side of the house facing the cemetery. This would block the doorway. However, having many tricks played on them, Mrs. Smith was upstairs looking out for any such event. We did not know this. As we were about to founder the wood, the contents of a kettle of boiling water came at us from above. Our little plan failed. We went back to his store, and packaged a week's groceries which we had Mr. Smith pick up the next day and haul home on his slide. The Smiths never knew who tried to play the trick on them. [MUNFLA 68-24: 130. This description is provided courtesy of Boyd Trask, whose reporting of Newfoundland customs provides some of the most sensitive and perceptive documents in the folklore archives.]

The Smiths seemed to know that along with the gift of firewood and food would come an attack – an attack that used the gift itself (the firewood) as a weapon: Mrs. Smith was specifically on the lookout for the attack. Although the prank was played by the merchant and his "gang," I suspect it must have had more general approval. Newfoundland outport houses are so close together that had the neighbors been outraged at the action they would have intervened. After the prank, although it failed, there was a second gift, as if becoming a victim were a form of reciprocity for the original gift, for which a further gift is due. The reciprocities of this transaction, in which the victim becomes an equal, are clearly indicated by the subtle changes in naming in the text: The story starts out with *Bobby* Smith – the name has been changed here but the diminutive form is equivalent – being on government relief and ends, via Mrs. Smith's counterattack, with *Mr.* Smith coming to collect his second gift. Central to the scoff, and to a slightly lesser degree to the cuffer, is also the equality of the victim and the victimizer, an equality that is defined at the outset by firm notions about who can participate in the custom, on either side; an equality that coexists with the inequality and, as it were, the unfairness of the act.

The other two stories both concern situations where reciprocity was

The politics of subsistence production

impossible. The first was reported by Professor Szwed, from his fieldwork in the village of "Ross" on the west coast in the early 1960s:

Jack Angus was having trouble hauling his winter's cut of wood out from his camp, several miles in the woods from the road. He had no tractor, and had recently lost his horse in an accident. Tom, a financially better-off wood cutter, offered to haul the wood out with his tractor. No bargain was struck in advance, and once the wood was out, Jack offered to pay for the work. Tom rejected the offer, however, accepting only a few bottles of home-brew in exchange for his efforts. There was no doubt that Jack still felt indebted to Tom, for he told of the kindness of the act at every opportunity he had. Similarly, he sought to do a number of small favors for Tom, such as offering first to help him cut some of his wood, and later to sell him some sheep at a very low price. Yet this did not discharge the debt, for as Jack Angus put it: "I'd like to do him a good turn like he done me, but he don't need anything I could do for him. He's after making a pile [going to make a lot of money] this winter, so his worries are over. Still, I feel as I'd ought to do something for him . . . I owes him a lot." [Szwed 1966: 93–4]

The third incident was told to me directly by the person it happened to – a resident of Placentia Bay, who grew up in Harbour Buffet, the same community as Victor Butler.

Toward the end of the depression, in 1939, this man, as a child of ten years, started working packing salt fish for the merchant, for four cents an hour. After working steadily for several hours, the first day at the job, bending over the entire time, he straightened up to rub his sore back. The merchant, watching, told him: "Go on home if your back is sore, and send your mom or grandma in your place." Forty years later this incident was still remembered with considerable bitterness. The year before, as a child of nine, he had lived in the merchant's house – lighting the fires before dawn each morning, running errands, doing small jobs: all in return for his food and a bed, and a new pair of canvas pants which was not part of the contract, but which the merchant gave him "extra."

In these two stories no form of reciprocity is possible – neither in the positive sense of a countergift, for Jack Angus felt he could not repay the kindness in the context of the inequality between them, nor in the negative sense, for the child could not protect himself, via a counterattack, against having his own values and sense of self-worth turned against him.

All these stories are immensely complex, the last one particularly so. Remember that in this incident the child and merchant knew each other well; the assault on the child seems destructive in ways for which intimacy is a precondition. I suspect that not only the "manhood" of the child was being assaulted but also, by implication, he was being confronted by the fact that his mother and grandmother – his own family – could not help him; could they have, they were not likely to have sent him to live with the merchant, for this was not anything that even remotely resembled an apprenticeship, nor the fostering of children to give them better opportunities and wider contacts. It was most likely just one less mouth for the mother to feed in the midst of the depression.

166

We must live in hopes

The central issue in the second story seems to me to be the diminished possibility for continuing social relations between the two men as the inequality between them was brought to the foreground by their present social relations. Similar to both the second and the third incidents is the isolation of the underdog, or the victim, that emerges from the conjunction of inequality and the pressure for reciprocity. This isolation is one of the enduring products of certain forms of exchange in which the victim (of circumstances, of the other) is not an equal, and perhaps it is part of the fragmentation of hope into hopes.

We must, in any case, be alert to the possibility that "exchange relations" – or, in a broader sense, the social intercourse of daily life in a community – can not only bind people together but can also fragment. On this basis, with the contingent outcomes of exchange relations in mind, we can turn to a comparison of scoffs and gifts.

Marcel Mauss separates the process of giving gifts into three component interactions, and in so doing provides the basis for an analysis of reciprocal interactions that characterize the whole twentieth-century anthropological understanding of egalitarian social relations. The gift, Mauss argues, can be understood as the socially engendered obligation to give, to receive, and to repay (Mauss 1967). In one of the most important of the recent elaborations on this process, Bourdieu points out that between the gift and the repayment there must always be an interval and a difference. To return the same thing that was given, or to make the return too quickly, is to mock the gift and to reject the social relationship implicit in the act of giving (Bourdieu 1977: 4–6). The importance of Bourdieu's observation is that it provides one way for seeing how temporality is structured into social relations.

The gift has a long-term temporal structure: It creates potentially enduring relations of gift and countergift. The scoff is short term: A one-night party, food taken, perhaps an act of revenge, of countertheft, and there the matter ends. The gift not only creates ties between the giver and the receiver but within the community as well, as people both contribute to their representative gift givers and give moral support and prestige to those who give and receive well – with style, flair, and a sense for the fully appropriate. The scoff creates some ties of good feeling and mutual support, but these are limited to those who have enjoyed the party, as the ill will seems limited to the victims. The gift, however, beneath the surface structure of good will and close and equal ties, contains a deeper structure that has the constant potential for inequality – for change and for history: gifts that cannot be repaid, obligations that cannot be discharged; changing statuses newly marked, or publicly reinforced. The gift can thus be the basis for the formation of long-standing relations of obligation and of service – ultimately labor service or political clientage – that crystallize in the domain of symbolic action and carry over into the social relations of work and production. The scoff, to the contrary, has beneath its surface of antagonism no potential to create ties of inequality or to generate the fundamental structural antagonisms created by such inequality. The scoff creates pleasure, anger, social distance, and isolation, but no ties of future service or obligation.

The scoff reinforces the competitive egalitarianism of similarly isolated, similarly situated families, without establishing any effective claims between – or within – them, or between the fisher families and the merchant. By suggesting to the fisher families that they are the authors of their antagonistic relations to one another, the party scoff might well indirectly support continued merchant domination. But it is also the community itself that defines who may scoff and from whom food may rightfully be taken: The antagonisms within the community thus also emerge as part of the unity and strength of the community. Not only, or not simply, a mystification of the source of antagonistic relations between families, the scoff is also simultaneously the expression of a community's capacity to define and create itself as a particular community of place and space.

Sooner or later, the victims of the scoff usually find out who took their food, although there is little they can do about it. The scoff, as is the case with other aspects of Newfoundland village culture, expresses a mixture of clarity and powerlessness, and this contributes to the historical flatness of this custom. But village culture as a whole is not historically flat. To show how it participates more actively in fashioning time and history, we must look further into the linkage of clarity and powerlessness.

IV

In the mid nineteenth century, fishermen on Fogo Island, just off the northeast coast of Newfoundland, petitioned the House of Assembly:

For a number of years back we have been struggling with the world, as we suppose, through the imposition of the merchants and their agents by their exorbitant prices on shop goods and provisions, by which means we are from year to year held in debt, so as not daring to find fault, fearing we may starve at the approach of every winter. We being at a distance of seventy leagues from the Capital, [and being] where we suppose they [the merchants] arrogate to themselves a power not warrented by any law, in selling to us every article of theirs at any price they think fit, and taking from us the produce of a whole year at whatever price they think fit to give. They take it on themselves to price their own goods, and ours also as they think most convenient to them. [Prowse 1895: 379]

The clarity of this text, of the fisherfolks' understanding of their own situation and the trap they were in, did not contribute to a capacity to alter their situation: Nothing, of course, came of the petition. Yet the clarity has not been abandoned. To the contrary, it became embedded in the idiomatic language of the outports. Of the many expressions that briefly and richly delineate their situation, I have chosen four for presentation and comment.

To "fade," in Newfoundland, is both to wither and die, when used with reference to natural objects, and to survive, when used in reference to people: "I spoiled [cut down] the tree because its going to fade now. It was blowed out of root. Well, 'twould fade in any case" (DNE: 166). "And though by no means did we live in luxury, we faded it out till Spring" (DNE: 166). In what I think is a related perception of the world, "poor" – which is used by outsiders to refer to the condition of the inhabitants – is not used in outport Newfoundland, or hardly used, to refer to an economic state. It refers to someone who is deceased. "Poor Tom," when mentioned in a story, means Tom who has died. People fade, but they survive, and their fading does not make them poor – that is, impoverished or dead. The idiom "to fade it out" shows a certain tragic strength.

The second idiom, or set of idioms, turns on the word "collar." A collar is, to begin, a rope around a dog's neck. It is also, and even more frequently, used to refer to tying a boat to ropes that are usually fixed to the shore or the fishing stage: Putting a boat "on the collar" means to tie the boat off the stage head, or to the land. The most dramatic use of the term, from the early nineteenth century to the present, is when people sign on to fish, or to seal: This is called "going in collar," or to "come to collar." The usage here is very precise. Almost always it refers specifically to the unpaid or unremunerative labor of setting up the boat and equipment for the season's voyages, although the contract or agreement would be for the whole season, including setting the boat up, fishing, and putting the equipment in storage for the winter. Hence: "Usually the first of May you'd go in collar. You'd sign on for the summer and you'd work around until everything was ready and the schooner was ready, and you'd go on again [fishing]"; "...in order to join their respective vessels on the first of March, when every man was expected to be in collar for the ice" (DNE: 109). Yet although "going in collar" usually referred to this preparatory period (and I think would only be used by sharemen working for a part share or crewing on a sealing boat for a small share, not by partners in the small-boat inshore fishery), the end of the whole fishing season was referred to as "breaking collar": "Fishermen broke collar about the end of October and the schooner was moored for the winter" (DNE: 109).

A "dieter" is a person who is fed by someone, usually for the winter, in return for a promise to work for him the following season, or else to pay him for the food at the end of the following season. "When the tenth of October (would) come the voyage was over, fish was sold, an' the collar was taken off an' every man was at liberty. Whoever had homes then would go to them, an' (those) who had no homes (would) go back with the same man, or he'd ship with the same man, or he'd ship with someone else; an then [in these last two cases, when he would be fed for the winter] he was a dieter" (DNE 140). A dieter could also be a person who worked as a shareman on a summer voyage, living with a family and being fed by them. The proverbial phrase that catches the eye – or the heart – is "Out dogs and in dieters." It is used in two contexts. The first is to refer to the unpenning of dogs in the spring, turning them out to forage for themselves from the capelin washed up on the beach and other refuse, about the same time that the dieters for the summer are taken on – go on the collar. The second sense is when people, particularly along the northeast coast where the timber has been cut back quite far the from shore and where the winters are particularly severe, move into huts in the woods to be near fuel in the winter; the same huts near which the dogs were kept penned in the fall, when wood was being hauled out, often by dog-slide, for fall heating (DNE: 140). Dogs, we should add, are frequently treated rather brutally in Newfoundland. Most are not well fed, except when they are working; they are usually not sheltered, and not being huskies often suffer frostbite; and they are frequently killed or starved to death when too old to work: "No animal in Newfoundland is a greater sufferer from man than the dog" (Tocque 1846: 93).

The fishermen, in sum, knew. They knew their own situation, clearly and unromantically. The communities they shaped and the communalities of their idiomatic expressions gave voice to this collective knowledge. If a "class" is formed not simply by a common position in the social relations of production, which makes it only an object of historical processes, but also by an understanding of their situation, then these communities are the equivalent of a class (the working class of industrial capitalism) in the particular context of merchant capital. The communities form into the equivalent of a class not simply by their common circumstances, their common poverty, or even by their common intentionalities, but also by their common understandings. These understandings are not mechanically derived from circumstances but are also contingent; contingent derivations from the social relations of outport life and the social relations of appropriation, and the customs and idioms that are rooted in, and express, these social relations.

Class systems, I noted in Chapter 1, do not form into neat packages with workers on one side and owners on the other. This structural inability to form into neat packages is essential to giving shape to the historical dynamic of what are loosely called class struggles. The term is loose and imprecise because it usually is taken simply to mean a struggle between classes: In the introduction, I noted that the struggles within classes, particularly concerning alliances with different classes, are equally important.

A similar lack of neat packaging can be found in Newfoundland in the context of exploring the notion that the communities of fisherfolk are the merchant-capital equivalent of a class. On the one side, to begin, we have the fisherfolk; on the other, at times, either the merchant, the state, or both. And either the merchants or the state will, at times, take the side of the fisherfolk.

V

When Newfoundlanders voted to renounce independence and confederate with Canada, they were doing more than abandoning a country that had done little for them; they were voting for – as they were repeatedly promised by Joey Smallwood, and as the terms of union guaranteed – a variety of transfer payments from Canada to Newfoundland families: "baby bonuses," old-age pensions, the possibility of unemployment insurance for fishermen (which was eventually realized), and so forth. For inshore fisher families from the 1950s through the 1970s, these transfer payments came close to the amount earned from fishing (probably exceeding it if the costs of fishing are deducted from earnings). Such payments directly support fisher families and indirectly subsidize the fishing industry, making possible otherwise impossibly low fish prices.

Two tables illustrate the general situation of inshore fishing families after Confederation. The first was compiled by Prince Dyke as part of a report to the Agricultural Rural Development Act Task Force, in Ottawa. Dyke grew up in the district of Bonavista North, on the northeast coast of Newfoundland, worked in the area on geographic and economic surveys, and on this basis constructed a "hypothetical" budget for a fishing family that consisted of "a couple with a grown-up son who resided in the household part-time, a grown up daughter working elsewhere, three children below sixteen years of age and one grandmother (on old-age pension)" (Table 2).

In the summer of 1963, T. F. Wise compiled from surveys of Newfoundland fisher families the income sources for families in several different areas of Newfoundland and Labrador. His figures show a lower proportion of transfer payments but the same general pattern (Table 3).

Newfoundland fisher families, in sum, depend upon the state to the point where it influences the ongoing structuring of families, giving the elderly a new power and prestige, as their pensions become crucial to the family income (see, e.g., Scammell 1973: 47–52). But however much the fisher families may depend upon the state, the state has not been very interested

Table 2. *"Hypothetical" annual family income (in Canadian dollars),*
Bonavista North, 1965

Gross returns from inshore fishery for two fishermen	796
Son's income from other employment, 2 months at $225	450
Total unemployment insurance benefits, father and son	760
Annual amount sent home by working daughter	120
Family allowance (one child under ten at $6 per month, two between ten and sixteen at $8 each per month	264
Old-age pension at $75 per month	900
Value of produce of garden, hunt, fish consumed, firewood produced by family, knitted goods, etc.	700
Amounts saved by outright ownership of house, in monthly payments or rent	1,000
Total annual income	4,990

Adapted from Brox 1972: 10.

Table 3. *Source of income (in Canadian dollars), heads of households in*
fishery, 1963

Source of income	Petty Harbour (Avalon Peninsula N)	Trespassy Area (Avalon Peninsula S)	Straits Area (near Labrador)	Catalina Area (Trinity Bay)	Port de Grave Area (Conception Bay)
Average fishing income for heads	838	837	823	722	1,665
Other income from wages, for heads	446	211	297	784	134
Average transfer payments per head of household[a]	852	867	732	731	888

[a]Transfer payments include unemployment-insurance benefits, pensions, family allowances, and welfare payments.
Adapted from Brox 1972: 11.

in their continuity in the fishery, preferring to transfer as many as possible to wage labor; if not the current fisherfolk, then at least their children. Relocation, it was admitted, would create a "lost generation" of current fishermen who would never work again, but their children were supposed to become firmly embedded in a "modern" economy.

In 1954 the Province of Newfoundland began a "Centralization Program" to assist people to move from "isolated settlements with inferior public services" (Copes 1972: 101) to other places in Newfoundland. This program had two motivations, both of which the government attempted to conceal: first, to close out smaller communities, which were very expensive to service (with mail, medical visits, schools, etc.) or were regarded as obstacles to the development of tourist parks (R. Matthews 1976: 53ff.), and which paid no direct taxes; and second, to create a factory labor force. As a rationale for relocation, the government emphasized "progress" and "opportunity," sought to conceal its more specific motivations, invited people to sign petitions for relocation, and pretended, as long as it could, that it was simply assisting people to do what they both wanted and needed to do. But when two communities on an island in Notre Dame Bay petitioned not for relocation but for a new central post office,

in his reply the [federal] minister . . . indicated that he could not seriously consider their request because . . . [they] were on a provincial government list of communities which were to be resettled. The provincial government had long maintained that there was no list of communities "slated for resettlement," and had argued that the decision to resettle was always a local decision. The federal disclosure therefore caused them considerable embarrassment. [R. Matthews 1976: 29. This incident occurred in 1969.]

The relocation "assistance" began as a cash payment of $150 per family in 1954 and rose to $600 per family by 1965, when the program was changed. This assistance to families was provided *only* if *every* person in the village agreed to move – that is, the program required that the outport be abandoned. During the time I lived in Dunville, Placentia Bay, among people who had been relocated from island communities in the bay, I was told over and over that the tensions this offer created, between those who wanted to leave and those who wanted to stay – between brothers and sisters; parents and children; neighbors; friends and kin – made life in the village so unhappy that "you might as well leave."

In 1965 a much more forceful Household Resettlement Program was begun, increasing the pressures to move and for the first time attempting to control where people moved. Under the former program it was sufficient that people left their outport; with the new program they were supposed to move to "growth centers" where factory wage labor was available, or was planned for some future time, in order to qualify for the money – though many exceptions were made to this condition to help get people out.

The Federal-Provincial Newfoundland Fisheries Household Resettlement Program that was introduced effective April 1, 1965, provided much stronger incentives toward resettlement. Each household . . . received an outright grant of $1,000 with a further $200 per member of the household. An additional payment was made to defray actual travel and removal expenses. . . . The stipulation of the Centralization Program, that all the households in a settlement had to agree to move, was replaced by a requirement that 90 per cent of the households had to agree (by petition) to resettlement. This was lowered soon after the beginning of the program to 80 per cent. . . . Much of the additional financing was made available by the federal government. [Copes 1972: 102]

173

The politics of subsistence production

In fact, when 90 or 80 percent of the people move, and the schools, post office, and medical services are withdrawn (services that are often diminished before people "agree" to move), it is not likely that anyone will stay behind. Moreover, when too few fishermen remain in an area the merchant will leave, and unless there is a freezing plant nearby that purchases fresh cod, the fishing is finished. Between 1954 and 1965, 115 communities, with 1,500 families and 7,500 people, were relocated. In the first five years of the Household Resettlement Program, 1965–70, 143 communities, with 3,000 families and 16,000 people, were moved, and the average population of the relocated outports had risen from 65 to 112 (Copes 1972: 106).

The scope for resettlement in Newfoundland is far from exhausted. . . . Using 1966 census data, [there are] 1,293 unincorporated communities with 48,615 households containing 245,633 individuals. Together they comprised 49.8 per cent of the Newfoundland population. . . . Three-quarters of all communities in the province had a population of less than 300. . . . The majority of Newfoundlanders still live in very small communities, most of which are potential candidates for resettlement. At the current rate of resettlement of 5,000 persons and 24 communities a year, a great deal of scope remains for the Second Resettlement Program and subsequent ones. [Copes 1972: 106]

In the summer of 1972 the Canadian Broadcasting Corporation interviewed several people who had been relocated. The two people whose interviews are transcribed below came from small outports on the south coast, and both were interviewed in Fortune, a south coast factory town centered on the open-ocean trawler fishery. Here factory-owned draggers, with hired labor, brought fish to a freezing plant.

Q. Mr. Smith, why did you leave Rencontre West?
A. Well, we didn't have any other choice. All the others was going. We couldn't stay there with just two families.
Q. Why were they going?
A. Oh, they were going, I suppose they were going because they could find better jobs, you know, and so forth.
Q. How did the idea start?
A. Well, they were going to take the post office out of it, and then close down the bait dipple [depot]. We were going to get no service, like no medical services, and all this stuff, that's how it started, one to the other.
Q. Whose idea was it, or was it just, just . . . ? [Here the question trails off, as if the interviewer started to ask about the government, and changed his mind.]
A. It was just a bunch around the harbor, that's all, as far as we know, it was just a bunch around the harbor.
Q. Why do you think the government wanted Rencontre West resettled?
A. Well, I couldn't answer that question, I couldn't.
Q. To save money?
A. I don't know. Could be, but I don't know that, but we are not making so much over here as we were on the other side. [Note that the answer changes government to personal finances.]
Q. What sort of a life did you have in Rencontre West?

174

We must live in hopes

A. We had a pretty good life over there. You own your own, you know, all that. Everything you had you was the owner of, but here you got nothing, "just the hoot you got on your boot," that's all.

Q. What about your home?

A. Well, we owned that, but we don't own this. We got so [such an] amount of time to pay this out, and by the time we get this paid out and I can tell you it's mine I'll be even too old to work.

Q. Could you describe your life in Rencontre West – how you made your living and where you got your food and that – the whole sort of works?

A. Our living came out of the water over there and off the hills. We was fishing, cod fishing, and in the winter time there was a lot of herring on the go, you could make a good catch of herring. And then, years a little later [before] you get squid, and we used to go to squid. And then, so far as living goes, you could get a license, kill a moose, put it in your cold storage for yourself; you would always have something to cook. The time of the year would come to go salmon fishing, and you could get a good catch of salmon. You wouldn't make a big pile of money, but you'd have no trouble to get by on [it]. But I don't know, I don't think that much of it over here. You get a bunch of hours here for nothing. Well, we got a raise here, they say we did. We get now – we used to be getting a dollar eighty three cents an hour, and now we'll get two dollars and six cents. Why you got to work eight hours now for $16.24. Why that's nothing, if you was going to compare it to fishing. That's only a little over 250 pounds of fish. And you don't have to do much fishing now to get 250 pounds, not in eight hours. Right down here now its six cents a pound, and Mr. Midge told us that he's going to pay eight cents a pound here in November. So that's $80 a thousand pound of fish. You can't make the monies around the plant that you can make on the water. Can't be done.

Q. What about the cost of living here?

A. Well, the cost of living is pretty high. You got to buy everything you eat here. Everything. Except a pound of fish, you can get that down here, sometimes. But over where we come from, over there, you had your license, and kill your meat, and you get your partridge license, you get some of them and put them in your cold storage, you'd have something to eat, anyway. But I wouldn't go hunting over here, anyway. I'm too scared . . . [afraid of getting shot by mistake]. So I don't care too much about it over here myself.

Q. What about your vegetables, and that sort of thing?

A. No, we didn't grow none of that over there. They did years ago, but not late years. There might be somebody have a few buckets of potatoes, or something like that, not nothing big.

Q. What sort of inconveniences did you have over in Rencontre West?

A. (silence)

Q. Why would people want to move?

A. Well, probably for the children. They get better education, and so forth. That's the only thing I know they had to move for. They didn't move because they couldn't make a living, not over [in] Rencontre where we came from. Every man over there owned his home, and if they go to the store for to buy a tub of trawl a ton of coal, or whatever it is, whatever the case might be, they could pay for it as soon as they had it, they didn't need to charge nothing. Here, I'm in debt for the rest of me life.

Q. How so?

A. Well, for the first beginning we got this house now. He was $10,923, and

175

that was just the shell. Then we had to pay another $2,850 for the finishing off. We pay $71 month, and we get 48 years paying out. So, I'm 32 now, time I gets another 48, when I'm out [of debt], I'll see the best of my days . . .

Q. What did you have to leave behind?

A. Well, sir, too much for to tell you. We left the house behind, three store-houses, stage, and a lot of me fishing equipment was left over there. But it's not there now. Other people was back in around there, they beat it up, stole it, carry it all away. So there's nothing to go back there for now. Not to look for anything I had for to use. I had a brand new dory and engine, I had to give that away. You can put it that way, I sold it down the way along for $200. New dory and engine. Because it's no good to bring it here and have it in Fortune. We was over in Marystown seven months while we was building this. So if I'd have brought it here in Fortune and left it here, time I came back for to use it there wouldn't be nothing left, according to what they've done since I've been here . . . [people steal propellers and shafts, etc.].

Q. What about working in the plant?

A. Well, I wouldn't work in the plant, anyway. I'm not working *in* the plant, I works outside, aboard a dragger, discharging, taking fish out of the dragger. That's not too bad of a job, I mean you're outside. But I wouldn't want to be buried up any more than that.

Q. What would you say about factory work, the sort of work you're doing now, compared to the sort of work you did as a fisherman?

A. I can't get interested in to it. It's not interesting. I mean, first to begin with, you're on night shift. We go to work 5 o'clock in the evening. Most evenings 5, some evenings it's 8. And you're down there 'til 7 the next morning. And 2 o'clock in the morning. Why you don't know nothing about your family, anyway. You go away in the evenings, 5 o'clock, and you work 'til 2 and you come home and turn in and you don't get up 'til dinnertime. By the time you come to yourself it's time to go back down to work again. And when you comes off 7 o'clock in the morning you meets your wife in the doorway coming out to get breakfast. So that's no good. (laughs)

Q. How long you been on night shift?

A. I went on night shift last year the twenty-seventh day of March. That's when I started night shift. But I was two and a half months on day shift while the wife was sick there and that was, well, very good, you know, nothing extra, but not so bad as night shift.

Q. Who gained by resettlement, anybody?

A. Not that I know of, sir. So far as I know we're all in the one boat. You hear everybody talking about it, you know. There's nobody likes it, so far as this night shift racket goes. There's a lot of people I've been talking to, they'd sooner be over where they come from. With one [. . . ?] day they'd be out. So they can't like it too much better than meself.

Q. What about being close to a doctor, and a road, and that sort of thing? [This is the exchange recounted above, here in context.]

A. Well, that's one thing, I suppose. If you got a car it's alright. But if you didn't have a car it'd be bad. You'd probably have to fool around getting a taxi, and half the time you can't get them. But if you got a car of your own, and somebody's sick belong to you, you can go right on with them, you know. But I didn't [have it] that bad over where I come from [with no road access]. We used to get anywhere from three to four steamers a week, and if you were sick they'd come right on after you. Carry you to Burgeo, or Harbour Breton, wherever they was going. . . .

stood directly, personally, and on an instance-by-instance basis. The lack of knowledge on the part of Mr. Smith about who was "behind" relocation in Rencontre West – who was encouraging people to sign the required petition – is startling. In fact, when asked about the government, he answers about individuals making money. This reply seems related to his comment about what would happen if someone got sick in Fortune. It might be argued that such responses are engendered by the dislocations of the forced move, but the response is not that different from his description of formerly hunting moose (an animal larger than most horses) for himself and his family.

The young woman, being dragged about by social forces seemingly beyond her control, responds "sensibly," but point by point, and in sum thus both illogically and, I think, tragically. Mr. Smith echoes, albeit skeptically, one of the major government public rationales for relocation – that it is good or necessary for the sake of "education" for the children. The young woman accepts education as a goal, but this leads her to break with her co-workers. For all her friends, her underlying isolation is indicated by her remark that working in the fish plant is "all right for some people that don't have any learning."

VI

Part Three opened with the title "The Politics of Subsistence Production." As is clear by now, however, Newfoundland fisher families are not "subsistence" producers in the usual, restricted sense of the term: people who primarily produce what they themselves consume. Not only are the fisher families commodity producers, but they also do not produce the bulk of their own subsistence goods directly; they purchase much of their food and clothing, as well as key production supplies, from merchants.

Subsistence has broader and here more relevant meanings. It implies people who are getting by without many extras, certainly the historic case in the Newfoundland fishery. It also points to a populace that, in addition to commodity production and unlike factory wage workers, produces a significant portion of its own consumption and production needs – growing and hunting food, building houses and boats, knitting nets, and so forth.

Newfoundland fisher families have been subsistence producers in a special, specific way; special to, but not uncommon in, the hinterlands of merchant and industrial capitalism. They have had some of the autonomy and self-direction implied by the narrow sense of the word subsistence; an autonomy based both on producing for themselves key portions of their own needs (a small but crucial amount of their food and much of their fishing equipment), and even more on the self-organization of their work processes.

179

The politics of subsistence production

The commodity production that they participated in organizing usually earned them only a bare subsistence return. This subsistence return was mediated by two central and dominant institutions: the fish merchant and the state. Fisher families could reappropriate a portion of the value that they created in their salt cod – reappropriate this value in the form of food, clothes, salt, twine – but they could do so only on terms set by the merchants' adjustment of the price allowed for fish and the price debited for supplies. What they had "as their own" was also influenced by state policy: directly, after Confederation, in the form of transfer payments that approximated earnings in the fishery; or the "dole" before Confederation, which functioned as a substitute for winter supply from the merchant and sustained the fish families and the fishery in times of crises. Also directly from the state came income and benefits from roadwork and wharf construction, which particularly since the mid nineteenth century provided a supplement and occasionally an alternative to fishing. Indirectly, again from the state, the specific material conditions of their daily lives depended on the laws and policies that influenced their access to land, the possibilities of agriculture, the conditions of alternative employment, and their bargaining power with fish merchants.

It was, I think, from this context – as commodity producers for a subsistence return; as subsistence producers whose subsistence was not directly determined by their own efforts, nor by the vagaries of nature, but rather was crucially mediated by merchants and the state (i.e., for fisher families and for the outport communities, the merchant and the state stood between production and consumption, often, but not always, seemingly side by side) – it was in this context, with the anger, despair, and self-reliance that it generated, that fisher families turned with increasing intensity in the twentieth century, to a willingness to go along with policies of industrialization and wage labor, even though they were time and again bitterly disappointed by the effects of these policies. The intensity of the hopes that were placed on industrialization – hopes I think that were in substantial part for a less mediated, less controlled existence, and not just for higher wages – did not diminish or soothe the feelings of ambivalence about such "progress," as industrialization is often called in Newfoundland. The slogan "Burn your boats, boys, there will soon be two jobs for every man" was appealing to people who had worked so hard for so little, and people did sign the petition for relocation thinking at least it would be better for their children. Yet the early post-Confederation factories in Newfoundland had to pay higher wages than they anticipated to get people to stop fishing and come to work, perhaps because giving up the autonomy of fishing took more pressure than expected. Even as late as 1973, when the possibilities for fishing (which had been severely diminished) turned upward at least briefly, a major fish plant had to give a 21 percent increase in plant wages, not demanded by their current workers, in order to attract more wage laborers (D. MacDonald 1980: 56). Relocation of whole communities made fisher families more like farmers: Once they left there was no going back, no starting over again. This partly "solved" the problem of needing to use wage inducements to obtain labor, but at extraordinary human cost.

While relocation was at its peak in the early 1970s, and a labor force was being created that had no other choice but factory wage labor, the fishery became unionized. The Newfoundland Fishermen, Food, and Allied Workers' Union was formed in 1970, with two locals – the trawlermen and inshore fishermen forming one, the fish-plant workers the other. Two major strikes in 1974–5 substantially improved the earnings of fishermen and plant workers and the working conditions aboard trawlers; by 1977 all the traw-lermen and about half the full-time, "professional" inshore fishermen were members of the union. (D. Macdonald 1980 presents an excellent history of this union and its relations to both companies and the state.)

In the attempt to unionize the inshore fishermen, the union felt that it would be in a stronger position if representation elections were held only among "full-time" fishermen; part-time or casual fishermen would be less likely to support unionization. The union thus pressured for a government licensing scheme, pushing part-timers out of the commercial fishery, as part of the process of defining a "fisherman" (who would be entitled to vote for or against union representation). In 1973 they were successful. No license is required for cod, which is the mainstay of the fishery, but cod alone will not support a fisher family; they must also, in particular, take some other kinds of fish: lobster, salmon, herring, scallops, shrimp, crabs, and so forth, for which licenses are required. A complex set of conditions controls who can get a license; these conditions are highly re-strictive and require continuity in the fishery (not leaving for a few years of industrial employment and then coming back, a history of fishing), and they impose restricted hereditability on licenses. Although the government claims that these restrictions ensure adequate income to the fishermen by dividing the potential harvest among fewer participants, this policy also engenders a factory labor force by making inshore fishing increasingly impossible; it indirectly supports low landing prices (for the number of people who can earn a living from a stock of fish depends in part on the prices paid); and it also – as an impression from my discussions with outport residents – engenders a great deal of bitterness between the remaining outporters over who can and cannot fish. Outports, classlike in some re-spects in the context of merchant capital, are being dragged willy-nilly into a modern class system, whether or not the residents are yet factory workers. And the fishermen's own efforts at unionization have contributed to this process.

The politics of subsistence production

In the introduction it was suggested that class has – must have – a political dimension; in what was intended as a related point, it was suggested that "culture enters the dynamic of class because it is where class becomes dynamic." We can now return to those points.

By class having a political dimension I mean more, or something more specific, than the familiar point in Marx and the marxist literature that makes the distinction between class *in* itself and class *for* itself: class as a conscious and acting participant in social stability and change. Nor is it adequate to suggest that class has a political dimension because it must (or should) express itself and its claims in the political arena, narrowly defined; I find both these perspectives too restrictive, even as supplements to a more basic materialist perspective, to enable us to understand the formation, development, and assertiveness – or lack of assertiveness – of classes in a social system.

If we start with a very broad definition of the "political process" – namely, the process of collectively reincorporating experience into social structure – we can then see classes, and the communities of merchant capital as illustrated here, as participants in the political process not only directly, consciously, and explicitly but also indirectly, only partly consciously, and often unintentionally – or with a substantial gap between partly formed, often-fragmented, contradictory intentions and partly grasped, partly realized effects.

We can also begin to see, if only dimly and in general terms at first, how culture comes to matter – how people come to understand and express their experiences and relations to one another, and to give voice to, or silence, these understandings. Whether people – classes or communities – act on their own behalf, forming and expressing substantial claims, or remain quiet and quiescent, the contradictions, paradoxes, and disjunctions between different understandings, plural hopes, and shifting alliances are a crucial part of the process. To see a class, or a collection of communities or "tribes" within merchant capital, as actors in history, or to see culture as an active participant in class or community struggles, it is not at all necessary, and it may be misguided, to give a class, a community, or a culture one voice, or even a clear voice.

The experiences of Newfoundland outport families both united and divided people, within and between families, creating a mixture of intimacy and antagonism that has been expressed and reshaped in a wide range of outport customs. The distinctive culture of Newfoundland outports marked a distance between fisher families and the elite, but it did not *separate* the fisher families from the elite, nor engender antagonistic confrontations. Not mummering or scoffing with the merchant or with representatives of the

182

government or the outside world (teachers, doctors, nurses, etc.), and having customs that belonged to the community of fisherfolk, created a partly separate social world, partly antagonistic, partly conjoined – and partly illusory. Within this partly separate world of the outport, the two major themes of interaction emerged.

1. The first was a focus on family and self – in the words of Mr. Smith, the moose meat "in your cold storage for yourself," "owning your own," being able to take care of people that "belong to you." But fisher families, individually or collectively, did not own key productive resources such as cod-trap berths, or the facilities for access to markets. They sometimes privatized some of these resources, for a while, by long-standing individual claims to trap berths and community fishing territories (Martin 1973), but in ways that often contributed to the antagonisms between fisher families. Sometimes they communalized access – for example, by lotteries for trap berths – but this was only a partial sharing of the resources and not, for example, a pooling of catch and cure. So the relatively intense cultural focus on "one's own," and one's own family, was partly self-deceptive and definitely in contradiction to one of the major realities of their situation: They did not, even to the extent that farmers do, own some of the resources that they needed to own to provide a material basis for their autonomy. To the contrary, they were harnessed not only to merchant capital in general, as we have discussed, but also to their specific merchant in particular and through him (via truck and tal qual), as well as directly, to each other. Their individuality was thus a source, or a focus, of their dignity – their sense of their own strength and abilities – and a weakness: an individuality found and expressed in the communities that brought individuals together, but that was ultimately mediated by the merchants and the state. Hence the difficulty of resisting relocation in those communities where sentiment seems to have run strongly against relocation (R. Matthews 1976): Resistance often depended on help from outsiders or from the merchant; the pressures and inducements to relocate all too easily fragmented families; and if the merchant was going to leave, with rare exceptions communities were not able to plan or develop cooperatives that would replace him. The extent to which such mediations penetrated daily life is perhaps best illustrated by an incident from the late 1960s (told to me by Louis Chiaramonte, personal communication): When the fisher families of a south coast community decided to withhold their fish in a demand for higher prices, the merchant cut off their food, and the strike was broken in a single day. On the other side of the coin is Victor Butler, rowing out to fish in February to support his family without resorting to the dole. Also on the other side is Elizabeth Goudie, though scarcely out of childhood herself, helping a neighbor deliver a baby; providing, under conditions of

183

severe hardship, food, clothes, and medical care for her family; and, like Victor Butler, having a quiet pride in her own ability (and a clearer sense of her own human weakness).

2. Connected to, but different from, this complex and contradictory individuality, was the second major theme of interaction: the very strong sense of dignity that emerges from the actions of fisherfolk, particularly in their dealings with power, which, however, merges uneasily with an incapacity to effectively resist the impositions of power. The first and most moving instance that comes to mind is again Elizabeth Goudie – one of whose sons rose to become a member of the Newfoundland provincial legislature – quietly renaming her first son Horace, though noting, with equal quietness, that the name on the hospital book remained Esau. Also, in the same style of dignity and powerlessness, an incident from the field-work of Professor B. McKay: A fisherman, seeking to discharge part of a debt owed to a merchant, offered a brace of freshly shot sea ducks. The offer was refused. He put them on the counter, anyhow, saying as he left, "I guess you'll have to try to pluck me instead," and probably knowing, as he said it, that this was precisely what would happen. It is perhaps out of this mixture of dignity and powerlessness that a certain kind of ideology is born: the ideology that asserts "We are only loggers" as a central part of a militant claim against the logging companies and, even more, against the state that sided so publicly and decisively with the companies, accusing the striking men of all sorts of evils; that adopted, in the days of the Fishermen's Protective Union, the fishermen's jersey as its badge and uniform – and the motto, "Suum Cuique" (to each his own) implying, on one level, that the producing fishermen deserved a fair return, but also implying much more.

VII

The sense of powerlessness, pervasive but far from total, conjoins also with an insightful clarity into their own situation. "We Newfs, we are all niggers, we are all indians, we are all eskimos." The man who said this to me was a highly paid construction worker, when he could find work, and had worked on a number of "development" projects. On each he had worked as hard as possible, hoping to be taken on "full time" after the construction finished. He was often successful at this, and each time he saw the plant go bankrupt and the work end. Most of the time he worked in construction, he had to leave his wife and children back in the town where people relocated from the outports were sent. Despite it all he still kept trying, which was his major antidote for a clarity that led nowhere.

In section IV of this chapter, I have shown some aspects of this clarity, expressed in petition and idiom: about merchant exploitation, about the "dog's life" working conditions, and about the capacity to survive. The clarity is not always accurate nor realistic – note Victor Butler referring to the people he and the merchant were preparing to abandon as his "friends" – but it is sufficient to rub against the grain of their current situation, their needs, and their hopes: a contradiction between knowing why and knowing what, on the one hand, and knowing themselves, on the other.

At its most profound level, the conjunction of clarity and powerlessness is not simply formed against elements of their circumstances, nor simply expressed in specific utterances – petitions, idioms, turns of phrase. It is, rather, rooted in and expressed throughout the basic conjunctions and contradictions of outport culture and social organization.

Cuffers, I have asserted, introduce history into contemporary social relations, not by telling stories of the past but rather by introducing a tension between past and present, and implicitly between past, present, and future. Scoffs engender tensions also, but tensions that are historically flat and that lack a significant temporal dimension. Mummering permits, in the midst of its tensions, the reorganization of social relations – the community doing what must be done to enter the new year – but not the restructuring of social relations; mummering did not form fisherfolk cooperatives or unions, but it was part of the creation of a community intimate enough to be able to buck food from one another and antagonistic enough to do it.

It is these contradictory elements of culture – the contradictions within each custom, as well as between them – that provide the doorway into the inner terrain of Newfoundland folk culture. What we find on the other side of the door is that tradition, no less than class, is a process. Tradition is not a process in the simple sense that it changes over time. Tradition becomes dynamic partly, we have argued, because of the diversity of social ties in which it is rooted and to which it gives voice (communities of place and space; communities of account). Further, tradition becomes dynamic because it becomes a vehicle for intentionality – which is often in opposition to current forms of social organization. Such intentions are not simply opportunistic (the claims of one family or group against another); they can also be fundamental. The "traditional" customs of outport Newfoundland – mummering, scoffing, cuffing, and so forth – are set at least partly against the fragmentation of social ties produced by the daily operation of merchant capital in the fishery.

The extraordinarily rich and vibrant customs of Newfoundland outports were developed in the past century and a half, at the longest. None are ancient relics; most are relatively recent. It is here suggested that the tensions, disjunctions, paradoxes, and contradictions within and between outport customs, intersecting with and partly rooted in diverse forms of social organization (the community of place and space and the community of account) and also intersecting with the imposed and the claimed connectedness between the people of the outports, kept folk culture being continually generated; newly created, not simply recreated anew. I think, for illustration of this merger of history and intentionality, of one fisherman prodding another to sing at an informal gathering – teasing, encouraging, pushing, tormenting – and then holding his hand while he sings, to ease the tensions and to meet the need. In those clasped hands, and not in any abstract intellectualized plans, are the hopes that come with and before the "supposed" despair. I said earlier in the chapter that Newfoundland people do not make general nouns plural. But they often make verbs plural – "We fishes as we will" – and the hope of "living in hopes" turns out to be a verb.

Conclusion

10

Merchant capital and the cross-handed triumphs of tradition

I

The technical sophistication of the trading methods, the ability to concentrate funds to finance (at usurious rates of interest) governments and landed aristocrats who were always short of easily realizable assets, the cultural patronage of these medieval merchant capitalists, has brought forth a chorus of admiration from their historians. None, however, has been able to alter the estimate which Marx made of their historic role, that their capital remained always within the sphere of circulation, was never applied either to agricultural or industrial production in any innovative fashion. The so-called commercial revolution in no way altered the feudal mode of production. [Hilton 1978: 23]

To claim, as do Marx and others, that merchant capital (in its emergence out of a decaying feudalism, in a more contemporary colonial or neo-colonial context, or even in the hinterlands of relatively advanced industrial nations) remains within the sphere of circulation, and in no significant way alters prior or more autonomous modes of production, is to miss the whole dynamic of social and cultural differentiation and inequality – which is not specifically class based – in the formation of the modern world. From this perspective, the history and sociology of merchant capital remain flat, finding their explanations for development and change in such tertiary phenomena as the "genius" of a people, geographic location, the accidents of naval victories, the mechanics of transportation (its schedules and costs) or, at the level of secondary phenomena, the mysteries of unexplained demographic growth.

One of the primary ways in which merchant capital has been seen as leaving the sphere of circulation to enter the social world of semiautonomous production and the hurly-burly of daily life is through the notion that merchant capital, still in search of fulfilling its mandate to "buy cheaply," in a context of increasing competition, will eventually seek to "penetrate"

189

the productive process. Its purpose in so doing is to drive down the unit costs of production by assembling large numbers of workers, and the diverse tasks of a complex work process, in one spot – increasing the division of labor, improving the tools of production, breaking worker ownership of productive tools, and driving down the frequency and intensity of village and family ceremonies and customs, the costs of which were formerly borne, in part, by the price of the product. Although such processes do seem to characterize broad and powerful long-term historical developments, and lend the blurred color of historical motion and the appearance of fundamental structural transformation to the analysis of at least the decline of merchant capitalism, the simultaneous coexistence of precisely the opposite directionality – a process called *deindustrialization*, which either destroys the putting-out system, leaving behind the remnants of a subsistence or market agriculture and widespread pauperization, or breaks up early and semideveloped manufacturing units in favor of either the less costly putting-out system or of other forms of kin- and village-based production ordinarily found in merchant capitalism – should alert us to the existence of more profound social processes than the "penetration of production" in the developing and changing connections of merchant capital to the social life and productive capacities of its producers.

We can find a first hint about the shape of this connection in the fact that processes of kin- and village-based production (including the production of labor power – people – for use elsewhere) that turn out to be less costly are so not simply, as is usually claimed, because the producers are "feeding themselves" and thus carrying part of the costs of their social reproduction themselves (e.g., Meillassoux 1975). The lower production costs are, as the Newfoundland data suggest, rather more significantly due to the social and cultural *domination* that merchant capital's structuring of the whole interregional process of production and distribution makes possible. This domination is the framework for driving down the claims that producers can make, or even formulate, on their own output. If merchant capital never dies, but has coexisted as a dynamic aspect of all postneolithic forms (including feudalism) and for a while was itself the dominant socioeconomic form, it is not because greed is universal, nor because there are always people who wish to buy cheap and sell dear, but rather because merchant capital makes possible processes of interregional articulation that other forms of economic organization cannot as easily achieve. The power of these processes lies in their breadth, in the wide range of social and cultural life that they include. If we say that merchant capital never leaves the sphere of circulation, then we must perforce say that everything else is drawn into this sphere. But there are more precise ways of posing the issues.

The penetration of merchant capital into the process of production –

coercing, rewarding, transforming, often associated with a highly intensified focus on the output of one, or a few specific kinds of commodities – must be understood from two perspectives. From "above," from the vantage point of merchant capital, we can see a process of incorporation of the producers into a "world" or interregional economy. Simultaneously, we can see an equally powerful, if more complex, set of processes distancing the producers – politically, economically, socially, and culturally – both from the metropolitan heartland of merchant capital and, usually, from each other. On the other side of the connection between merchant capital and the producing communities – from "below," as it were – we find the simultaneous processes of integration with larger structures, and heightened differentiation – particularly cultural differentiation – of ethnic groups and regions, "tribes," and villages, from one another and sometimes within each one. The distinctiveness and cultural distance from domination can be intensified in situations where people seek to use their distinctive ways of life as a moral or political rallying point either to organize resistance to further incorporation, or to compete, perhaps violently, for a more favorable position within a system of increasing domination and inequality, or simply as a framework for organizing productive labor and for constructing the most satisfying possible life in the midst of the imposed antagonisms of merchant capital (a social life not without its own tensions and antagonisms). Because this increasing differentiation of producing communities is so often increasingly antagonistic between and also within producing groups, it can become an obstacle to, as well as a rallying point for, resistance to further domination.

There is, in sum, a double bond between merchant capital and its producers. One bond is formed in the domain of production, the other in the domain of culture. A new and more historically dynamic perspective on merchant capital and the social worlds that have formed under its domination thus becomes an especially appropriate task for anthropology – but an anthropology that goes beyond the study of the *content* of local cultural (and social-organizational) particularity first to an analysis of the historical specificity of this cultural particularity – its ties to the changing and partly diverse contexts of daily life and production – and then shifts to an enquiry into the existence of cultural particularity itself: the role of culture in history.

II

On the south coast of Newfoundland, where the sea bottom is too rocky to set cod traps, men have fished with drift or gill nets – a smaller-scale operation – rowing out to fish in dories with the long oars needed to pull a loaded boat through the waves. When a man cannot get a partner to fish with him, he does not use shorter oars, nor can most men pull such long oars when alone in a boat. So they set the oar ends inboard, crossing them over to get greater leverage on the blades, and cross their hands to grasp the oars. This is rowing "cross-handed" – alone. The same phrase is used to describe a man whose wife is away or a person who travels alone: "He slept cross-handed last night"; "He went to Toronto cross-handed" – in sum, to describe engaging in any activity alone that should be done together (Gaffney 1977). "Cross-handed" is thus a particularly interesting term, combining a reference to and perhaps a triumph over necessity with a subtle and gentle prodding of the victims of necessity: a metaphor not only for a variety of solitary actions but by extension perhaps also for "traditional" culture itself.

The emergence, development, and flourishing of this "traditional" outport folk culture occurred during the period when Newfoundland was clearly fully part of the world capitalist system, selling its fish on world markets and paying world-market prices for importing its supplies. From the market transactions for fish and supplies a great deal of wealth was derived, but not of course by the fisher families. This wealth was ultimately converted into capital – into the means to employ wage labor in productive organizations. Most of the investments that converted wealth into capital were not made in Newfoundland but in Britain, mainland Canada, and the United States.

Newfoundland is thus an instance, fairly common in the hinterlands of advanced industrial regions, of capital-formation-at-a-distance. The point is as important for an understanding of hinterland folk culture as it is for economic structures. During this same period, Manchester factory workers, for example, by laboring for less than the value they created, helped to form the capital that often displaced them or transformed their situation. Capital formation occurred right over their heads, as it were, and they could see and be conscious of its direct effects on their lives. Because in Newfoundland capital formation occurred at a distance, people could live their lives for a time without directly dealing with its effects. The isolation of Newfoundland outports and the "traditionalism" possible in this isolation, however humanly satisfying and however much it might have been claimed and created by the people themselves through their own efforts, was thus fundamentally illusory, existing in a space that lasted only until the capital that they helped to create came rushing back, in the mid twentieth century, to overwhelm their social practices and relations.

One dimension – only one, but an important one – of the traditional culture that develops in the hinterlands in the context of incorporation into merchant capital is the isolation from the larger social formation that the traditional culture suggests to its participants and that it helps to create.

This isolation has many facets, from its hidden illusory quality to its defensive and even assertive potential. But whatever facet is turned to the light, they all together comprise a reflection of domination and integration.

Yet the "traditional" culture, with its illusory isolation, is capable not only of contributing substantially to the organization, over extended periods of time, of a work force for commodity production for the market (as with mummering), and capable not only of expressing, within itself, the tensions that derive from imposed social relations (e.g., the scoff) but capable also of confronting, in particular, the conjunction of work and appropriation and especially the attempt to extend appropriation beyond the domain of work into the daily life of the communities. One important and hard-fought demand of the fishermen's union is that the trawler boats tie up long enough in the winter for them to enjoy the Christmas season with their families – the far end of a process of culture confronting domination that began with the Yule customs of Captain Cartwright's servants. With the cultural isolation of the village from larger structures of domination and incorporation – illusory, defensive, assertive, partly self-defeating – and with such small and yet significant victories as this midwinter shutdown, we have returned to the cross-handed triumphs – not triumph – of tradition.

I have sought to show that village culture could be both adaptive to conditions of imposed pressure and fragmentation and simultaneously a form of collective self-assertion, part of the struggle against domination and appropriation. It is precisely this adaptiveness and these struggles, *taken together*, that situate culture within the social relations of daily life and production and that thus enable contradictions to emerge within culture, between culture and daily life, and between culture, the state, and production.

From this perspective, we can begin to understand "culture" as the locus of mediations between daily life and appropriation. It is not the content of culture but its contradictions, and the contradictions of and between multiple cultural forms in class societies, that conjoin culture to production and the state on the one hand and to daily life on the other. When people organize on their own behalf, shaping new experiences, their culture is as relevant as their class, as understandable, as rooted in prior and current experiences, and as autonomous: What makes this so is the salience of the cultural contradictions. But for all this, traditional culture is often not notably effective as a locus of substantial claims against domination by capital or by the state, for more reasons than the force that is brought to bear against the people.

Although folk cultures, "peasant" or "tribal," can have an explosive potential, violently confronting domination – a potential perhaps partly

193

rooted in the same conjunction of clarity and powerlessness seen in New-foundland – Newfoundland presents a different directionality of development.

The wellspring of outport culture was formed with the shunting aside of custom as a locus of direct confrontation over inequality. The culture developed through the local manifestations of three very widespread features of merchant capitalism, beginning with the harnessing of communities of producers to extremely specific commodity production, which exposed these communities to the impact of massive variations in supply and price, and so drove them back upon their own resources as they were increasingly embedded in the world market. The inability of subsistence production to meet needs, and the contradictions between the social relations of commodity and subsistence production, not only forced these communities to turn outward to the state for aid but were also a central part of a number of social processes that served to individualize experience and intentionality, and thus to undermine the political assertiveness of outport culture.

This individualized intentionality, expressed within and through village culture, made the folk culture increasingly less collectively confrontational and thus contributed to its apparently traditional and apparently backward-looking orientation, despite its recency and fluidity (see Berger and Mohr 1975 for southern European and Mediterranean examples). This individuation – within, not apart from, folk culture – has been a major obstacle to the use of culture as a vehicle for developing assertiveness.

Yet direct "ideological" appeals, which are not as rooted in current experience and intentionality as are "traditional" folk customs, have not been found to be very appealing. For those concerned with the future well-being of "marginalized" and "traditional" communities – an important concern not just in capitalist but also in socialist societies, whose records of treating their aboriginal and hinterland populaces are often rather dismal – the task is to help discover and develop frameworks for collective intentionality that are as rooted in the shaping of experience and as directly relevant to ongoing social life as are the supposedly routine and archaic customs and social rituals.

It is the strategic purpose of this analysis to suggest that developing this collective intentionality requires first developing the linkages between people, in daily life and production. Without these linkages, there is little basis for developing oppositional cultures or a class consciousness that can confront the expanding and intensifying conjunction of production and appropriation.

References

Abbreviations

Institutions and archives
MUN   Memorial University of Newfoundland
ISER   Institute of Social and Economic Research, MUN
MUNFLA   Memorial University Folklore and Language Archives
NLPA   Newfoundland and Labrador Provincial Archives

Frequently cited works
DNE   Dictionary of Newfoundland English. See Story, Kirwin, and Wid-
           dowson 1982
CO 194   See Great Britain 1696–1782
CMND 4480 See Great Britain 1933
CMD 8867   See Great Britain 1898
JHA   Journal of the House of Assembly (Newfoundland)
JLC   Journal of the Legislative Council (Newfoundland)

Alexander, David. 1977. *The decay of trade: an economic history of the Newfound-
    land saltfish trade, 1935–1965*. St. John's: ISER, Newfoundland Social and
    Economic Studies no. 19.
Andersen, Raoul (ed.). 1979. *North Atlantic maritime cultures*. The Hague: Mouton.
Andersen, Raoul, and Cato Wadel (eds.). 1974. *North Atlantic fishermen: anthro-
    pological essays on modern fishing*. St. John's: ISER, Social and Economic
    Papers no. 5.
Anspach, Lewis. 1819. *A history of Newfoundland*. London: Sherwood, Gilbert
    and Piper.
Antler, Ellen. 1974. Brief prepared for the report of the Committee on Federal
    (fish) Licensing Policy. On file at ISER.
    1977. Women's work in Newfoundland fishing families. *Atlantis* 2 (2), part II:
    106–13.
    1981. Fisherman, fisherwoman, rural proletariat. Ph.D. dissertation, anthropol-
    ogy, University of Connecticut.
Antler, Ellen, and James Faris. 1979. Adaptation to changes in technology and
    government policy. In Raoul Andersen (ed.) 1979: pp. 129–54.

195

References

Antler, Steven. 1975. Colonial exploitation and economic stagnation in nineteenth century Newfoundland. Ph.D. dissertation, economics, University of Connecticut.

Berger, John, and Jean Mohr. 1975. *A seventh man*. Hammondsworth: Penguin.

Bonnycastle, Sir R. H. 1842. *Newfoundland in 1842*. London: H. Colburn.

Bourdieu, Pierre. 1977. *Outline of a theory of practice*. Cambridge: Cambridge University Press.

Brox, Ottar. 1972. *Newfoundland fishermen in the age of industry: a sociology of economic dualism*. St. John's: ISER, Newfoundland Social and Economic Studies no. 9.

Buchanen, Archibald. 1785. Concerning landed property in Newfoundland. British Museum ms., Add. 38347, Liverpool Papers ff. 373–88, vol. clviii, Aug.–Dec. (Microfilm copy also at MUN).

Butler, Victor. 1975. *The little nord easter: reminiscences of a Placentia Bayman*. Edited, with an introduction, by Wilfred Wareham. St. John's: MUNFLA Publications, Community Studies Series no. 1. Republished in 1980 by Breakwater Books, St. John's, with a much abbreviated introduction by Wilfred Wareham.

1977. *Sposin' I dies in d'dory*. St. John's: Jesperson.

1982. *Buffett before nightfall*. St. John's: Jesperson.

Cammett, John. 1967. *Antonio Gramsci and the origins of Italian communism*. Stanford: Stanford University Press.

Canada, Economic Council of. 1980. *Newfoundland: from dependency to self-reliance*. Hull, Quebec: Canadian Government Publishing Centre.

Cartwright, George. 1792 (repr. 1911) *A journal of transactions and events, during a residence of nearly sixteen years on the coast of Labrador*. 3 vols. Newark: Notts. My page references are to the more readily available abridged 1911 reprint, *Captain Cartwright and his Labrador journal*, ed. C. W. Townsend. Boston: D. Estes.

Cell, Gillian T. (ed.). 1981. Introduction to *Newfoundland discovered*. London: Hakluyt Society.

Chadwick, St. John. 1967. *Newfoundland: island into province*. Cambridge: Cambridge University Press.

Chiaramonte, Louis. 1969. Mumming in "Deep Harbour": aspects of social organization in mumming and drinking. In Halpert and Story (eds.) 1969: pp. 76-103.

1970. *Craftsman-client contracts: interpersonal relations in a Newfoundland fishing community*. St. John's: ISER, Newfoundland Social and Economic Studies no. 10.

Clark, Rex. 1984. Review of Victor Butler, *Buffett before nightfall*. *Newfoundland Quarterly* 80 (1): 42–3.

Copes, Parzival. 1972. *The resettlement of fishing communities in Newfoundland*. Ottawa: Canadian Council on Rural Development.

Crabb, Peter. 1974. Cheap power – an expensive failure: hydroelectric power and industrial development in Newfoundland. *Water Resources Bulletin* (American Water Resources Association) 10 (1): 42–53.

Davis, John. 1973. *Land and family in Pisticci*. Ithaca: Cornell University Press.

Evans, Allen. 1981. *The splendour of St. Jacques*. St. John's: Harry Cuff.

Faris, James C. 1968. Validation in ethnographic description: the lexicon of "occasions" in Cat Harbour. *Man* 3 (1): 112–24.

1972. *Cat Harbour: a Newfoundland fishing settlement*. St. John's: ISER, Newfoundland Social and Economic Studies no. 3.

196

References

Firestone, Melvin. 1967. *Brothers and rivals: patrilocality in "Savage Cove."* St. John's: ISER, Newfoundland Social and Economic Studies no. 5.

Gaffney, Michael. 1977. Crosshanded: work organization and the developmental cycle of the south coast Newfoundland domestic group. Paper read at Northeastern Anthropological Association meetings, 1977. On file at ISER.

Geertz, Clifford. 1973. Ideology as a cultural system. In *The interpretation of cultures*, pp. 193–233. New York: Basic Books.

Gluckman, Max. 1955. *Custom and conflict in Africa.* Oxford: Basil Blackwell.

1963. *Order and rebellion in tribal Africa.* New York: Free Press.

Goody, Jack. 1962. *Death, property and the ancestors.* Stanford: Stanford University Press.

Gordon, H. S. 1954. The economic theory of a common property resource: the fishery. *Journal of Political Economy* 62 (April): 124–42.

Goudie, Elizabeth. n.d. "A Labrador Trappers Wife." Manuscript in collection of Newfoundland Center, Queen Elizabeth II Library, MUN.

1973. *Woman of Labrador*, ed. David Zimmerly. Toronto: Peter Martin Assoc.

Gramsci, Antonio. 1971. *Prison notebooks.* New York: International.

Great Britain. 1696–1782. Colonial Office Records, Newfoundland, series 194. London: Public Record Office.

1841. Minutes of evidence taken before the select committee appointed to enquire into the state of the colony of Newfoundland. British Museum Library Catalog no. 9555.9.9.

1898. British parliamentary papers, CMD 8867. *Newfoundland correspondence relative to a contract for the sale of the Government Railway*, no. 26.

1933. British parliamentary papers, CMND 4480. *Newfoundland Royal Commission, report; chairman*, Lord Amulree.

Gunn, Gertrude. 1977 (orig. pub. 1966). *The political history of Newfoundland, 1832–1864.* Toronto: University of Toronto Press.

Gwyn, Richard. 1972. *Smallwood: the unlikely revolutionary* (rev. ed.). Toronto: McClelland and Stewart.

Halpert, Herbert, and George M. Story (eds.). 1969. *Christmas Mumming in Newfoundland.* Toronto: University of Toronto Press.

Handcock, W. Gordon. 1977. English migration to Newfoundland. In John J. Mannion (ed.) 1977: 15–48.

Hay, Douglas. 1975. Property, authority and the criminal law. In Douglas Hay, Peter Linebaugh, John Rule, E. P. Thompson, and Cal Winslow (eds.), *Albion's fatal tree*, pp. 17–64. New York: Pantheon.

Head, C. Grant. 1976. *Eighteenth century Newfoundland.* Toronto: McClelland and Stewart, Carleton Library no. 99.

Hiller, James K. 1971. A history of Newfoundland 1874–1901. Ph.D. dissertation, Kings College, Cambridge University.

1980. The railway and local politics in Newfoundland. In J. Hiller and S. Neary (eds.) 1980: 123–47.

Hiller, James K., and Peter Neary (eds.). 1980. *Newfoundland in the nineteenth and twentieth centuries.* Toronto: University of Toronto Press.

Hilton, Rodney. 1975. *The English peasantry in the later Middle Ages.* Oxford: Clarendon.

(ed.). 1978. Introduction, in *The Transition from Feudalism to Capitalism.* London: Verso.

Hobsbawm, Eric, and Terence Ranger (eds.). 1983. *The invention of tradition.* Cambridge: Cambridge University Press.

197

References

Innis, Harold A. 1954. *The Cod Fisheries* (rev. ed.). Toronto: University of Toronto Press.

Kriedte, Peter, Hans Medick, and Jurgen Schlumbohm (eds.). 1981. *Industrialization before industrialization*. Trans. Beate Schempp. Cambridge: Cambridge University Press; Paris: Editions de la Maison des Sciences de l'Homme.

Leach, Edmund. 1954. *Political systems of Highland Burma*. Boston: Beacon Press.

Lévi-Strauss, Claude. 1969. *The raw and the cooked. Introduction to a science of mythology* I. New York: Harper & Row.

Lodge, Thomas. 1935. Newfoundland today. *International Affairs* 14 (5): 635–53.
1939. *Dictatorship in Newfoundland*. London: Cassell.

Lounsbury, Ralph Greenlee. 1934. *The British fishery at Newfoundland: 1634–1763*. New Haven: Yale University Press. Reprinted by Archon Books, New York, 1969.

MacDonald, David. 1980. *Power begins at the Cod End*. St. John's: ISER, Newfoundland Social and Economic Studies no. 26.

McDonald, Ian. 1980. W. F. Coaker and the balance of power strategy: the Fishermen's Protective Union in Newfoundland politics. In Hiller and Neary (eds.) 1980: 148–80. Ian McDonald's Ph.D. thesis on the Fishermen's Protective Union, not now available for circulation, is being prepared for posthumous publication by James K. Hiller.

McLintock, A. H. 1941. *The establishment of constitutional government in Newfoundland*. London: Longmans, Green, Imperial Studies no. 17.

Mannion, John J. (ed.). 1977. *The peopling of Newfoundland*. St. John's: ISER, Social and Economic Papers no. 8.

Martin, Kent O. 1973. "The Law in St. John's Says . . . ": space division and resource allocation in the Newfoundland fishing community of Fermeuse. M.A. thesis, anthropology, MUN.

Marx, Karl. 1963 (orig. pub. 1844). On the Jewish question. In *Karl Marx: early writings,* ed. T. B. Bottomore, pp. 1–40. New York: McGraw Hill.
1971 (written 1857–8). *The Grundrisse: foundations of the critique of political economy,* ed. and trans. David McLellan. New York: Harper & Row.
1976 (orig. pub. 1859). *Preface and introduction to a contribution to the critique of political economy.* Peking: Foreign Languages Press.
1967a (orig. pub. 1867). *Capital,* vol. I. New York: International Publishers.
1967b (orig. pub. 1894). *Capital,* vol. III. New York: International Publishers.

Mathias, Philip. 1971. *Forced growth: five studies of government involvement in the development of Canada.* Toronto: James Lorimer.

Matthews, Keith. 1973. Lectures on the early history of Newfoundland. Rexograph, Maritime History Group, MUN.
1974. Historical fence building: A critique of the historiography of Newfoundland. Rexograph, Maritime History Group, MUN.
1977. The class of '32: St. John's reformers on the eve of representative government. *Acadiensis* 6 (2): 80–94.

Matthews, Ralph. 1976. *"There's no better place than here."* Toronto: Peter Martin Associates.
1980. Class interests and the role of the state in the development of Canada's east coast fishery. *Canadian Issues* 3 (1): 115–24.

Mauss, Marcel. 1967. *The gift.* New York: Norton.

Meillassoux, Claude. 1975. *Femmes, greniers, capitaux.* Paris: Maspero.

Mitchell, Harvey. 1958. The constitutional crises of 1889 in Newfoundland. *Canadian Journal of Economics and Political Science* 24 (3): 323–31.

198

References

Moreton, (Rev.) Julian. 1863. *Life and work in Newfoundland: reminiscences of thirteen years spent there.* London: Rivingtons.

Moulton, E. C. 1967. Constitutional crises and civil strife in Newfoundland, February to November 1861. *Canadian Historical Review* 48 (3): 251–72.

Murray, J. 1895. *The commercial crises in Newfoundland.* St. John's: J. M. Withers, Queen's Printer.

Neary, Peter (ed.). 1973. *The political economy of Newfoundland, 1929–1972.* Vancouver: Copp Clark.

1984. Clement Atlee's visit to Newfoundland, September 1942. *Acadiensis* 13 (2): 101–9.

Nemec, Thomas. 1974. I fish with my brother: the structure and behavior of agnatic-based fishing crews in a Newfoundland Irish outport. In Andersen and Wadel (eds.) 1974: 9–35.

Newfoundland, Dominion of. 1916. *Decisions of the Supreme Court of Newfoundland, reports, 1817–1828,* ed. B. Dunfield. St. John's: J. M. Withers, Queen's Printer.

Newfoundland and Labrador, Province of. 1955. Report of the Newfoundland Royal Commission on Agriculture. St. John's: David R. Thistle, Queen's Printer.

1980. *Managing all our resources.* St. John's: Newfoundland Information Services.

Newfoundland and Labrador Federation of Labour. 1978. *"Now that we've burned our boats . . .". The report of the people's commission on unemployment, Newfoundland and Labrador.* St. John's: Creative Printers and Publishers.

Noel, S. J. R. 1971. *Politics in Newfoundland.* Toronto: University of Toronto Press.

Overton, D. J. B. 1976. Underdevelopment and merchant capital: the case of Newfoundland. Rexograph, Center for the Development of Community Initiatives, Queens College, MUN.

Palliser, (Gov.) Hugh. 1769. British Museum, Colonial Office Papers, CO 194/162ff.

Pedley, (Rev.) Charles. 1863. *The history of Newfoundland from the earliest times to the year 1860.* London: Longmans, Green.

Prowse, D. W. 1895. *A history of Newfoundland from the English, colonial and foreign records.* London: Macmillan. Reprinted by Mika Studios, Belleville, Ont., Canada, 1972.

Reeves, John. 1793. *History of the government of the island of Newfoundland.* London: printed for J. Sewell. Reprinted by Johnson Reprint, New York, 1967.

Rogin, Michael P. 1975. *Fathers and children: Andrew Jackson and the subjugation of the American Indian.* New York: Random House.

Ryan, Shannon. 1971. The Newfoundland cod fishery in the nineteenth century. M.A. thesis, history, MUN.

1980. The Newfoundland salt cod trade in the nineteenth century. In Hiller and Neary (eds.) 1980: 40–66.

Sanger, Chesley W. 1977. The evolution of sealing and the spread of settlement in northeastern Newfoundland. In Mannion (ed.) 1977: 136–51.

Scammell, A. R. 1973. *My Newfoundland.* Montreal: Harvest House.

Schmitt, Jean-Claude. 1981. Les traditions folkloriques dans la culture medieval: quelques reflexions de methode. *Archives de Sciences Sociales des Religions* 52 (1): 5–20.

Sider, Gerald M. 1976. Christmas mumming and the new year in outport Newfoundland. *Past and Present* 71: 102–25.

References

1980. The ties that bind: culture and agriculture, property and propriety in the Newfoundland village fishery. *Social History* 5 (1): 1–39.

1984. Family fun in Starve Harbour, Newfoundland. In *Material interest and emotion: essays on the study of family and kinship*, ed. Hans Medick and David Sabean, pp. 340–66. New York: Cambridge University Press.

1986. When parrots learn to talk, and why they can't: dominance, deception and self-deception in Indian–White relations. Forthcoming.

Slade/Kelson Letters, Trinity. 1809–25. NLPA P7/A6/box 30, folder 2.

Staveley, Michael. 1977. Population dynamics in Newfoundland: the regional patterns. In Mannion (ed.) 1977: 49–76.

Stiles, Geoffrey. 1973. Reluctant entrepreneurs: organizational change and capital management in a Newfoundland fishery. Ph.D. thesis, anthropology, McGill University.

Story, George M. 1969. Newfoundland: fishermen, hunters, planters, and merchants. In Halpert and Story (eds.) 1969: 7–33.

1980. "Old Labrador": George Cartwright 1738–1819. Lecture delivered to the Newfoundland Historical Society, 9 Oct. Rexograph.

Story, George M., W. J. Kirwin, and J. D. A. Widdowson (eds.). 1982. *Dictionary of Newfoundland English*. Toronto: University of Toronto Press.

Szwed, John F. 1966. *Private cultures and public imagery: interpersonal relations in a Newfoundland peasant society*. St. John's: ISER, Newfoundland Social and Economic Studies no. 2.

1969. The mask of friendship: mumming as a ritual of social relations. In Halpert and Story (eds.) 1969: 104–18.

Thompson, Edward P. 1974. Patrician society, plebeian culture. *Journal of Social History* 7 (4): 382–405.

1978. Folklore, anthropology and social history. *Indian Historical Review* 3 (2): 247–66.

Thornton, Patricia. 1977. The demographic and mercantile basis of initial permanent settlement in the strait of Belle Isle. In Mannion (ed.) 1977: 152–83.

Tocque, (Rev.) Philip. 1846. *Wandering thoughts, or solitary hours*. London: T. Richardson.

Trask, Boyd. 1968. "Mischief nights." MUNFLA 68-24.

Wareham, Wilfred W. 1975. Introduction to Victor Butler, *The little nord easter*. St. John's: MUNFLA.

1982. Towards an ethnography of "times": Newfoundland party traditions, past and present. Ph.D. thesis, folklore, University of Pennsylvania.

Widdowson, J. D. A., and H. Halpert. 1969. The disguises of Newfoundland mummers. In Halpert and Story (eds.) 1969:

Williams, (Gov.) Ralph. 1913. *How I became governor*. London: J. Murray.

Williams, Raymond. 1976. *Keywords: a vocabulary of culture and society*. New York: Oxford University Press.

1977. *Marxism and literature*. New York: Oxford University Press.

Index

"admiral" (fishing), 16, 11, 122
"after," 74–5
agency, 9–10, 103
agriculture, 114–15
anthropology
  ecological, 20–1
  functional, 9–10

Brooking, Thomas H., 59–60, 135–6
"bucking," 78–9, 185
Butler, Victor, 101–3, 106, 107–8

capital formation, 22–3, 33, 108–9, 127, 145
Cartwright, George (Captain), 53–5
Catholic–Protestant relations, 133–8, 140–1
Chamberlain, Joseph (Colonial Secretary)
  148–9
class, 5–9, 170–1, 182–4
  class struggle, 7–9
  in Newfoundland, 117–18
codfish, curing, 13–14, 41–4
common-property resources, 28–29
community
  of account, 71–2, 92
  of place and space, 70–2, 92
contradictions, 7
culture, 3, 4, 5–7, 9–11, 45, 109–10, 120–2,
  193–4
  capital formation and, 108–9
  class and, 6–7, 10
  contradictions (paradoxes, disjunctions)
    and 75, 94–5, 101, 154–7
  distinctiveness and, 29, 30, 93–5
  historical specificity and autonomy of, 94
  merchant capital and, 38
  social structure and, 72
custom, 30, 53–5, 56–7, 93–4
"cuffer," 161–4, 185

"dealers," 58
deception, 68–70
"dieters," 169–70
"drink of water," 71

economic development, *see* government,
  forced growth and
equality, among fisherfolk, 68
experience, *see* agency

"fade," 169
fisher families
  income, 171–2
  organization for fishing, 80–6
  tensions within, 84–6

government
  confederation with Canada, 100
  crises, 26, 99–100, 129–33
  finances, 99
  fiscal crises of, 129–30
  forced growth and, 21–2, 100, 142, 144–
    5, 148–9, 151–3
  "Representative," 130–2
  "Responsible," 129, 132–7, 140–1
  revenues, 139
  sectarianism and 131, 133–7, 140–1
  social reproduction and, 128, 144–8
Goudie, Elizabeth, 158–61, 183–4

hegemony, 89, 109, 119–28
history
  anthropology and, 4–5
  cuffers and, 161–4, 185
  gifts and, 164–8
  scoffs and, 168
"honesty" and "industry," 68–70
hydraulic methodologies, 4

Index

ideology, 57, 100, 152–5, 194
inshore fishery, organization, 46, 80–5, 127
intentionality, 3, 10, 94–5
intimacy and distance, 75, 85–6, 105–6, 108–9, 183–4
isolation, 178–9

judiciary, 110–12, 115–116, 122, *see also* "admiral"

Landergan petition, 115–17
Lodge, Thomas, 149
logic (of social systems), 22

Meillassoux, Claude, 44
merchant capitalism, 34–8, 57, 144–8, 189–91
  "putting-out" system and, 23–4, 146–7,
Moreton, Julian (Reverend), 74, 117–18, 122, 158, 161
mummering, 75–7, 88–93, 94–5
  urban, 89–90, 93, 138–9

Nowlan v. *McGrath*, 48–9

Palliser, Hugh (Governor) 50–1, 113
paternalism, 53–5
pauperism, 141–3, 151
peasant social systems, 27, 30, 193–4
planters, 16, 17, 47–56, 69
  and labor discipline, 50–5
poor relief, 99, 147–8
political economy, 145
political process, 182
press-gang, 16
property, 109–10, 112–14
Protestant–Catholic relations, *see* Catholic–Protestant relations

railroad, 148–9
reciprocity, 79, 164–8
relocation, *see* resettlement
reproduction (social), 10, 23–5, 128, 144–8, 156–7

resettlement, 105, 144, 172–9, 181
residents, 18
resource base, 27–9
roads 20, 116, 117

"scoff," 77–80, 88, 91–3
sealing, 13, 25, 139
servant
  contract, 47–9
  fishery, 32
  guaranteed wage, 47–52
  lien, 51–3
settlement patterns, 15, 16, 19, 20
  and demography, 18
"ship's room," 14
Slade and Kelson, plan, 60–7
Smallwood, Joseph R. (Premier), 106, 148, 150, 152
social structure, 45
"stage," 14, 41
Story, George, 53, 54
subsistence production, 37, 179–80
Sumer, proverbs, 121
supplying system, 70

"tal qual," 87–8, 91–2
Thompson, E. P., 4, 9–10
time, 74–5, 118
"times," 75, 79–80
tradition, 23, 24, 26–8, 32, 35–6, 44–5, 53–5, 57, 73, 94–5, 191–3
  class and, 45
  time and, 3
"tribal" social systems, 27–31, 193
"truck," 18–23, 58–9, 72–3, 86–8, 92, 146–8, 168

unions, 126, 155, 181, 184

Williams, Sir Ralph (Governor), 124–5, 126
winter supply, 22, 26, 60, 104, 151

Yule customs, 89–90

CAMBRIDGE STUDIES IN SOCIAL ANTHROPOLOGY

Editor: Jack Goody

1. The Political Organisation of Unyamwezi
   R. G. ABRAHAMS
2. Buddhism and the Spirit Cults in North-East Thailand*
   S. J. TAMBIAH
3. Kalahari Village Politics: An African Democracy
   ADAM KUPER
4. The Rope of Moka: Big-Men and Ceremonial Exchange in Mount Hagen, New Guinea*
   ANDREW STRATHERN
5. The Majangir: Ecology and Society of a Southwest Ethiopian People
   JACK STAUDER
6. Buddhist Monk, Buddhist Layman: A Study of Urban Monastic Organisation in Central Thailand
   JANE BUNNAG
7. Contexts of Kinship: An Essay in the Family Sociology of the Gonja of Northern Ghana
   ESTHER N. GOODY
8. Marriage among a Matrilineal Elite: A Family Study of Ghanaian Senior Civil Servants
   CHRISTINE OPPONG
9. Elite Politics in Rural India: Political Stratification and Political Alliances in Western Maharashtra
   ANTHONY T. CARTER
10. Women and Property in Morocco: Their Changing Relation to the Process of Social Stratification in the Middle Atlas
    VANESSA MAHER
11. Rethinking Symbolism*
    DAN SPERBER, translated by Alice L. Morton
12. Resources and Population: A Study of the Gurungs of Nepal
    ALAN MACFARLANE
13. Mediterranean Family Structures
    Edited by J. G. PERISTIANY
14. Spirits of Protest: Spirit-Mediums and the Articulation of Consensus among the Zezuru of Southern Rhodesia (Zimbawe)
    PETER FRY
15. World Conqueror and World Renouncer: A Study of Buddhism and Polity in Thailand against a Historical Background*
    S. J. TAMBIAH
16. Outline of a Theory of Practice*
    PIERRE BOURDIEU, translated by Richard Nice
17. Production and Reproduction: A Comparative Study of the Domestic Domain*
    JACK GOODY
18. Perspectives in Marxist Anthropology*
    MAURICE GODELIER, translated by Robert Brain
19. The Fate of Shechem, or the Politics of Sex: Essays in the Anthropology of the Mediterranean
    JULIAN PITT-RIVERS

203

Cambridge Studies in Social Anthropology

20. People of the Zongo: The Transformation of Ethnic Identities in Ghana
    ENID SCHILDKROUT
21. Casting Out Anger: Religion among the Taita of Kenya
    GRACE HARRIS
22. Rituals of the Kandyan State
    H. L. SENEVIRATNE
23. Australian Kin Classification
    HAROLD W. SCHEFFLER
24. The Palm and the Pleiades: Initiation and Cosmology in Northwest Amazonia
    STEPHEN HUGH-JONES
25. Nomads of South Siberia: The Pastoral Economies of Tuva
    S. I. VAINSHTEIN, *translated by Michael Colenso*
26. From the Milk River: Spatial and Temporal Processes in Northwest Amazonia
    CHRISTINE HUGH-JONES
27. Day of Shining Red: An Essay on Understanding Ritual
    GILBERT LEWIS
28. Hunters, Pastoralists and Ranchers: Reindeer Economies and their Transformations
    TIM INGOLD
29. The Wood-Carvers of Hong Kong: Craft Production in the World Capitalist Periphery
    EUGENE COOPER
30. Minangkabau Social Formations: Indonesian Peasants and the World Economy
    JOEL S. KAHN
31. Patrons and Partisans: A Study of Politics in Two Southern Italian *Comuni*
    CAROLINE WHITE
32. Muslim Society*
    ERNEST GELLNER
33. Why Marry Her? Society and Symbolic Structures
    LUC DE HEUSCH, *translated by Janet Lloyd*
34. Chinese Ritual and Politics
    EMILY MARTIN AHERN
35. Parenthood and Social Reproduction: Fostering and Occupational Roles in West Africa
    ESTHER N. GOODY
36. Dravidian Kinship
    THOMAS R. TRAUTMANN
37. The Anthropological Circle: Symbol, Function, History*
    MARC AUGE, *translated by Martin Thom*
38. Rural Society in Southeast India
    KATHLEEN GOUGH
39. The Fish People: Linguistic Exogamy and Tukanoan Identity in Northwest Amazonia
    JEAN E. JACKSON
40. Karl Marx Collective: Economy, Society and Religion in a Siberian Collective Farm*
    CAROLINE HUMPHREY
41. Ecology and Exchange in the Andes
    Edited by DAVID LEHMANN
42. Traders without Trade: Responses to Trade in Two Dyula Communities
    ROBERT LAUNAY

Cambridge Studies in Social Anthropology

43. The Political Economy of West African Agriculture*
    KEITH HART
44. Nomads and the Outside World
    A. M. KHAZANOV, *translated by Julia Crookenden*
45. Actions, Norms and Representations: Foundations of Anthropological Inquiry*
    LADISLAV HOLY *and* MILAN STUCHLIK
46. Structural Models in Anthropology*
    PER HAGE *and* FRANK HARARY
47. Servants of the Goddess: The Priests of a South Indian Temple
    C. J. FULLER
48. Oedipus and Job in West African Religion*
    MEYER FORTES
    with an essay by ROBIN HORTON
49. The Buddhist Saints of the Forest and the Cult of Amulets: A Study in Charisma, Hagiography, Sectarianism, and Millenial Buddhism
    S. J. TAMBIAH
50. Kinship and Marriage: An Anthropological Perspective†
    ROBIN FOX
51. Individual and Society in Guiana: A Comparative Study of Amerindian Social Organization*
    PETER RIVIERE
52. People and the State: An Anthropology of Planned Development*
    A. F. ROBERTSON
53. Inequality among Brothers: Class and Kinship in South China
    RUBIE S. WATSON
54. On Anthropological Knowledge*
    DAN SPERBER
55. Tales of the Yanomami: Daily Life in the Venezuelan Forest
    JACQUES LIZOT, *translated by Ernest Simon*
56. The Making of Great Men: Male Domination and Power among the New Guinea Baruya
    MAURICE GODELIER, *translated by Rupert Swyer*
57. Age Class Systems: Social Institutions and Polities Based on Age*
    BERNARDO BERNARDI, *translated by David I. Kertzer*
58. Strategies and Norms in a Changing Matrilineal Society: Descent, Succession and Inheritance among the Toka of Zambia
    LADISLAV HOLY
59. Native Lords of Quito in the Age of the Incas: The Political Economy of North-Andean Chiefdoms
    FRANK SALOMON
60. Culture and Class in Anthropology and History: A Newfoundland Illustration
    GERALD SIDER

* Also available in paperback
† Paperback available in USA only